SPRING AND SUMMER DAYS

Rowland Purton

SPRING AND SUMMER DAYS

Basil Blackwell · Publisher

First published 1983

Published by
Basil Blackwell Publisher
108 Cowley Road
Oxford OX4 1JF

British Library Cataloguing in Publication Data

Purton, Rowland W.
Spring and summer days.
1. Encyclopedias and dictionaries
I. Title
032'. 02 AE6

ISBN 0–631–13203–1

Typset in eleven point Palatino by Oxford Publishing Services
Printed in Great Britain

Contents

Acknowledgements

The author and publisher are grateful to Messrs. Evans Bros. & Co. for permission to reproduce the poem 'June' by Irene F. Pawsey (p. 116) from 'The Book of a Thousand Poems'.

If the use of any other material has unwittingly infringed copyright the author tenders his sincere apologies and, if notified, will gladly rectify any such omissions in future editions.

Thanks are expressed by the author to the many people who have supplied information and offered encouragement in the compilation of these books, not the least being his wife Sylvia, who has spent very many hours in the preparation of the books.

Introduction

These two books, *Autumn and Winter Days* and *Spring and Summer Days*, have been written both for general interest and as resource books for teachers. The books have been so arranged that the former covers the first half of the school year and the latter the second half.

For ease of reference, the books have been comprehensively indexed, having a general index and an index of related themes (pp. 229–245), in which many entries have been listed by theme with main and sub-headings linking subjects that may be associated in projects.

As books of days there is much of general interest — births, deaths, events, sayings, quotations, folklore and customs for every day of the year.

Every effort has been made to ensure accuracy but discrepancies regarding some dates appear even in otherwise reliable sources. There is the added confusion of dates, Russian for example, which differ, some being indicated as 'O. S.' (Old Style), a result of the change in the calendar. Further complications arise, as with the first moon landing, when a few hours deviation of time records that they landed on one day according to U. S. Eastern Daylight Time but on the following day according to Greenwich Mean Time.

Apart from the calendar dates, monthly themes open each month and a list of movable or variable dates is given at the end, including local customs and shows. A list of shows, giving locations, dates and names of local secretaries is published annually by Agricultural Press Ltd., Information Service, Surrey House, 1 Throwley Way, Sutton, Surrey SM1 4QQ, who will be pleased to send a copy on request (S.A.E. please).

The British Tourist Authority's magazine *In Britain*, available from booksellers, lists forthcoming events. Also available from booksellers, or from the publishers, TEE Publishing, 216 Coventry Road, Hinckley, Leics LE10 ONG (1983–4, £1.10) is the Steam Yearbook, a guide to preserved transport and industrial archaeology with a diary of events.

Local information officers are also only too pleased to give information about events in their immediate neighbourhood. There are many such events and ceremonies which bring the past to the present, adding colour and interest to any study of 'days'.

R.P.

MARCH

March

March takes its name from the Latin Martius, the month of Mars, who was not only the god of war but the protector of crops. The Anglo-Saxons dedicated their third month to the goddess Hretha — so this was Hrethmonath.

March has a reputation for a wild blustery start but changing to much milder weather before the end of the month, as suggested in the old saying:

March comes in like a lion and goes out like a lamb.

The first three days of March are St. David's Day (1st), St. Chad's (2nd) and St. Winwaloe's (3rd). Hence the verse

First comes David,
Then comes Chad,
And then comes Winneral
As though he were mad!

And is it just the weather that is mad? It is sometimes said that a person is as mad as a March Hare. Hares certainly give the impression of being mad, jumping up and down, twisting their bodies in the air and thumping the ground with their powerful back legs. The March Hare is one of the well-known characters in *Alice's Adventures in Wonderland.*

March comes in with adders' tails and goes out with peacocks' feathers.

March may have its wild moments but it is also the time when people begin to notice the awakening of nature.

It is the first mild day of March:
Each minute sweeter than before,
The redbreast sings from the tall larch
That stands beside our door.

There is a blessing in the air,
Which seems a sense of joy to yield
To the bare trees, and mountains bare,
And grass in the green field.

William Wordsworth

Mild days and blustery days may be expected at any time, for March can be unpredictable. There may still be heavy falls of snow and frosts are quite common. A very mild spell early in the year may mean early growth of plants and blossom but sharp frosts will destroy it. Even the following verse is not quite accurate as late May frosts can still ruin the crop.

If apples bloom in March
In vain you'll for them search;
If apples bloom in April
Why then they'll be plentiful;
If apples bloom in May
You may eat them night and day.

This is true of the plant world in general. Early growth gives small return, but a cold March holds back the growth:

March flowers make no summer bowers.

A dry, cold March never begs its bread.

Whatever the weather, there are signs of activity in the animal world, with some creatures emerging from hibernation and others beginning their preparations for spring.

On the first of March
The crows begin to search.

On March the fifteenth come sun and swallow.

The sun and the swallow are two of the many signs that spring is near. The Spring, or Vernal Equinox, the day on which day and night are of equal length, falls on 21 March.

It is only natural that the birth of spring should be regarded by some people as the beginning of a new year. The ancient Roman calendar began on 1 March until Julius Caesar added January and February. Although the calendar was changed in this way, making March the third month, the Feast of the Annunciation, 25 March, was regarded as New Year's Day until 16th Century. It is now generally known as Lady Day, one of the English Quarter Days.

People of the Zoroastrian and Bahá'í religions regard 21 March as the start of their new year.

Lent

Lent has always been regarded as one of the important periods in the calendar of the Christian Church and part of it always falls during the month of March. Often the whole of March is within the forty days of Lent. This is the period of fasting before the great festival of Easter and, as the date of Easter varies from year to year, so does the period of Lent.

The first day of Lent is Ash Wednesday, which may be as early as 3 February or as late as 9 March. Easter, which ends Lent, may fall on or between 22 March and 25 April.

Nowadays few people change their life-style during Lent, though there may still be some form of self denial. At one time there was strict fasting throughout Lent and some foods were forbidden altogether. Hence the jollifications of Shrovetide, the days that precede Lent, and the eating up of forbidden foods such as eggs and fats as pancakes.

The one day in Lent on which people were allowed freedom from some of the restrictions was the fourth Sunday, known also as Mid-Lent Sunday or Mothering Sunday. The latter name came from the custom of people in outlying hamlets to visit the mother church of the parish to make offerings.

Mothering Sunday had nothing to do with Mother's Day, which is an idea that started in America in 1907. Nevertheless it did become customary on Mothering Sunday to have happy family reunions and for young people to return home to visit parents. As far back as the 17th Century, or even earlier, servants and apprentices were allowed time off work to go 'a-mothering' and take a present, traditionally some flowers such as violets or primroses, flowers sometimes given on Mothering Sunday to this day.

The lad and lass on Mothering Day,
Hie home to their mother so dear;
'Tis a kiss for she, and a kiss for they,
A chine of pork and a sprig of bay,
A song and a dance — but never a tear!

'Shakespeare's Greenwood' G. Morley

Mid-Lent Sunday is also known as Simnel Sunday because it was also the custom for simnel cakes to be taken home to mother on that day. There are three types of simnel cake, named after the towns in which they were first made. The Bury simnel was a round, flat cake, filled with dried fruit, peel and spices; the Shrewsbury a dark cake topped with a crown of almond paste; and the Devizes a star shaped cake. No one can be quite sure how the name simnel originated, though it may have come from a Latin word for flour. Records exist of simnel cakes being made over nine hundred years ago.

Another Mid-Lent treat was a bowl of frumenty, a dish made by soaking grain in a warm oven for about three days.

The following Sunday, the fifth Sunday in Lent, is Passion Sunday, so called because of the Passion of Jesus Christ. It is also known in some parts as Carling Sunday from the old custom of eating carling nuts, which are a kind of pea, fried in butter, made into a pancake and seasoned with salt and pepper.

The last Sunday in Lent is Palm Sunday, on which the story is recalled of Jesus Christ riding into Jerusalem and welcomed by people waving branches of palm trees.

It was once the custom for people to go 'a-palming' on the days before Palm Sunday, gathering greenery to decorate both church and home. There are no palms in Britain to be gathered but a favourite then, and still today, is the sallow willow with its fluffy catkins. In some churches, worshippers are given crosses made from palm leaves.

Palm Sunday is also known, in some parts of the country, as Fig Sunday, possibly in remembrance of the story of Jesus and the fig tree. Even the poorest families tried to obtain a few figs, which were either eaten as raw fruit or cooked in puddings or pies. The custom was dropped by the beginning of the present century.

Another custom that died out about the same time was that children put pieces of Spanish liquorice, sweets and sugar into a bottle which was filled with water, probably from a local holy or wishing well. The liquid was then consumed with obvious delight. So, for some, Palm Sunday was also 'Spanish Sunday'.

The week beginning with Palm Sunday is called Holy Week and in it are recalled the events in the last week in the life of Christ. The Thursday is known as Maundy Thursday. It commemorates the Last Supper shared by Christ and the twelve apostles. At this supper, Jesus gave them 'a new command to love one another'. The Latin for command is *mandatum* and it is believed to be from this that the word maundy comes.

Because, on that occasion, Jesus washed the feet of his disciples, it became customary for pious people, and even for kings, to wash the feet of twelve poor people as a sign of humility. Gifts of money were sometimes given at the same time, linked, perhaps with the age or circumstances of the king. In 1212, when King John had reigned for 13 years, he gave 13 pence to 13 men. When King Edward III was 50 years old, in 1361, he gave 50 poor men a pair of slippers each.

Nowadays on Maundy Thursday there is the interesting ceremony of Distributing the Royal Maundy at which especially minted coins are given, usually by the sovereign in person, to old people, corresponding in number to the sovereign's age.

The following day is Good Friday, solemnly observed in many churches with vigils and services in remembrance of the Crucifixion. It is also the day on which various local customs are observed, some of them associated with the Easter story. Of course, many people have Hot Cross Buns for breakfast.

There are also active sporting events here and there, and the culmination of the Marbles season with the championship at Tinsley Green (p. 42). In some southern counties of England, the Marbles season lasted from Ash Wednesday until noon on Good Friday, which was also know as Marbles Day.

Lent was also the season for spinning tops, which traditionally were taken out on Shrove Tuesday and put away on Good Friday.

Tops are in, spin 'em agin:
Tops are out, smuggin' about.

'Smugging' was legitimately stealing tops that were played with out of season. There were many kinds of top: whipping, peg, humming, teetotums (spun with the fingers), mushrooms, boxers, Japan, French, Klondykes and others — all providing light relief in an austere season.

Leeks and daffodils will be seen in many places this morning as Welsh people display their national emblems to commemorate the day of their patron saint, St. David, or Dewi. He lived in the 6th Century in the South-west of Wales, now known as Dyfed, but then as Menevia, of which he became Archbishop. There now is the city of St. Davids with its ancient monastic buildings and cathedral.

From one cathedral to another. It was on 1 March 1962, that a tapestry from Felletin, France, was delivered to the new cathedral built in Coventry to replace the one destroyed during World War II. It was the tapestry 'Christ in His Majesty', which had been designed by the artist Graham Sutherland, to hang behind the altar. A strikingly modern work of art, measuring 72ft x 39ft (21.94m x 11.88m), it is the largest single piece of tapestry ever to have been woven.

Each year on 1 March there is an interesting festival in Lanark, Scotland, known as Whuppity Scoorie. No one really knows how it came by its name or how it began. It was probably one of the many ancient customs, intended to drive away evil spirits by making a loud noise.

By 6 pm the children of Lanark have gathered at the Lanark Cross, each carrying a paper ball on the end of a piece of string. Then, as the church bell is tolled for the first time in four months, the children process three times round the church before hitting each other with these paper balls, then scramble for pennies thrown to them. It is great fun!

It wasn't much fun for tanker driver Bob Kelly, whose brakes failed as he drove down-hill through Farnham, Surrey, on 1 March 1979. He could have jumped out but Farnham was busy with shoppers. With lights flashing and horn blaring in warning, he avoided people until the tanker crashed into a shop front and overturned. It was a brave act.

Sir Samuel Romilly was born on 1 March 1757. He was a lawyer who was keen to see changes in the law to reduce the severity of punishments, such as capital punishment for minor offences. In 1806 he became Solicitor General.

This is the feast day of St. Chad, who died of plague on 2 March 672. With his brother, St. Cedd, he was educated under St. Aidan at the Abbey of Lindisfarne on Holy Island off the coast of Northumberland.

Chad is chiefly remembered as the man responsible for the conversion to Christianity of the people of the ancient English kingdom of Mercia. At Lichfield he built a church and a monastery and this became the centre of his work as bishop. He is remembered for his great zeal and for the great amount of travelling he did, mainly on foot, as he took his faith throughout the Midlands.

Another who travelled a great deal many years later was John Wesley. He was a clergyman of the Church of England but, because of his teachings, he was barred from preaching in the Anglican churches. So he preached outside, travelling on horseback throughout England to do so. 'I look upon the world as my parish', he said. In fifty years he preached some 40,000 sermons and travelled ten times as many kilometres to do so. He died on 2 March 1791.

It is difficult for us today to imagine what it must have been like to travel always on foot or horseback. Today we are used to speed and comfort. On 2 March 1969, the supersonic luxury jet air-liner *Concorde* made its first test flight, introducing a new high standard in the air.

Travelling was somewhat slower for Sir Vivian Fuchs in 1957–8. He commanded the British Commonwealth Trans-Antarctic Expedition, which made the first crossing of Antarctica from the Weddell Sea to the Ross Sea, where they arrived on 2 March 1958. It had taken 100 days to travel nearly 3,500 km in Sno-cats and other tracked vehicles.

Deep snow can cause problems for farmers and animals in Britain. Imagine how surprised a farmer in Strath Brora, Scotland, was to dig out alive, on 2 March 1978, two ewes that had been buried under the snow for 33 days.

Bedrich Smetana, composer, was born on 2 March 1824.

Some of the most dreadful schoolgirls imaginable were the girls of St. Trinians, whose escapades were fiendish to say the least. They first appeared in 1941 and continued to be encountered until 1953, after which they appeared in four films. The girls were cartoon characters created by Ronald Searle, whose humorous drawings and cartoons have been enjoyed by many. He has also published more serious drawings such as those of his experiences as a prisoner of war of the Japanese after the fall of Singapore. Ronald Searle first contributed to *Punch* in 1949 and he joined its staff in 1956. This is his birthday; he was born on 3 March 1920.

Robert Adam created characters of a different kind. Born in Kirkcaldy, Scotland, he grew to be one of the greatest architects and designers of the 18th Century. He was recognised as a leading designer of furniture and of interiors of great houses in what became known as 'the Adam style'. He died in London on 3 March 1792.

This was the birthday, in 1847, of another Scotsman who made a great contribution to the world. He was Alexander Graham Bell, the son of a teacher who specialised in teaching children who were deaf and dumb. As he grew older, he helped his father but he became ill and the family emigrated to Canada, where it was thought he might get well again. He did and then moved to Boston, USA, where he opened a school for training teachers of the deaf. He invented a number of devices to help deaf people, but his most important invention was the telephone, which he patented in 1876. It was in March of that year that his assistant, Thomas Watson, in another room, heard Bell say, 'Mr Watson, will you please come up here. I want you.' These were the first words spoken and transmitted by electrical means. It is difficult today to imagine a world without telephones. They have meant so much to millions of people.

Sir Henry Wood was born on 3 March 1869. He was an organist and conductor but he is especially remembered as the founder of the Promenade Concerts in 1895, which are still performed in London each year and are very popular.

We begin today with a mystery. On 4 March 1918, the USS *Cyclops*, with about 300 people on board, disappeared. She was a naval collier carrying a cargo of manganese ore from Rio de Janeiro to Norfolk, Virginia. What happened to her? Nobody knows.

Many ships are lost at sea without trace and are forgotten. *Cyclops* is remembered because she is the largest ship to have been lost in the Bermuda Triangle, an area of sea to the south-east of the United States with its corners at Bermuda, Puerto Rico and the Gulf of Mexico. Not only ships but aircraft have been lost without trace in the Bermuda Triangle. No doubt there are simple explanations but, for many people, the mere fact that they have happened in the Bermuda Triangle is an indication that something mysterious or uncanny has occurred.

This was the birthday, in 1394, of a man who sent many sailors into unknown waters on voyages of discovery. He was Prince Henry, the Navigator, of Portugal, who made a name for himself as an army leader but preferred more peaceful pursuits. He studied astronomy and mathematics, founded the Order of Jesus Christ, and sent brave captains who would seek a route to India and take Christianity to any peoples they encountered on the way. Henry the Navigator has been called 'the originator of modern discovery'.

Another with an interest in the sea was Sir William Hillary, soldier, traveller, writer and later a regular member of the crew of the lifeboat at Douglas, Isle of Man. It was on 4 March 1824, that he met some people in London, who, together, formed the National Institution for the Preservation of Life from Shipwreck, which later became the Royal National Lifeboat Institution.

The Constitution of the United States of America came into force in 1789 and the Comintern (Communist International) was formed in 1919.

Also on 4 March. . . .

Saladin, Muslim leader against the Crusaders, died in 1193;
Sir Henry Raeburn, Scottish portrait painter, was born in 1756;
The Forth railway bridge was officially opened in 1890.

Peace came to Europe in May 1945 with the ending of World War II. The allies had defeated their common enemies but they, themselves were poles apart. To the west of Germany were the nations that had been fighting for democracy and freedom : to the east was the Soviet Union, a vast totalitarian communist state opposed to most of the standards of the western world. On 5 March 1946, Sir Winston Churchill, speaking at Westminster College, Fulton, USA, said, 'An iron curtain has descended across the Continent.' That invisible 'iron curtain' has remained.

To the east of the iron curtain were various communist lands. The USSR had come into existence following the Bolshevik Revolution led by Lenin. On his death, in 1924, control passed to Josef Vissarionovich Dzhugashvili, whose adopted name was Stalin ('Man of Steel'). He had been editor of the Bolshevik newspaper *Pravda*: he became a cruel, ruthless dictator, destroying all who stood in his way. Some ten million peasants died in the 1930s and there was a blood-bath of former leaders. Officers in the army were replaced by low-ranking soldiers. At the end of World War II, his territories were larger than before. He died on 5 March 1953.

To the west of the iron curtain were nations with a passionate desire for freedom. British people had long enjoyed stirring national songs and found encouragement in words such as:

Rule, Britannia, Britannia rule the waves;
Britons never, never, never shall be slaves.

The music for this was written, in 1740, for the masque *Alfred*, by Thomas Arne, who died on 5 March 1778.

This day, in 1790, saw the death of Flora Macdonald, whose loyalty to Bonnie Prince Charlie in assisting him to escape in 1745 disguised as her maid, is legendary.

Gerardus Mercator, the Flemish mathematician, who gave us Mercator's Projection for maps, was born on 5 March 1512.

Count Alessandro Volta died on this day in 1827. He was the Italian physicist who invented the dry battery and after whom the electric unit, the volt, was named.

If people knew how hard I have to work to gain my mastery, it would not seem wonderful at all.

Although Michelangelo had this to say of himself, there are few who would not agree that he was a genius. Born in Florence on 6 March 1475, Michelangelo di Lodovico Buonarroti Simoni was to become one of the greatest painters and sculptors of his age besides being an architect and poet.

Early in life he went to Rome, where he sculptured many works, the most famous being his 'Pieta', now in St. Peter's Basilica. Returning to Florence, he sculptured 'David' from a huge block of marble which had stood 40 years awaiting a sculptor.

When an artist was needed to paint the ceiling of the Sistine Chapel, who better to commission than Michelangelo? It took him 4 years, lying on his back on scaffolding 100 ft (30.5m) above the floor. He then worked on the Pope's monument with its magnificent statue of Moses. Statues he sculptured for the Medici tomb are some of his greatest achievements.

Visitors to Rome to this day are impressed by the great dome of St. Peter's. Who designed it? Michelangelo. He was the chief architect of that building and of others in Rome.

Michelangelo may have attributed his success to hard work but the results are certainly wonderful.

Gottlieb Daimler put his mind to creativity of another kind. He lived during the 19th Century, when people were experimenting with engines. He patented one of the first high-speed internal combustion engines in 1885 and invented a carburettor so that petrol could be used as fuel. Petrol engines were fitted to a cycle, a four-wheeled carriage and a boat. Daimler, who died on 6 March 1900, was one of the great pioneers in the history of the motor car industry.

For creativity of different kinds: Louisa May Alcott, author of *Little Women* and other books, died in 1888; John Philip Sousa, composer of marching music, died in 1932; and David Sheppard, cricketer and bishop was born in 1929, all on this day.

In 1836, Davy Crockett, frontiersman and politician, was among those killed when the Alamo fell to the Mexican army.

Richmal Mangnall was born on 7 March 1769. Her name may not be familiar to many today but it must have been known in the past to thousands of schoolgirls. Miss Mangnall, an English teacher who became headmistress of a ladies' school near Wakefield, published a book called *Questions*, which reached its 84th edition in 1857 and was even reprinted thirty-five years after that.

A world best-seller is, of course, the *Bible*, available now complete or in part in over 1,500 languages and dialects. This has been the work of the world's Bible Societies, of which one is the British and Foreign Bible Society. Founded on 7 March 1804, its aim was to produce and supply Bibles in as many languages as possible at prices which people could afford. It adopted as its emblem a picture of a sower scattering the seed broadcast, knowing that some of the seeds of the Gospel will fall on good ground and produce results.

For many years we have been used to the broadcasting of news and many kinds of entertainment by means of radio. In recent times, local commercial radio stations have grown in popularity. The first three of these, Radio Leicester, Radio Merseyside and Radio Sheffield were formed in 1967, the announcement being made in Parliament on 7 March of that year. They were the first radio stations to be financed by advertising.

This day was also the beginning for Sir John Herschel, the astronomer, who was born on 7 March 1792.

Ten years later, this was the birthday of Sir Edwin Landseer, whose pictures of animals were very popular. He was the designer of the lions in London's Trafalgar Square and was Queen Victoria's favourite artist.

This was also the birthday, in 1875, of Maurice Ravel, the French composer of *Bolero*, other orchestral and piano music and songs.

Tomáš Masaryk, chief founder and first president of Czechoslovakia (1918–35), was born on 7 March 1850.

Admiral Lord Collingwood died at sea on 7 March 1810. He took part in many naval victories in the time of Nelson and was buried alongside Nelson in St. Paul's Cathedral.

On the west bank of the River Nile, in the Aswan region of Nubia, Egypt, stood the two temples of Abu Simbel, outside which were four colossal statues of the Egyptian king, Ramses II. Carved out of a sandstone cliff, the four seated figures were 67 feet (20m) high. A little further down river, work began on building the new Aswan High Dam, to provide much-needed water for Egypt. When the dam was completed, the reservoir behind it would flood the temple, which would then be lost for ever.

On 8 March 1960, the United Nations Educational Scientific and Cultural Organization (UNESCO) and the Egyptian government launched an appeal to save the site. More than fifty nations provided the funds which enabled a team of engineers and scientists to take the temples and statues to pieces, then reassemble them on high ground, well clear of the water, where they can remain for future generations to appreciate.

Most countries have some treasures which they like to preserve. An old iron bridge may seem little compared with an ancient temple yet the one at Ironbridge, Salop, is of great historical interest for it was the earliest iron bridge to be built (1777–9) and now forms part of the museum area, a reminder of the iron industry begun in Coalbrookdale by the first Abraham Darby, who died on 8 March 1717, and which was continued by his son.

The Duke of Bridgewater, who died on 8 March 1803, is usually regarded as the founder of the British canal system. He employed James Brindley to construct a canal from his estates in Worsley to Manchester, a distance of 10 miles (16 km), so that his coal could be transported cheaply. Canals were a very important aspect of the Industrial Revolution.

A different kind of revolution began on this day in 1917, when the Russian people rose against the Tsar, Nicholas II, and his government. The Revolution was to have far-reaching results for Russia and for the rest of the world.

Today . . . in 1858, Ruggero Leoncavallo, Italian opera composer, was born; . . . in 1869, Hector Berlioz, French composer, died; . . . in 1929, Rev. G. A. Studdert-Kennedy ('Woodbine Willie') died; . . . in 1961, Sir Thomas Beecham, conductor died. died.

From a very early age, I had imbibed the opinion, that it was every man's duty to do all that lay in his power to leave his country as good as he had found it.

William Cobbett, who was born on 9 March 1763, did not want to see England spoiled by the Industrial Revolution. He became editor of the *Political Register,* through which he was able to express his opinions on the need for social and parliamentary reform. His *Rural Rides* showed his concern about the effects of industrialisation.

This was the birthday, in 1451, of a man who was to have a whole continent named after him. He was a merchant from Florence named Amerigo Vespucci, who had a business in Seville, Spain. As he supplied seafarers with their needs, he listened to accounts of their travels. One was Christopher Columbus. Later he sailed on two voyages to the new world, one sponsored by Spain and one by Portugal. On the second of these, he sailed along the coast of South America. A few years later, in 1507, the whole continent was named America.

On 9 March 1862, off the American coast, two unusual looking ships engaged in battle. The Confederate States *Merrimac* was covered with iron armour-plating. The Union *Monitor* was also an ironclad but had a revolving turret in which were two large guns. The *Monitor* drove off her opponent and introduced an idea, the movable turret, which was to remain a feature of warships for many years.

Mary Anning liked to walk along the beach with her father near their home at Lyme Regis, Dorset. Father was a cabinet maker who enjoyed looking for fossils. When she was only twelve, Mary made an important discovery, the fossilised remains of an Ichthyosaurus, which had lived millions of years ago. Mary's searchings later revealed a Plesiosaurus and a Pterodactyl. She died on this day in 1847.

David Rizzio was secretary to Mary Queen of Scots. He was murdered on 9 March 1566, by Lord Darnley and accomplices.

How many people live in Britain? The official figures are based on a census. The first census in Britain began on 10 March 1801, and there has been one in every tenth year since then with the exception of 1941 (wartime).

For Londoners it sometimes seems as though most of the population of Britain are trying to crowd into the underground trains during the rush hours. It was on this day, in 1906, that one of these railways, the Bakerloo Line, opened.

In the United States, before the Civil War, there was another Underground Railroad — a secret network of routes by which slaves who had escaped were helped to reach Canada and safety. One of the most famous 'conductors' was Harriet Tubman. As an escaped slave who had been aided by people on the 'railroad', she returned to help others. She became known as the 'Moses of her people', successfully guiding over 300 of them to safety in spite of the huge rewards offered for her capture.

Harriet Tubman was a devout Christian, who counted many of the leading abolitionists amongst her friends. In one of his letters, John Brown referred to her as 'one of the best and bravest persons on this continent — General Tubman as we call her.' During the Civil War she served the Federal army as a nurse and a spy. She died, aged over 90, on 10 March 1913.

Giuseppe Mazzini was something of a rebel, too. Early in life he had been stirred by the sight of refugees after a rising in Piedmont in 1821. He decided to work for a united, independent Italy and became a revolutionary. From then on he was a 'wanted', or perhaps unwanted man, being exiled from his own and from other countries. He was a great organiser, planning revolts and taking part in some. He died, after seeing a united Italy, on this day in 1872.

Jan Masaryk was a statesman who loved his country, Czechoslovakia, and served as its Foreign Minister in exile in London during World War II. In 1948, when the Communists took control, he jumped from an upper window on 10 March. Was it suicide? Or was he made to jump, as has been suggested by some?

Often when we buy a hot drink in a cafe or restaurant we are given a packet containing a couple of lumps, or cubes, of sugar. It is much easier to use cubes than loose sugar. The sugar cube was the invention, in 1872, of Sir Henry Tate, who became a very wealthy Liverpool sugar refiner.

Sir Henry founded the University Library at Liverpool and presented his private collection of paintings to the nation. They were housed in the Tate Gallery, which was built in London and which today houses a fine collection of British paintings as well as sculptures and some modern art forms. Today was Sir Henry Tate's birthday, in 1819.

This was the birthday, in 1904, of one of the 20th Century's controversial painters, Salvador Dali. Born at Figueras, Spain, he studied art at Madrid before going to Paris, where he became a leading Surrealist painter. After settling in the United States, he began painting on religious themes. One of his outstanding works is his *Christ of St. John of the Cross* with its unusual view of the cross from above.

One of the greatest Italian poets of the Renaissance was Torquato Tasso. This was his birthday, in 1544. This was also the birthday, in 1885, of Sir Malcolm Campbell, who became the land and water speed record holder in cars and craft named *Bluebird* in the 1930s. In 1916, this was the birthday of British Prime Minister Sir Harold Wilson.

Two great explorers died on 11 March. Sir Alexander Mackenzie, a native of Stornoway in the Hebrides, went to Canada, where he traced the course of the Mackenzie River and explored many other parts of Canada. He returned to Scotland, where he died on this day in 1820.

In 1957, Richard Byrd died. He was an American naval officer and aviator, who flew over both the North and South Poles and carried out important polar explorations.

Also on this day. . .

Sir Alexander Fleming, discoverer of penicillin, died in 1955;
London's first daily newspaper, *The Daily Courant*, appeared in 1702;
German troops marched into Austria in 1938.

Today is the Feast of St. Gregory the Great — Pope Gregory I, who died on 12 March 604. Born in Rome, he entered a monastery there after giving his wealth to the poor. It was in Rome that he saw Anglo-Saxon youths being sold as slaves and determined that he would go to teach their people about Christianity. He set out but was recalled and later unanimously chosen to be Pope. As such he proved to be one of the greatest administrators that the Roman Church has had. He had much to do but he had not forgotten the Anglo-Saxon people. Unable to go to England himself, he entrusted that mission to St. Augustine.

John Bull died on 12 March 1628 — not the jovial, stoutish gentleman who is pictured wearing a top hat and a Union Jack as a waistcoat but a handsome young man who became a doctor of music of both Oxford and Cambridge universities, organist of the Chapel Royal and a musician held in high esteem by Queen Elizabeth I and James I. Amongst his many compositions, he is credited with an early version of the British National Anthem.

On the subject of national music, we remember, today, the birth on 12 March 1710, of Thomas Arne, composer of the music for 'Rule Britannia', Shakespeare's songs and various theatre productions. His music was described by the music historian, Charles Burney, as 'the standard of all perfections at our theatres and public gardens'.

A man who did much for modern Turkey was born on 12 March 1881. Mustafa Kemal led the nationalist movement from 1909, was a general in World War I and, as President from 1923 to 1938, introduced many reforms. He took the name Ataturk — 'Father of the Turks'.

The father of the Chinese Republic died in Peking on this day in 1925. He was Sun Yat-sen, the revolutionary who became, in 1912, the first president of the republic.

It was on 12 March 1829, that the first uniformed police force came into being — in Paris. In Britain, on this day in 1935, the 30 mph speed limit was first introduced.

Edmund Halley, who was Astronomer Royal from 1719 to 1742, is always remembered in connexion with Halley's Comet, the comet that was named after him. In 1705, he worked out that the comet he had seen in 1682 was the same one that had appeared in 1531 and 1607. Its next appearance, he calculated, would be in 1758. It was, and, in fact, on 13 March of that year, reached its perihelion, or point nearest the sun.

Sir William Herschel was also an astronomer, and so was his wife Caroline. She discovered eight comets and she helped her husband with his many calculations and cataloguing of stars and star-clusters. On 13 March 1781, Sir William discovered the planet Uranus.

Percival Lowell, who was born in Boston, USA, on 13 March 1855, was a writer and traveller but became interested in astronomy in the 1890s. He set up his own observatory at Flagstaff, Arizona, where he studied the planets, plotted the irregular course of Uranus and organised a search by his staff for a 'Planet X'. They found it, on this day, 13 March 1930, some fourteen years after Lowell's death, and named it Pluto.

So to a star of a different kind. Richard Burbage, the star attraction of the Elizabethan stage, died on this day in 1619. He was very popular by the age of 20, starring in Shakespeare's plays, and was in great demand for other plays too.

Starring in his own show was Daniel Lambert, the fattest man, who made an exhibition of himself (p. 178). He was born on 13 March 1770.

Also born today were Sir Joseph Priestley, the scientist who discovered oxygen, in 1733; and Sir Hugh Walpole, novelist and dramatist, in 1884.

On this day, in 1813, William Hedley patented the steam locomotive. Later he built the *Puffing Billy*.

On 13 March 1904, people of Argentina and Chile assembled for the unveiling of *The Christ of the Andes*, a huge statue standing on the mountains between these countries.

Most photographers have at some time used a Kodak camera or film. Perhaps they have wondered what 'Kodak' means or how the name originated. It was a name invented by George Eastman, the American photography pioneer, because it had no meaning in any language. Eastman controlled nearly the whole photography market in America. In 1924, he gave away half of his fortune, over 75 million dollars. In one sense this is one of the great success stories of the century — but on 14 March 1932, George Eastman shot himself.

On this day, in 1757, shots rang out across Portsmouth harbour. Admiral John Byng fell dead on the deck of his own ship, executed by a firing squad for neglect of duty after fighting a half-hearted battle against the French and then retiring, leaving Minorca to the enemy. Some saw the trial and execution as a cover-up by the government for its own short-comings. Voltaire, the French author, in *Candide,* commented that the English found it necessary, from time to time, to shoot an admiral 'in order to encourage the others'.

This was the birthday of Johann Strauss, the Elder, in 1804. He was one of the principal composers of Viennese waltzes — a tradition continued by his son — as well as polkas, galops, quadrilles, other dances and marches.

In 1844, Sir Thomas Brunton was born on 14 March. He became a physician who studied circulation and discovered that the pain of angina could be relieved by amyl nitrite.

Albert Einstein was also born on 14 March in 1879. He ranks as one of the most brilliant physicists in history. His *General Theory of Relativity* brought him world-wide fame. In 1921, he was awarded the Nobel Prize for Physics. A German Jew, he left Hitler's Germany to settle in the USA.

Also on this day. . . .

1748 Field-Marshal Wade, military road builder, died.
1883 Karl Marx, Communist revolutionist, died in London.
1925 The first transatlantic broadcast was made.
1961 *The New English Bible* was published.
1964 Rachel Carson, writer and conservationist, died.

One of the most famous names in history is that of Julius Caesar, Roman general and statesman, who became the most powerful man in the world in his day. After having made a name for himself in Rome, where he became chief magistrate, he led his armies into Gaul where, for nearly ten years, he fought and conquered. These wars are described in his book *De Bello Gallico* ('The Gallic Wars').

Julius Caesar had gained his successes in Rome by various plots and intrigues. Whilst he was away, others were plotting. So he returned to Rome, was received as a conqueror and given great power. Soon he had defeated all rivals and was undoubtedly head of the whole Roman Empire.

He did many things to help his people and he is remembered for many good reforms. However, the plots continued and there were those, even amongst his friends, who thought he was too powerful. They decided to assassinate him. 'Beware the Ides of March', a soothsayer says, according to Shakespeare. It was on the Ides of March (15th) that Julius Caesar went to the Senate building, where he was stabbed to death.

If the assassins thought to curtail the powers of the Emperor, they were mistaken. Future Emperors were to have even greater powers as absolute rulers.

Henry Bessemer had the golden touch. He developed a means of making 'gold' powder from brass for use in paints and this business proved quite prosperous. He is remembered chiefly for his Bessemer Converter, the means he invented of making good steel very cheaply. Bessemer patented his invention, received a royalty on all steel made by this method, and died a millionaire on 15 March 1898.

Visitors to London from many parts of the world head for Oxford Street to shop at one of the largest and most famous department stores, Selfridge's. It was the brainchild of the American businessman, Harry Gordon Selfridge, who moved to London in 1906. Selfridge's opened on 15 March 1909.

On the other side of the world, on 15 March 1876, in Melbourne, Australia, cricketing history was made with the first Test Match. It was a three-day match in which Australia beat England by 45 runs.

Nowadays one of the sporting highlights in England is the F A Cup Final at Wembley, attended by many thousands of football enthusiasts. It has been at Wembley since 1923, before which it was held at various places. The first Cup Final was on 16 March 1872, when a mere 1,000 spectators saw the Wanderers beat the Royal Engineers 1–0 at Kennington Oval, London.

Footballers, and other sportsmen, know the value of keeping fit and especially of not carrying more body weight than is necessary. Other people are not always as careful; many suffer from obesity; and many suffer body disorders because of overweight. In 1862, a London undertaker, William Banting, went to see a doctor because of deafness. He was told, as many patients are today, that he needed to lose weight. He was only 5 feet 5 inches in height but weighed 202 pounds (91.6 kg).

The surgeon, William Harvey, put Banting on a diet of lean meat, fish and dry toast: fats and carbohydrates were strictly forbidden. During the following year Banting lost 46 pounds (20.8 kg) and his health improved. He was so pleased that he published a pamphlet giving details of his problems, his diet and his improvement in health, — the fore-runner of many such publications and diet sheets produced today by dietitians and slimming organisations to help people to lose weight. William Banting died, an octogenarian, on 16 March 1878.

Captain Oates turned to his companions on 16 March 1912, and said, 'I am just going outside and may be some time'. His friends knew they would never see him again. They were the remaining members of Captain Scott's expedition to the South Pole, now trapped in their tent in a blizzard. Oates, very badly frostbitten, knew he could only be a burden to his friends, so he walked to his death. It was the action of a very brave man — and a true friend.

This was the birthday, in 1787, of Georg Ohm, the German physicist, whose researches into electricity resulted in his name being give to the ohm, the unit of electrical resistance.

The Long Parliament, summoned in 1640, was finally dissolved on 16 March 1660.

17 March

Most people know 17 March as St. Patrick's Day, celebrated by Irish people the world over in honour of their patron saint. Taken to Ireland as a captive, Patrick escaped to Gaul but later returned to carry the Christian faith to the court of King Laoghaire. Later he became Bishop of Ireland.

It is not so well known that today is also the feast day of St. Joseph of Arimathaea. He it was who requested the body of Jesus Christ after the crucifixion and placed it in the tomb. Was Joseph a traveller too? There is a legend that he travelled to Glastonbury, Somerset, taking with him the Holy Grail.

In much more recent times, 17 March marked the climax not only of one voyage but of years of expectation. In 1959 the USS *Skate*, a nuclear submarine, broke through the ice to surface at the North Pole. The idea of travelling to the North Pole by submarine had first been suggested by Sir Hubert Wilkins, an Australian, who had made a name for himself as an Arctic explorer. He had set out in 1931 in an old submarine on a voyage that proved impossible: the submarine needed to surface often for air and could not because of the ice.

It was not until August 1958 that the USS *Nautilus* was able to pass under the North Polar ice. She had nuclear propulsion, and did not therefore need to surface.

Sir Hubert Wilkins did not live to see the fulfilment of his dream. He died on this day, 17 March 1958, having asked that his ashes should be scattered at the North Pole. So it was most appropriate that the USS *Skate* should break through the ice on the first anniversary of his death and that his request should be granted.

It was on 17 March 1766, that the Stamp Act, which caused such bad feeling among the American colonists, was repealed and ten years later to the day that British troops were compelled to leave Boston, toward the end of the War of Independence.

Also today. . . .

1846 Kate Greenaway, artist and illustrator, was born.
1959 The Dalai Lama, spiritual leader of Tibet, fled to India.

Ivan the Terrible, the first tsar of Russa, died on 18 March 1584, having done much to build up the state of Russia by conquest and treaty. The last twenty years of his reign were ones of terror: several thousand were executed on suspicion of treachery and many others oppressed. Even so, Ivan is remembered for many reforms and for encouraging Russian commerce and culture.

One who contributed to Russian culture in later years was Nikolai Rimsky-Korsakov, born on 18 March 1844. He was a composer, teacher and editor, who did much to encourage Russian national music. His music, for opera and orchestra, is enjoyed by many and is very colourful musically.

Guido di Pietri liked beautiful things. At the age of 20 he entered a Dominican monastery but the last ten years of his life were spent in Rome. He gave the world many fine frescoes and other paintings. The beauty of his angelic figures gave him the name by which he is remembered — Fra Angelico. He died on 18 March 1455.

Four centuries later, across the Atlantic, Henry Ward Beecher saw little that was beautiful around him and was outspoken against slavery in the days before the Civil War. A leading Congregationalist preacher of his day, he died on 18 March 1887.

One of the leading English statesmen of the early 18th Century was Sir Robert Walpole, often referred to as Britain's first Prime Minister, for it was under him that power was transferred to the House of Commons and he, as First Lord of the Treasury, presided at Cabinet meetings. He died on this day in 1745.

Rudolf Diesel was born on 18 March 1858. He is remembered as the inventor of the internal-combustion engine which bears his name. Diesel's life was full of ups and downs. Eventually he disappeared without trace from a cross-channel steamer in 1913. Nowadays huge tankers carry crude oil for refining to 'feed' the millions of diesel and petrol engines. It was on this day, in 1967, that one, the *Torrey Canyon*, was wrecked off Lands' End, polluting the sea and beaches and highlighting the need for strict anti-pollution measures.

Today is St. Joseph's Day. Of the references to him in the Bible several refer to his journeyings — from Nazareth to Bethlehem when Jesus was born, to the temple at Jerusalem and to Egypt. So perhaps today is a good day to think of travelling.

Sir Richard Burton was born on 19 March 1821. He served in the Indian army and found it easy to learn foreign languages. In fact he learned thirty-five. He also enjoyed disguising himself as native people and was so successful that he was able to get into the forbidden city of Mecca disguised as a man from Afghanistan. He then turned to exploring Africa. With J.H. Speke he discovered Lake Tanganyika. Later he served as British Consul in several parts of the world and he wrote no less than 43 volumes about his travels and exploration, besides translating many books written in eastern languages.

Another traveller in Africa was also born on this day in 1813. He was David Livingstone, born in Blantyre, Scotland. In 1840, he went as a missionary to South Africa. He believed the best way to stamp out slavery was to open up the unknown parts of Africa. He explored the great rivers, discovered the Victoria Falls and Lake Nyasa and eventually died in Africa. He was buried in Westminster Abbey.

On 19 March 1687, Robert Cavelier, Sieur de la Salle was murdered by one of his men in Texas. La Salle had settled as a fur trader in Canada but he began to explore the Great Lakes and several rivers including the Mississippi, as well as the surrounding lands, which he claimed for France and named Louisiana after King Louis IV.

Six men made an unwilling journey to Australia in 1834. They were the Tolpuddle Martyrs, six farm labourers from that Dorset village, who were sentenced on 19 March to penal servitude for forming an illegal society of agricultural labourers.

To help modern travellers, Sydney Harbour Bridge was opened in 1932 and the Great St. Bernard Tunnel through the Alps in 1964, both on 19 March. And for a 'journey into space', the London Planetarium opened on this day in 1958.

I do not know what I may appear to the world, but to myself I seem to have been only like a boy playing on the sea-shore and diverting myself in now and then finding a smoother pebble or a prettier shell than ordinary, whilst the great ocean of truth lay all undiscovered before me.

Whatever Sir Isaac Newton may have thought of himself, the world certainly regards him as one of the greatest physicists and mathematicians, whose work laid the foundations upon which many others have been able to build. His observation of a falling apple led to his working out the laws of gravity. He followed this with the laws of motion. He explained how white light can be divided into the seven colours of the spectrum. He was a brilliant mathematician. He made a reflecting telescope to help his studies of astronomy. His book, *Mathematical Principles of Natural Philosophy,* is regarded by some as the greatest science book ever written.

Newton was honoured and respected during his lifetime. Before he was thirty, he was elected a Fellow of the Royal Society. He became a Member of Parliament and was Master of the Mint from 1699 until his death on 20 March 1727.

Home life ceases to be free and beautiful as soon as it is founded on borrowing and debt.

Perhaps these words of Henrik Ibsen in *A Doll's House* reflected his own experience. He was born on 20 March 1828, into a prosperous Norwegian household but his father went bankrupt. Ibsen studied to be a chemist and gained experience as a theatrical producer before writing such important works as *Peer Gynt* and *Hedda Gabler,* which showed him to be one of the greatest dramatists of all time.

Brendan Behan, Irish playwright, died on 20 March 1964.

On stage, one of the greatest Italian operatic tenors was Beniamino Gigli. This was his birthday in 1890. His last concert appearance was in 1955, two years before his death. He is remembered for his powerful mellow voice.

Also on this day. . . .

There was a total eclipse of the sun in England in 1140.
The Dutch East India Company was formed in 1602.
Napoleon began his 'Hundred Days' in 1815.

That leaving here a name, I trust
That will not perish in the dust

A couple of lines from 'My Days among the Dead' by Robert Southey, who died on this day in 1843. They are obviously true of all the following, who were born or died on 21 March:

Archbishop Thomas Cranmer, burned at the stake in 1556;
Johann Sebastian Bach, composer, born in 1685;
Benito Juarez, Mexican national hero, born in 1806;
Modest Mussorgsky, composer, born in 1839;
William Scoresby, scientist and Arctic explorer, died in 1857;
Aleksandr Glazunov, Russian composer, died in 1936.

This day, in 1617, saw the final act of a story that captured the imagination of people of those times and ever since. It began ten years before, when John Smith landed in America to form a new colony. That winter, he was captured by Indians, who were about to kill him when Pocahontas, the daughter of Chief Powhattan rushed forward, cradled Smith's head in her arms and appealed for his life to be spared.

In time, John Smith returned to England. Pocahontas met and married a young farmer named John Rolfe, who had gone to Virginia from Norfolk. She became Christian, was christened Rebecca, and went with Rolfe to London, where she was the centre of attraction and met many important people, including the Queen.

After a while she became ill. Rolfe blamed the London weather and took her onto a ship to return to Virginia but the little Indian princess died of pneumonia off Gravesend and, on 21 March 1617, she was buried there in the chancel of St. George's Church, near which a statue of her was erected.

The Scottish National Gallery, was opened in Edinburgh on this day in 1859.

This was a sad day, in 1960, in the history of South Africa. A large number of black people gathered at Sharpeville to demonstrate against the pass law, by which all black people had to carry passes. Attempting to disperse the crowd, the police opened fire, killing 67 and wounding 186. It is known as the Sharpeville massacre.

He never wants anything but what's right and fair;
Only when you come to settle what's right and fair,
it's everything that he wants and nothing that you want.

We all know people like that and we also know people who are just the opposite, for the world consists of people of many different kinds. Put some of them, all boys, together in a public school and you have the makings of a situation in which the bully, the weakling, the extrovert and introvert show up in their respective colours. Such was the picture painted in *Tom Brown's Schooldays*, from which the quotation comes. The author, Thomas Hughes, who based the book on his experience at Rugby School, wrote a sequel, based on his life at Oxford, but *Tom Brown at Oxford* was not such a success. Hughes, who studied law and later became a Q.C., County Court Judge and Liberal Member of Parliament, died on 22 March 1896.

Put together such a group of grown men in a small ship in the Royal Navy in a wartime situation, add to it the violence of the North Atlantic weather, the tension of enemy action and the traumatic decisions that must be made. The result may be that found in *The Cruel Sea*, the popular novel which was made into an exciting film. It was one of the novels written by Nicholas Monsarrat, who was born on this day in 1910.

One of the greatest names in world literature is Johann Wolfgang von Goethe. He was not only a deep thinking creative writer but a poet, dramatist, philosopher, educationalist, journalist, critic, artist, scientist, theatre manager and much more besides. He died on 22 March 1832.

A prolific Flemish artist of the 17th Century was Sir Anthony Van Dyck (or Vandyke), whose birthday was 22 March 1599. He painted subjects of a religious or mythological nature but is chiefly remembered for his portraits of royalty and the aristocracy of Europe.

It was on this day, in 1945, that the Arab countries of the Middle-East formed the Arab League, through which they might be able to work together.

Give me liberty or give me death

These words were spoken on this day in 1775 by Patrick Henry, the brilliant American orator, who played an important part in the American Revolution. He was twice governor of his home state of Virginia.

It was the Stamp Act, imposed on the American colonists by the British parliament ten years earlier, which, although repealed in the following year, was one of the causes of the revolution.

It was the liberty and freedom of the wide open spaces that led many people to leave a rather squalid life and make their home in the undeveloped new colonies overseas. It was on this day, in 1848, that the first officially organised settlers landed at Dunedin in New Zealand.

Donald Campbell was a man who needed the wide open spaces of land and water, not for making a home but for creating world speed records. He was born on 23 March 1921, the son of Sir Malcolm Campbell, himself a speed king.

He was the first to use a jet-propelled hydroplane for an officially timed run on Ullswater, Cumbria, in 1955, when he set up a world water speed record of 202.32 mph (325.6 km/h). Later, after raising it several times on Coniston Water, he went to Australia and created a new record, on Dumbleyung Lake, of 276.33 mph (444.7 km/h). Also in Australia, on Lake Eyre Salt Flats, he raised the world land speed record to 403.1 mph (648.7 km/h). In 1961, on Coniston Water, he was travelling at over 300 mph (480 km/h) when his jet-propelled *Bluebird K7* broke up and he was killed.

Roger Bannister, another record-holder, was also born on this day, in 1929. His was not the great speed of Donald Campbell but that of the athlete. He has the distinction of being the first man to run a mile in less than four minutes, accomplished on 6 May 1954 (p. 88).

There was nothing fast about the trams that ran on the first London tramway between Notting Hill Gate and Marble Arch, dating from this day in 1861.

William Morris was born on 24 March 1834, at Walthamstow, then a village on the edge of Epping Forest. At the age of eight, he was taken to Canterbury, where the cathedral greatly impressed him. Later he began to study architecture but then took up painting. With some friends, he established a decorating firm, which designed carvings, tiles, house decorations and stained-glass windows. Morris then turned to fabric designing and the use of vegetable dyes. He had an eye for anything beautiful and was horrified to see anything of beauty destroyed. He set up the Society for the Protection of Ancient Buildings. The more he travelled, the more he wanted to see the beauty of the English countryside preserved. So William Morris, the poet, wrote:

Forget six counties overhung with smoke,
Forget the snorting steam and piston stroke,
Forget the spreading of the hideous town;
Think rather of the packhorse on the down,
And dream of London, small and white and clean,
The clear Thames bordered by its gardens green.

William Morris fell in love with and lived in Kelmscott Manor, near the banks of the Thames in Oxfordshire. It lent its name to the Kelmscott Press, which he established toward the end of his life to produce some of the finest of all British decorated books. The extent of his work was astonishing — not a jack but a master of all trades — a man of boundless energy, who left the world a much more beautiful place.

Henry Wadsworth Longfellow, the American poet, died on 24 March 1882, leaving *Hiawatha* and many other well-known poems. From *Tales of a Wayside Inn*:

Ships that pass in the night, and speak each other in passing;
Only a signal shown and a distant voice in the darkness;
So on the ocean of life we pass and speak one another,
Only a look and a voice; then darkness again and a silence.

And so, in passing . . . . on 24 March the Dutch Admiral Michiel de Ruyter was born in 1607; and these all died —
Queen Elizabeth I in 1603.
John Harrison, inventor of the marine chronometer, in 1776.
Jules Verne, science fiction writer, in 1905.
Field Marshal Viscount Montgomery of Alamein, in 1976.

For my own sake I do not regret this journey, which has shewn that Englishmen can endure hardships, help one another, and meet death with as great a fortitude as ever in the past. We took risks, we knew we took them; things have come out against us, and therefore we have no cause for complaint, but bow to the will of Providence, determined still to do our best to the last.

So wrote Captain Robert Falcon Scott in the icy wastes of Antarctica, when it was clear that all hope of survival was gone. Exploration in Antarctica in 1901–4 had led him to make an attempt to reach the South Pole. He reached it on 17 January 1912, only to discover that Amundsen had been there earlier. Within a few miles of a depot, the party was halted by blizzards and there they died. Scott's last diary entry, on 25 March 1912, read; 'For God's sake look after our people.'

Arturo Toscanini was a perfectionist. He was satisfied with nothing less from himself or those who formed his team — the members of the orchestra which he was conducting. He was a truly remarkable man, described as the greatest conductor of his day. Born on 25 March 1867, he was playing the 'cello at the age of nine. Ten years later, at a concert in Brazil, the conductor, who was jeered by the audience, walked out. Young Arturo stepped forward, picked up the baton, and conducted the whole opera from memory. Later he became conductor at the La Scala Opera House, Milan and of famous orchestras.

This day in 1881 was the birthday of another musician, Béla Bartók, the Hungarian composer who based his compositions on Hungarian folk music. It was also the birthday, in 1947, of Reginald Dwight, who was to become famous as the millionaire pop musician, Elton John. Claude Debussy, the French composer, died on 25 March 1918.

Also on 25 March. . . .

John Drinkwater, poet and playwright, died in 1937.
London Airport, Heathrow, was opened in 1948.
In 1957, the Treaty of Rome was signed by the Six.
King Faisal of Saudi Arabia was assassinated in 1975.
In 1980, Dr. William Runcie was enthroned 102nd Archbishop of Canterbury.

Simple and fresh and fair from winter's close emerging
As if no artifice of fashion, business, politics had ever been,
Forth from its sunny nook of shelter'd grass — innocent, golden, calm as the dawn,
The spring's first dandelion shows its trustful face.

It is about this time of year, as the world is awakening from its winter sleep, that we may notice the first dandelion. This is one of the shorter poems of Walt Whitman, the American poet and journalist. At various times a teacher, printer, editor, stationer and office worker, he died on 26 March 1892.

Sir Noel Coward died on 26 March 1973, leaving behind him a wealth of music, plays, films, songs and happy memories. After appearing in a play at the age of 12, the theatre became his life. He acted and wrote plays and comedies including *Bitter Sweet* and *Blithe Spirit*. He acted himself in the film he wrote about the Royal Navy, *In Which We Serve*, whilst his *Brief Encounter* became a British cinema classic. He also composed hundreds of songs.

Ludwig van Beethoven also died on this day, in 1827. He too, left behind a great heritage for future generations. Recognised as one of the greatest musicians of the western world, he wrote great symphonies and concertos as well as chamber music and one opera, music for orchestra and for the piano — and some of the finest of it toward the end of his life when he was totally deaf.

David Lloyd George, the fiery Welsh politician, died on 26 March 1945. A Member of Parliament for 65 years, he was Prime Minister from 1916 to 1922 and laid the foundations for the modern welfare state.

Cecil Rhodes also died on this day, in South Africa, in 1902. He mined diamonds and gold, formed the British South Africa Company, entered politics and had Rhodesia (now Zimbabwe) named after him. After a very full and active life, his last words were

So little done, so much to do.

Most people have been thankful, at some time, that a doctor has been able to see inside their bodies by means of an X-ray. X-rays, first known as Röntgen rays, were an accidental discovery by a German physicist, Wilhelm Konrad von Röntgen, who placed an electric tube on a book in which there was a key. The whole happened to be resting on a photographic plate on which Röntgen later discovered a 'picture' of the key, which had been photographed through the book. The discovery of X-rays gained Röntgen a Nobel Prize for Physics in 1901. This day was Röntgen's birthday in 1845.

Today we remember another physicist who gave us an article that most people have found useful. Sir James Dewar was a Scottish physicist and chemist who studied gases and found a means of liquifying gases such as oxygen and hydrogen at low temperatures, for which purpose he invented a double-walled vacuum flask. Encased in a metal container, such a flask has been marketed as the Thermos flask. Sir James Dewar, who also worked with Sir Frederick Augustus Abel to develop the explosive, cordite, died on 27 March 1923.

Some other famous people who died on 27 March. . . .

King James I of Great Britain was the first Stuart King of England and the first king to rule both England and Scotland. He died in 1625.

John Bright died in 1889. A Quaker from Rochdale, Lancashire, he became one of the leading statesmen and orators of the 19th Century. He entered Parliament in 1843 and, but for a brief interruption, remained there for the rest of his life, serving as a Cabinet Minister under Gladstone. He was a founder member of the Anti-Corn Law League.

Arnold Bennett, the novelist, who is best remembered for his books about the 'Five Towns' now forming Stoke-on-Trent, died on 27 March 1931.

Yuri Gagarin, the first man to orbit the earth in space, was killed in an air crash in 1968.

Sir Arthur Bliss, English composer, died in 1975.

The first Rugby international, in which Scotland beat England at Edinburgh, was played on 27 March 1871.

Never do anything that you cannot do in the presence of all.

Wise words from a wise woman. This was the birthday, in 1515, of one who came to be known as St. Teresa of Avila, a young woman who devoted her life to the service of God and her neighbours, who travelled Spain founding convents, and whose writings have influenced many people.

Another young woman who made a place for herself in history but for an entirely different reason was Peg Woffington, a talented Irish actress whose beauty, wit and vivacity endeared her to audiences in Dublin and London. She became ill when aged about 43 and died three years later, on 28 March 1760. In 1902 this was the birthday of Dame Flora Robson, the English actress who became famous for her roles portraying historical characters. Today, too, we recall two very famous names from the days of the silent film. Mary Pickford and Douglas Fairbanks were married on 28 March 1920.

This day saw the deaths of two great Russian musicians. Modest Mussorgsky gave up a military career to allow himself more time for composing. He is remembered mainly for his opera *Boris Godunov* and his songs. He died on 28 March 1881, some eight years after the birth of Sergei Rachmaninoff, composer of symphonies, concertos and other orchestral works. Rachmaninoff left Russia in 1917, at the time of the Russian Revolution, and made his home in the United States. He died at Beverley Hills, California, on 28 March 1943.

About that time an American general was making a name for himself commanding US armies in Europe during World War II. Dwight D. Eisenhower later became supreme commander of NATO. In 1952 he was elected President of the United States and four years later was re-elected. Affectionately known as 'Ike', he died on 28 March 1969.

Also on this day. . . .

Sir Joseph Bazalgette, civil engineer, was born in 1819.
Virginia Woolf, English writer, died in 1941.
The Crimean War began in 1854.

Thomas Coram was a Dorset shipwright who settled first in Massachusetts and then London. He is remembered for helping many people in different ways such as forming a colony in Nova Scotia for unemployed artisans. He was very concerned about many abandoned children in London, for whom he founded the Foundling Hospital. Thomas Coram was more thoughtful for others than he was for himself, so that he would have died a pauper had it not been for the care of his friends. He died on 29 March 1751.

Another philanthropist who died on this day, in 1972, was J. Arthur Rank. A member of a flour milling family, he became interested in the film industry and did much to promote British films when Hollywood seemed to have a monopoly. He was chairman of Gaumont-British and of other cinema and television groups linked under the umbrella of the Rank Organisation. He was made a peer, Baron Rank, in 1957. He was also keenly interested in social problems and was an active supporter of the Methodist Church.

Today saw the passing of one of the earliest Methodists. Charles Wesley, who died on 29 March 1788, is remembered especially as a hymn writer. He wrote about 5,500, many of which are well-loved and frequently sung today. He was the brother of John Wesley, the founder of Methodism, and, like his brother, an ordained clergyman in the Church of England. Another Anglican hymnwriter who died on this day, in 1866, was John Keble, vicar of Hursley, near Winchester. He was also a writer and scholar. Keble College, Oxford, was named in his memory.

Another scholar and writer on religious matters to die on 29 March 1772, was Emanuel Swedenborg, a Swedish mathematician who had curious dreams which convinced him that he had special spiritual insight. He made no attempt himself to form a new sect but others did so on the basis of his teachings.

Also on this day. . . .

In 1869, Sir Edwin Landseer Lutyens, architect, was born.
The Royal Albert Hall, London, was opened in 1871.
Sir William Walton, English composer, was born in 1902.

When William Seward, the US Secretary of State, bought Alaska from the Russians on 30 March 1867, for nearly 1½ million pounds there was an outcry from people who thought it a waste of money. Some of them began to think otherwise when gold was discovered there some thirty years later. The gold alone has produced wealth more than fifty times the price paid for Alaska. Add to that the silver, lead, tin, platinum, oil and a useful site for military bases. Seward's purchase was, indeed, a bargain.

George Brummell also spent a fortune, but not so wisely. After a brief army career, he inherited a fortune and entered upon a life as a leader of fashion, earning himself the title of Beau Brummell. His success was phenomenal until he quarrelled with the Prince Regent in 1813. A few years later his fortune had gone and gambling debts forced him to flee to France. It was there that he died in the pauper lunatic asylum at Caen, on 30 March 1840.

Today also saw the death in France, in 1707 of Marshal of France, Sebastian de Vauban, a French military engineer who built many defences round France and played an important part in some military actions.

Marie Le Brun painted numerous portraits of the French royal family in the late 18th Century and her work was very fashionable. Perhaps wisely she left France at the outbreak of the French Revolution, returning in 1805 to Paris. She died on 30 March 1842.

This was the birthday of two very famous artists. Francisco José de Goya, the Spanish artist, known simply as Goya, was the son of a poor farmer but rose, with encouragement, to become a great artist, lithographer and engraver. He was born in 1746. A little over a century later, in 1853, Vincent van Gogh, recognised as one of the greatest Dutch painters, was born.

Anna Sewell painted pictures in words. Her *Black Beauty* is undoubtedly one of the most famous books about a horse. This was her birthday in 1820.

The Moving Finger writes; and having writ
Moves on: nor all thy Piety nor Wit
Shall lure it back to cancel half a Line,
Nor all thy Tears wash out a word of it.

Nothing we do can ever erase or change what has been done. These words are from *The Rubá'iyát of Omar Khayyám*. The words of the 12th Century Persian poet were freely translated by Edward Fitzgerald, whose birthday this was in 1809. It is now regarded as a classic of English literature.

Another English classic is *Jane Eyre,* written by Charlotte Brontë, the eldest of the three daughters of the rector of Hawarth, Yorkshire. Charlotte died on 31 March 1855.

John Donne, who died on 31 March 1631, was the leading poet of the 17th Century and an outstanding churchman and preacher, who attracted huge congregations to the old St. Paul's Cathedral in London. A most unlikely person to become a great preacher was Rodney Smith, born on this day in 1860 in a gypsy caravan in Epping Forest. He grew up to be Gypsy Smith, the evangelist, whose preaching attracted great crowds in Britain and America.

One of the world's greatest athletes, J.C. ('Jesse') Owens, died on 31 March 1980. In May, 1935, he succeeded in breaking six world records in four events within a 45-minute period. In the Berlin Olympics, in 1936, he won four gold medals.

Also on this day. . . .

John Constable, regarded by many as the greatest English artist, died on this day in 1837.

Franz Josef Haydn, the best-known composer in Europe in his day, was born in Austria on this day in 1732.

Robert Wilhelm Bunsen, the German chemist who gave us the Bunsen burner, was born on 31 March 1811.

The Eiffel Tower, the remarkable 300-metre tower in Paris, was completed on 31 March 1889. Its builder, Alexandre-Gustave Eiffel was thereafter nicknamed 'magician of iron'. Another man concerned with iron was the second Abraham Darby of Coalbrookdale, Salop, who died on 31 March 1763.

Some March Events and Commemorations

(see also pp 3–6)

Near middle of Lent Ufton, Berkshire: Bread Dole. Bread is distributed at Ufton Court to residents of the parish.
Third Thursday Market Weighton, Yorkshire: Kiplingcotes Derby, probably the oldest horse race in the world, has been run each year since 1515. It is run through 5 parishes and finishes at Kiplingcotes Farm. Riders, who must weigh more than 10 stone (63.5 kg), are weighed before the race.
22nd Croydon, Surrey: Founder's Day of almshouses of which the foundation stone was laid on 22 March 1618. Occupants of the almshouses, with teachers and boys of Whitgift School, attend the parish church, where a wreath is laid on the tomb of Archbishop Whitgift.
25th Tichborne and Cheriton, Hampshire: Distribution of the Tichborne Dole each year on Lady Day. The 800-year old bequest originated as a request from the dying Lady Mabella Tichborne that her husband would set aside land to provide money for a distribution of bread to the poor. He agreed to give whatever she could traverse whilst a faggot burned. She crawled round 20 acres and this land, still known as The Crawls, provides money to distribute flour to the villagers.
Palm Sunday Hentland, Sellack and King's Capel, Herefordshire: Pax Cake Distribution after morning service attended by the villagers of all three parishes. Each cake, marked with an impression of the Paschal Lamb, is handed out with the words, 'God and Good Neighbourhood'.
During month Stockbridge, Hampshire: Court Leet to appoint officers to control the common land.
Old Bolingbroke, Lincolnshire: Candle auction at the annual parish assembly to allocate grazing rights.

EASTER If Easter is early, the Easter events listed on pages 42–4 and 76 will take place at the end of March instead of during April.

SOME MARCH FAIRS Easter fairs if Easter is early.
First Tuesday St. Buryan, Cornwall.
7th Hingham, Norfolk: Fair by Royal grant of 1264.
Second Thursday Leicester: Cattle fair.

APRIL

April

April is the season when trees and flowers begin to open, so the Romans called this month Aprilis, the name coming from the verb *aperire* (to open). There is a suggestion, too, that it may have come from the name of the goddess Aphrodite. Certainly the Anglo-Saxons named this month after a goddess. It was Eosturmonath, the month of Eostre, goddess of the dawn.

April is renowned for its changeable, showery weather:

April, April,
Laugh thy girlish laughter;
Then, the moment after,
Weep thy girlish tears!

'April', Sir William Watson (1858–1936)

The girlish tears, the April showers, are important for the growing crops, as the old saying reminds us:

March winds and April showers
Bring forth May flowers.

Some farmers may welcome a cold April or may watch the weather about Easter time, which often falls in April. A cold April holds back the crops but fair weather from then onwards should lead to good harvests.

A cold April
The barn will fill.

Fair weather from Easter to Whitsuntide,
Butter will be cheap with cream on the side.

A good deal of rain upon Easter Day
Gives a lot of good grass but little good hay.

It is not only farmers who watch the April weather. This is the month in which many people like to get out into their gardens to begin digging.

April is a month for bird migration. Winter visitors will have made for the colder lands, whilst swallows, martins, nightingales and cuckoos will be arriving from warmer climes.

When will the first cuckoo be heard? For many years, people have listened for the sound of the cuckoo, usually regarded as the herald of spring and the warmer weather.

In April the cuckoo shows her bill,
In May she sings all day.
In June she alters her tune,
In July she'll fly away.

But when in April? One old saying goes:

On the 3rd of April the cuckoo comes in and the nightingale

However, 14 April is often known as 'First Cuckoo Day', when, according to tradition, the cuckoo is released by the Old Woman from her basket at Heathfield Fair, Sussex, to fly up England carrying the warmer days with her.

In the month of Averil
The gawk comes o'er the hill,
In a shower of rain;
And in the middle of June
He turns his tune again.

Welcome as she may be, the name cuckoo has come to indicate one who is foolish. Perhaps it is because of the cuckoo's nesting habits. But is it the cuckoo that is the fool? Or is it the bird left 'holding the baby'? April starts with the day of fools!

April may have its many moods but it is the month when so much of nature is beginning to emerge after winter. Robert Browning (1812–1889) begins his *Home Thoughts from Abroad* by reflecting on April in his homeland.

Oh, to be in England
Now that April's there,
And whoever wakes in England
Sees, some morning, unaware,
That the lowest boughs and the brushwood sheaf
Round the elm tree bole are in tiny leaf,
While the chaffinch sings on the orchard bough
In England — now!

Easter

Easter frequently falls during the month of April. The date is dependent upon the moon and is a day known in the Church as a 'movable feast'. The earliest it can be is 22 March and the latest is 25 April. It comes at the end of the forty-day period known as Lent, formerly a period of strict fasting.

Although it is the most important of the Christian festivals, Easter has many of its roots in ancient pagan customs, which were associated with the spring equinox and sun worship. The name of the festival comes from Eostre, the goddess of Spring.

On Good Friday it is customary to eat Hot Cross Buns which are accepted today as a reminder of the death of Jesus Christ on the cross. But, long before Christian times, spiced bread was eaten to bring good fortune. The ancient Greeks stamped theirs with a horned symbol as an offering to Astarte. It has long been considered lucky to eat at least one spicy Hot Cross Bun on Good Friday.

Services are held in many churches on Good Friday, some lasting three hours, the duration of Christ's suffering on the cross. Elsewhere, passion plays may be performed or perhaps a Pace-egg Play. This is a mummers' play associated with Easter. The hero, St. George, battles against evil characters. A comic character, Tesspot carries a basket into which, at one time, eggs were put. Nowadays money is given instead. The Pace-egg play is performed in several places in Yorkshire.

Good Friday morning is the time for the Marbles Championship at Tinsley Green, Sussex, the survivor of a popular pastime once played in many villages. Forty-nine marbles are placed in a six-foot concrete ring covered with sand. Each competitor in a team of six tries to knock out of the ring as many as possible with his glass 'tolley'.

The championship is played under the rules of the British Marbles Control Board, which are the same rules as those used at the beginning of the seventeenth century, including ending promptly at noon.

Many of the recreational activities of Easter take place on Good Friday or Easter Monday but, here and there, one can find on the Saturday, a special event. In Bacup, Lancashire, it is the day when the Britannia Coconut Dancers perform over a distance of seven miles across the town. Theirs is a form of Morris dance but they have wooden discs, or 'nuts', which are clapped together as they dance. They blacken their faces and wear red, white and black costumes.

In some places, late night vigils are kept on Holy Saturday and fires kindled. As Easter Day dawns, a paschal candle is lit and the people shout for joy, 'Christ is risen'. For Christians it is the resurrection of Jesus Christ that makes Easter the most joyful and most important festival of the year.

Easter Day is the time for exchanging Easter eggs. The egg has always been regarded as a symbol of new life and it was only natural that this should become associated with the Easter story. Eggs had once been one of the foods forbidden during Lent, which was why they were eaten up in pancakes. So, at the end of Lent, people gave eggs as presents to their friends and servants. They were usually decorated, which was thought to bring good fortune. Nowadays we give chocolate eggs in bright wrappings instead. There are interesting customs in many lands concerning Easter eggs.

Sometimes people have chocolate Easter bunnies. This is a modern error. The animal should be the hare, which was the animal sacred to the goddess Eostre.

It is also the custom for many people to put on new clothes for Easter. People of many religions do this at their festivals as a sign of renewal. Perhaps, too, it was a very good idea in the past to put on new clothes at Easter after going unwashed and sprinkled with ashes during Lent.

Some of the greatest displays of clothes are those to be seen at the Easter Parades in London, Atlantic City and New York City, where people display the latest fashions and Easter bonnets in parades of floats, bands and other attractions which continue to create a colourful, carefree occasion.

Easter Monday, the holiday following the festival, was naturally a time for activities of various kinds, many of them associated with the Easter story.

Egg-rolling is an old-established Easter pastime and usually takes place on Easter Monday, though sometimes on the Sunday. Children and young people gather at the top of a grassy slope armed with brightly-coloured hard-boiled eggs which are then rolled down the slope. As the eggs crack they are withdrawn from the game and eaten. The winner is the one whose egg travels furthest or remains unbroken for the longest time. One of the biggest egg-rolling events is in Avenham Park, Preston, there oranges are rolled as well as eggs. There is another orange-rolling event on Dunstable Downs on Good Friday. It is believed that these events originated as symbols of the rolling away of the stone from the tomb of Jesus Christ.

A favourite Easter Monday pastime up to the end of the nineteenth century was Lifting or Heaving, supposedly commemorating the rising from the dead of Jesus; though this may be an example of Christianising a pagan rite which was intended to encourage crops to grow tall.

Village lads carried a decorated chair to each house, where each woman was made to sit on the chair and be lifted three times into the air, for which she paid with money or a kiss. The ladies had their turn to reverse the roles on Easter Tuesday.

However, the charming custom became marred by hooliganism and lifting provided an excuse to grab, lift and kiss any unfortunate woman on the Monday or man on Tuesday.

There are surviving Easter Monday games and customs here and there but nowadays it is more a day for football matches or other sporting fixtures.

The second Monday and Tuesday after Easter form the season of Hocktide. It was once a time when men on one day and women on the other captured members of the opposite sex and demanded as a ransom, money, which was paid into the parish funds. Such celebrations declined and died out long ago, the one surviving reminder of this happy holiday being at Hungerford in Berkshire.

1 April

The first of April, some do say,
Is set apart for All Fools' Day,
But why people call it so,
Nor I nor they themselves do know.
Poor Richard's Almanack (1760)

Today is All Fools' Day, the day on which, for many years, people have played tricks on others so that they could cause them to be 'April Fools'. How the custom began is uncertain. It is possible that it may have been the last day of festivities when the New Year began on 25 March. It has been suggested, too, that it was a protest at moving New Year from March to the middle of winter. In some parts of the country the April Fool is an April Noddy, a cuckoo or gowk. In Scotland this day may be called Huntigowk Day.

The greatest April Fool hoax took place in 1860, when several hundred people received invitations to attend the ceremony of washing the White Lions at the Tower of London. Admission to the ceremony would be by the White Gate. The crowds arrived, only to discover that there were neither a White Gate nor White Lions. They were all April Fools.

However, all such activities end at mid-day. After that it is the joker who becomes the fool.

April Noddy's past and gone,
You're the fool an' I'm none.

On 1 April 1573, William Harvey was born. After medical training at Padua, Italy, he became a physician at St. Bartholomew's Hospital, London and he served as the personal physician to King James I and King Charles I.

He is remembered especially for his work which proved that blood circulated round the body with the heart acting as a pump. His book, *Essays on the Motion of the Heart and Blood in Animals,* is one of the most important medical books.

Prince Otto von Bismarck, the 'Iron Chancellor', founder and first Chancellor of the German Empire, was born on 1 April 1815.

On 1 April 1918, the Royal Flying Corps and the Royal Naval Air Service amalgamated to form the Royal Air Force.

On 2 April 1801, Nelson raised his telescope to his blind eye and said, 'You know I have only one eye — I have a right to be blind sometimes. I really do not see the signal.' The signal was an order given by the admiral, at the Battle of Copenhagen, to break off the action. Nelson destroyed the Danish fleet and so continued to build his reputation as a successful naval officer.

Today is the birthday of a number of people whose lives are differing success stories. Charles, son of Pepin the Short, was born on 2 April 742. He became Charles I, King of the Franks, conqueror and fighter for Christendom, who gained the titles of Charlemagne ('Charles the Great') and Holy Roman Emperor.

Hans Christian Andersen was born in Odense, Denmark, on 2 April 1805. He came from a poor family, had little education and not enough talent for the theatre, which he would have enjoyed making his career. A play he wrote and two novels were failures but the wealth of folklore learned at an early age proved the basis for his success as a writer of fairy tales.

William Holman Hunt, who was born in London on 2 April 1827, was not a success as a painter at first but he made his reputation in 1854 with his famous portrayal of Christ, 'The Light of the World'.

Emile Zola, born in Paris on 2 April 1840, who came from a poor family, worked as a clerk and in the sales department of a publishing house. He became a controversial but very successful novelist and critic.

Sir Alec Guinness, born in London on 2 April 1914, was a copywriter for an advertising agency. He gave it up for a stage career in 1934 and became one of the greatest recent British actors of stage and screen.

Richard Cobden, the politician who fought for the repeal of the Corn Laws, died on 2 April 1865.

On 2 April 1982, Argentinian troops invaded the Falkland Islands. British forces liberated the islands by 15 June.

This day, in 1882, marked the end of a legend in America. Robert Ford pulled a gun and shot Thomas Howard in the back of the head. Thomas Howard was none other than the legendary outlaw and bank robber Jesse James; and the killer was one of his former gang, who wanted the 10,000 dollar reward that had been offered. Jesse James began his life of crime after the American Civil War and remained an outlaw for 16 years, robbing banks, trains, stage-coaches, stores and individuals. His gang boasted, however, that they never robbed a friend, a preacher, a Southerner, or a widow. Many of the stories of Jesse James were exaggerated or romanticised for the benefit of those who liked to read a blood-thirsty tale of the Wild West.

Another legend of the Wild West began on this day in 1860. The first Pony Express riders set out to carry their messages from St. Joseph, Missouri to Sacramento, California. Riders covered the 1,800 mile (2,897 km) journey in about 10 days, changing horses six to eight times between each of the 157 stations. Two of the most famous riders were 'Buffalo Bill' Cody and 'Pony Bob' Haslam. The Pony Express lasted only 18 months. There were not enough subscribers, many riders were killed and the new transcontinental telegraph system proved a much quicker method of sending messages.

> *It has been a matter of marvel to my European readers, that a man from the wilds of America should express himself in tolerable English. I was looked upon as something new and strange, in literature.*

Washington Irving, the 'father of American literature', who was born on 3 April 1783, wrote this of himself.

The first Prime Minister of Britain, Sir Robert Walpole, took up this office on 3 April 1721; and on this date in 1978 the first broadcast direct from the House of Commons was made.

Also on this day. . . .
George Herbert, poet and hymn writer, was born in 1583.
Bishop Reginald Heber, hymn writer, died in 1826.
Sir James Clark Ross, Arctic and Antarctic explorer, died in 1862.
Johannes Brahms, German composer, died in 1897.
Haile Selassie was proclaimed Emperor of Ethiopia in 1930.

Spectators at the finish of the Paris-Bordeaux road race in 1895 were very interested in one of the cars. It had not won the race but it did have something that the other cars hadn't — pneumatic tyres. It was the idea of the two brothers André and Edouard Michelin, who had set up as tyre manufacturers and established the Michelin Tyre Company in 1888 to make cycle tyres. They were the first to use demountable pneumatic tyres on cars and the first to market them successfully. By the time André died on 4 April 1931, Michelin was an international name in the motoring world.

Two years earlier, on 4 April 1929, another motoring pioneer died. He was Carl Benz, the engineer who designed and built the first practical motor car to be driven by an internal-combustion engine. This three-wheeled vehicle first ran in 1885. The company Benz founded built its first four-wheeled car in 1893 and a racing car six years later. In 1929, the Benz and Daimler companies merged to form Daimler-Benz, makers of Mercedes-Benz cars, which have a high reputation for quality.

Karl Wilhelm Siemens was born in Germany on 4 April 1823. He studied chemistry, physics and mathematics before moving to London, where later he became Sir William Siemens. He invented a water heater and a new kind of furnace. In 1863, he opened a cable-making factory and his firm laid the first cable, in 1875, between Britain and the United States.

Grinling Gibbons, one of the world's greatest decorative wood carvers (p. 199), was born in Rotterdam on 4 April 1648.

Around the world. . . .

That is just what Sir Francis Drake did. After his voyage round the world he was knighted by Queen Elizabeth I on his ship, *Golden Hind* at Deptford, London, on this day in 1581.

On 4 April 1968, in Memphis, Tennessee, Martin Luther King, American civil rights leader, was shot dead by an assassin.

Also in America, on this day in 1949, the North Atlantic Treaty (setting up NATO) was signed in Washington.

The first BBC broadcast for schools was on 4 April 1924.

5 April

Today is the end of the fiscal year in Britain, when government and local government accounts are closed and a clean sheet started tomorrow.

It was appropriate that Sir Winston Churchill should choose such a day to resign as Prime Minister in 1955. He had a very distinguished parliamentary career after his first election to Parliament in 1900, holding many important offices. His finest hour was during World War II when, as Prime Minister, he inspired people, instilling courage and determination. He had been Prime Minister again for the four years up to his resignation, after which he continued as a Member of Parliament.

Another Prime Minister to resign on 5 April was Sir Harold Wilson. He became a Labour Party MP in 1945 and was Prime Minister from 1964 to 1970 and 1974 to 1976, the year in which he resigned. He, too, retained his seat in the House of Commons after his resignation.

One of the French revolutionary leaders had no opportunity to resign: he was guillotined on 5 April 1794. Georges Danton once dominated the revolutionary government but became increasingly moderate, disapproving of the Reign of Terror. This led to his arrest and death.

Some of today's people. . . .

Elihu Yale, benefactor of Yale University, born in 1649.
Ludwig Spohr, violinist, composer and conductor, born 1784.
Robert Raikes, Sunday-school pioneer, died in 1811.
Joseph, Lord Lister, surgeon, medical scientist, born in 1827.
Algernon Swinburne, poet and humanist, born in 1837.
Booker Washington, educator and reformer, born in 1856.
Pandita Ramabai, Indian women's champion, died in 1922.
Howard Hughes, aviator and film producer, died in 1976.
Edward Young, poet, dramatist and author, who died on this day in 1765, left these words of wisdom:

Be wise with speed; a fool at forty is a fool indeed.

Be wise today; 'tis madness to defer.

Richard I, the Lion-Heart, King of England, died on 6 April 1199, of wounds received during the siege of a castle in Aquitaine. He is seen as one of the most romantic of English kings due to his many battles in the crusades and elsewhere. However, of his ten years as king, only a few months were spent in his kingdom and his adventuring cost his country a fortune.

Raffaello Sanzio was born on 6 April 1483 and was to become one of the greatest painters and architects of the Italian Renaissance period. He is usually known simply as Raphael. He spent some time in Siena and Florence but was called by Pope Julius II to Rome, where he spent the rest of his life, working on the reconstruction of the Basilica of St. Peter and producing some fine works of art. He died on the anniversary of his birth on 6 April 1520.

Meanwhile, one of the greatest German artists of this period was also busy, producing many forms of art. Albrecht Dürer sought perfection in all his art forms and the results were outstanding. His watercolours of flowers and grasses are truly masterpieces. His engravings and woodcuts became widely acclaimed and his 'Praying Hands' is seen in many homes. Dürer also painted in oils and was Germany's leading portrait painter. He was an illustrator and designer, ready to paint anything, however humble, that was a part of God's creation. Toward the end of his life, he wrote, 'What beauty is I do not know. No one can tell what beauty is but God.' Albrecht Dürer died of fever on 6 April 1528.

From art to music. Oscar Straus, conductor and composer of *The Chocolate Soldier* and other operettas, was born in Austria on 6 April 1870. Igor Stravinsky, leading 20th Century composer of ballet and other music, died on 6 April 1971. André Previn, outstanding modern conductor, was born this day in 1929.

Also on this day. . . .

In 1849, the Koh-i-noor diamond was presented to Queen Victoria. It became the central stone in the queen's state crown in 1937.

In 1874, Harry Houdini, magician and escapologist was born.

In 1909, Robert Peary reached the North Pole.

Let's begin today with a few well-known things — a box of matches for example. Today there are many different matchbox labels, collected by 'phillumenists'. One Japanese phillumenist has collected over half a million different labels. The first box of matches was sold on 7 April 1827, by John Walker of Stockton-on-Tees.

How many people began the day with a plate of Kelloggs — Corn Flakes or one of the other breakfast cereals with that name on the packet? W.K. Kellogg was born on 7 April 1860. For a time he worked with his brother, a physician and health-food pioneer, who developed the idea of dry breakfast cereals. He then went into business, marketing Corn Flakes in a small way but this grew into a large international concern from which W.K. Kellogg became rich. He gave large sums of money for child welfare, schools and other good causes.

After breakfast many people get into a car to drive to work. A Ford perhaps? Henry Ford died on 7 April 1947, having revolutionised the car industry and established one of the largest car manufacturing companies in the world. Mass production methods enabled him to sell his first car the Ford Model T (1908) in large numbers at a low price. He sold 15 million of them up to 1928.

Today's Ford driver may have his problems but he is not likely to be stopped by a highwayman as were coach drivers in days gone by. One of the most famous, Dick Turpin, was an Essex thief and highwayman. Many stories about him are romantic legend. One fact that is certain is that he was hanged for a crime in York — on this day in 1739.

Born on 7 April. . . .
In 1506, St. Francis Xavier, Jesuit missionary to the East.
In 1770, William Wordsworth, Poet Laureate 1843–1850.
In 1891, Sir David Low, outstanding political cartoonist.

And two who died. . . .
In 1614, 'El Greco', Cretan artist, at Toledo, Spain.
In 1891, Phineas T. Barnum, American showman.

Whether or not they like his style of painting, most people would agree that one of the greatest and most influential artists of the 20th Century was Pablo Picasso. From childhood, his drawings showed exceptional artistic talent. From his home in Malaga, he went to study in Barcelona and Madrid before going to live in Paris, where he became famous.

At first he used various styles of art but then developed a new form known as Cubism. His subjects were no longer true to life but greatly distorted. Other artists also produced surrealist paintings but Picasso led the field. His famous large painting 'Guernica', inspired by the Spanish Civil War, was painted in tones of black, grey and white. His 'Dove' lithograph became the symbol of the 1949 World Peace Congress. Picasso died on 8 April 1973, leaving works of art valued at hundreds of million pounds.

An artist of a different kind also died on this day, in 1950. He was Vaslav Nijinsky, whose artistry in ballet made him one of the most famous ballet dancers in Europe. Born in Kiev, he began dancing at the age of nine. In 1909 he joined the ballet of Sergey Diaghilev, travelling to Paris and other European capitals. Nijinsky was a sensation. His leaps were legendary, especially the one in *Le Spectre de la Rose*, in which he disappeared through a window. He danced in all the major ballets, had others written especially for him, and became a choreographer himself. Following a period of captivity in World War I, he became mentally ill and was unable to dance after 1919.

Sonia Henie, who was born on 8 April 1912, also trained as a ballet dancer but she used her artistic talents in a different way giving spectacular performances on ice. She won the world amateur figure skating championship for women for ten consecutive years from 1927 to 1936 and gained three Olympic gold medals. She then toured Europe and America in ice shows and starred in ten movie films.

On 8 April 1941, an experimental aircraft took off. It was the first jet-propelled flight and a triumph for the inventor of the jet engine, Sir Frank Whittle.

In 1513, Ponce de Leon, Spanish explorer, discovered Florida.

On a wintry March day in 1626, Francis Bacon went out to stuff a chicken with snow to see whether this would prevent the flesh going bad. He caught a cold and was taken to a friend's house, where he died on 9 April. To the end, he was searching after knowledge, which was one of his aims in life. In a letter to Lord Burghley in 1591, he wrote; '. . . I have taken all knowledge to be my province.'

Francis Bacon, Baron Verulam, Viscount St. Albans, was one of the cleverest men in the time of Elizabeth I. He was a lawyer, courtier and statesman, with a fine command of the English language. He was a very able prosecutor and, after holding various legal posts, was appointed Lord Chancellor. However, accused of bribery, he was banished from parliament and court. He spent much of the rest of his life in writing books and essays.

A man who made engineering his province was born on 9 April 1806. He was Isambard Kingdom Brunel, a man who had great ability and big ideas. He worked on the Thames Tunnel; he designed bridges and docks; and he became a great railway engineer of the Great Western Railway. He was responsible for building over 1,000 miles (1,609 km) of railway in Britain and used the broad gauge which had the rails 7ft (213 cm) apart. He was also a pioneer of shipping. His *Great Western* (1837) was the first steamship to provide a regular transatlantic service; his *Great Britain* (1843) was the first large vessel to be driven by a screw propellor; and his *Great Eastern* (1858) was the largest vessel yet built. His engineering projects also included improved guns and a complete prefabricated hospital, which was shipped to the Crimea in 1855.

Across the Atlantic, on 9 April 1865, Robert E. Lee, General of the Confederate armies in the American Civil War, surrendered by Appomattox Courthouse to Union General Ulysses S. Grant, so bringing the war to an end.

This was the birthday, in 1898 of Paul Robeson, a popular American Negro actor and singer. He played in *Othello,* the musical *Show Boat* and in films, as well as giving recitals notably of Negro spirituals throughout the world. He fell from favour in America, because of his racial and political ideas.

There are many things that we come to rely upon and perhaps take for granted. There must be millions of people who have tuned in to the chimes of Big Ben when they have wanted to set the time on their own watches and clocks, for the chimes of Big Ben have a reputation for accuracy. Yet it is not Big Ben that is accurate but the clock on the tower of the Houses of Parliament, of which Big Ben is the bell. Big Ben, which took its name from the Commissioner of Works, Sir Benjamin Hall, was cast on 10 April 1858.

Many millions of people have also come to rely, for lots of different reasons, upon a very much smaller object — a safety pin. The patent for the safety pin was taken out in the United States in 1849 by William Hunt and safety pins were first manufactured in New York City on 10 April. Maybe it was not a very spectacular invention but it was a very useful one.

Much more spectacular was the cinematograph, the motion picture camera and projector. Two pioneers were Auguste Lumiére, who died on 10 April 1954, and his brother Louis. Amongst their other achievements, they presented the first newsreel in 1896.

One of the most famous names in the news world is Pulitzer. Pulitzer Prizes have been awarded annually since 1917 for fiction, biography, poetry and other subjects as well as eight for special achievement in journalism. A gift for this purpose was made by Joseph Pulitzer, a Hungarian, born on 10 April 1847, who emigrated to America and, by buying and selling newspaper companies, became one of the most influential and respected American journalists.

News of a different kind was proclaimed by General William Booth, who founded the Salvation Army and took the Good News of Jesus Christ, as well as a great deal of compassion and help, to the poor and needy. This was his birthday in 1829.

This was also the birthday, in 1929, of Mike Hawthorn, who became the first British world champion racing driver. He won a motor cycle race at 18 and turned to sports cars at 21. He retired from racing in 1958 following his world championship but was killed in a road accident soon afterwards.

11 April

One of the great names in the history of Wales is Llywelyn ap Iorwerth, often referred to as Llywelyn the Great. He was a grandson of Owain Gwynedd, the powerful ruler of Gwynedd in North Wales. He had been sent into exile as a child by his uncle, David, but later he deposed David and gained control of nearly the whole of North Wales.

He married the daughter of King John of England but that did not prevent John from invading Wales when he thought that Llywelyn was threatening his possessions in South Wales. Most of Gwynedd was overrun by John but Llywelyn soon won it back. He then sided with the English barons over the sealing of the Magna Carta.

Within a couple of years, the English accepted that Llywelyn controlled almost the whole of Wales but later he was made to withdraw to the North. As an old man Llywelyn passed the reins over to his son, David. When Llywelyn died, on 11 April 1240, he was then described as Prince of Wales — not strictly accurate but most appropriate.

This is also the anniversary of the death, in 1447, of one of the most powerful men in England for almost half a century. He was Cardinal Beaufort. He was the son of John of Gaunt and cousin of Richard II, in whose reign he became Chancellor of Oxford University and Bishop of Lincoln. When his half-brother became Henry IV, Beaufort's power increased. He became Chancellor of England and Bishop of Winchester, one of the richest sees in the country. He made himself even richer by lending money to the crown at good rates of interest.

His prowess in the church was increased when he was made a Cardinal by the Pope. Henry VI came to the throne at the age of eight months and he grew up mentally unstable. Beaufort was, firmly in control of the government from about 1435 until 1443, when he retired from political life.

This was the day, in 1814, when Napoleon Bonaparte, following the defeat of France, abdicated before his exile to Elba.

Also on this day, in 1861, the fall of Fort Sumter led to the outbreak of the American Civil War between the Union (23 Northern States) and the Confederate States (11 Southern States).

Every position must be held to the last man: there must be no retirement. With our backs to the wall, and believing in the justice of our cause, each one of us must fight on to the end.

On 12 April 1918, World War I was at a critical stage and this Order to the British troops was sent out by Earl Haig, Field Marshal and Commander-in-Chief of the British forces.

The pages of history are filled with battles that have been fought not just for conquest but to protect one's possessions or stand by one's ideals.

During the American War of Independence, France and Spain thought to take the opportunity of seizing Britain's colonies in the West Indies. But on 12 April 1782 their combined fleet of 35 warships and 150 merchantmen, commanded by the Comte de Grasse, was intercepted in Saintes Passage between Dominica and Guadeloupe by Admiral Sir George Rodney with 36 ships. The Battle of the Saintes was an important victory for Britain.

It was a strong feeling about slavery and civil rights that led to the outbreak of the American Civil War on 12 April 1861.

One American with his own personal battle to fight was Franklin Delano Roosevelt. A man tipped to be President of the United States, he was struck down with polio and all seemed to be lost. But by sheer determination he fought back and, in 1933, became President. That same fighting spirit enabled him to lead his country through very hard times. He was re-elected President three times and died on 12 April 1945.

Another American of great determination and zeal was Adoniram Judson. Sent as a missionary to Burma, he worked as preacher, evangelist, and translator, establishing churches and schools. At one time he suffered extreme torture in Burmese gaols but later continued his work for the Burmese people until his death on 12 April 1850.

This was also a day of courage and conquest in 1961, when Major Yuri Gagarin of the Russian Air Force became the first person to travel in space. His spacecraft, *Vostok I*, travelling at a maximum speed of 18,000 mph (28,968 km/h), took 89 minutes for the single orbit. Today is celebrated in the USSR as Cosmonauts' Day.

Superstitious people may regard 13 as an unlucky number. It may, of course, be coincidence that things sometimes happen which suggest this to be so. The United States moon missions were undertaken under the name *Apollo*. No doubt some people raised their eyebrows on 13 April 1970, when an explosion in an oxygen tank on *Apollo XIII* brought to an end the mission and nearly cost the lives of the astronauts. On the other hand, perhaps the three considered themselves lucky still to be alive!

This was a good day, in 1962, for millions of seabirds, fish and other marine creatures, for an international agreement was signed by 40 countries to stop oil pollution of seas and beaches. Many millions of creatures have died horribly as a result of oil spillages, especially those resulting from the loss of huge super tankers carrying thousands of tonnes of oil.

It often pays to think of the little things in life. Frank Winfield Woolworth, who was born on 13 April 1852, developed a chain of stores in the United States at which everything was priced at 5 or 10 cents. When Woolworths stores opened in Britain they were 3d and 6d stores. The plan of selling a lot of small, cheap articles paid off so that, when Woolworth died in 1919, his estate was worth about 27 million dollars.

How many people have been greatly moved by the great music and stirring tones of Handel's *Messiah* performed by a large choir? For the first performance of the oratorio, in Dublin on 13 April 1742, Handel had placed at his disposal the entire choirs of two cathedrals — a total of fourteen men and six boys!

The prize for any boxer winning a British championship fight is a Lonsdale Belt, awarded by the National Sporting Club. It takes its name from Lord Lonsdale, the sporting Earl, who died on 13 April 1944.

Richard Trevithick, the Cornish engineer and inventor, who developed steam railway locomotives, was born on 13 April 1771.

Sir Robert Watson-Watt, the Scottish scientist who developed RADAR, was born on this day in 1892.

Richard Neville, Earl of Warwick, was one of the great nobles of the 15th Century. He was exceedingly rich, owner of vast estates and had innumerable retainers. He dressed magnificently and was very popular. His action on the battlefield endeared him to his followers and the capture of some huge Spanish ships made him a hero. He was courageous without a doubt but he was also careful and could hardly be described as loyal. He made a point of owing large sums of money to the citizens of London so that he always had some people anxious for his welfare.

Those were the days of the Wars of the Roses between the House of Lancaster and the House of York. In 1461, Warwick secured the crown for the Yorkist Edward IV. A few years later, he restored the Lancastrian Henry VI. Warwick earned himself the title 'The Kingmaker'. But it was the former who put an end to Warwick's intrigues: the troops of Edward IV killed Warwick at the Battle of Barnet, on 14 April 1471.

Abraham Lincoln was enjoying an evening with his wife at a theatre on 14 April 1865, a few days after the Civil War in America had ended. Lincoln, as President, had led the North in those dark years and was looking forward to rebuilding the nation. It was not to be. A fanatical actor, John Wilkes Booth, shot him in the head. Lincoln, one of the greatest and best-loved American presidents, died the following morning.

This day, in 1951, saw the death of one of the most powerful British trade union leaders of the first half of the 20th Century, Ernest Bevin. He helped organise the General Strike of 1926 and later became a politician, serving in the Cabinet during the war years as Minister of Labour and National Service and, from 1945, as Foreign Secretary.

George Frederick Handel, composer of operas, oratorios and orchestral music, died on 14 April 1759.

This was the birthday, in 1629, of the Dutch mathematician, physicist and astronomer, Christiaan Huygens.

The Highway Code was first published on 14 April 1931.

Early in the morning of 15 April 1912, the Atlantic liner *Titanic* sank on her maiden voyage from Southampton to America. She was the last word in passenger liners and declared to be unsinkable. Radio messages had warned of icebergs ahead and, shortly before midnight on 14 April, one was sighted. But it was too late. The *Titanic* hit the iceberg and began to sink. Because the ship was thought to be unsinkable, there were not enough lifeboats for everyone. A distress signal was not heard by the nearest ship because the radio operator was asleep. By the time the *Carpathia* arrived on the scene, the *Titanic* had disappeared beneath the waves and more than 1,500 of the 2,218 passengers and crew were already lost.

There was not much fear of the naval ships of Portsmouth sinking on this day in 1797. Their crews refused to weigh anchor as a protest against pay and conditions. The Spithead Mutiny was one of several mutinies about that time.

One man who was good at sinking, and no doubt gave others that sinking feeling, was Joe Davis, who spent much of his life sinking billiard and snooker balls, winning the world professional snooker championship a record 15 times, 1927–40 and 1946. This was his birthday in 1901.

Earl Godwin of Wessex, the most powerful man in 11th Century England, died on 15 April 1053; Matthew Arnold, poet, critic and inspector of schools, died this day in 1888; and, in 1925, the great portrait painter, John Singer Sargent died. He once said, 'Every time I paint a portrait I lose a friend.'

Many people lost a friend on 15 April 1889. They were the lepers on the Hawaiian island of Molokai: the friend was Father Damien, who went to help them and died of leprosy himself. He showed something of God in a 'God-forsaken' place.

Guru Nanak, was once told by a Muslim that he was insulting Allah because he slept with his feet toward Mecca. Nanak replied,

> *If you think I do wrong by pointing my feet toward the house of God, then turn them in some other direction where God does not dwell.*

Guru Nanak, founder of the Sikh religion, was born on 15 April 1469.

On 16 April 1245, a fat sixty-year-old Franciscan friar began a journey that could have been very off-putting for a much younger man. He was sent by Pope Innocent IV on a mission to Central Asia to meet the Great Khan, whose people, the Mongols, had invaded Christian lands. The friar, Giovanni da Pian del Carpini, and his companions were received by Güyük, who had just been elected Khan. They handed him a letter from the Pope and received a reply to take back. On the return journey they suffered great hardship from the weather but reached Kiev in June 1247. Carpini's account of his journey, *Mongolia and its people,* is a valuable record of that time by the first European traveller of importance to go there.

This day was the birthday of some people who made a useful contribution to the world.

John Hadley, born on 16 April 1682, was a mathematician and inventor, who produced the first reflecting telescope that was sufficiently accurate to be useful in astronomy.

Sir John Franklin, born in 1786, was the British explorer who proved the existence of the North-west Passage, the Canadian waterway linking the Atlantic and Pacific oceans.

Anatole-François Thibaut, known simply as Anatole France, was born in 1844. One of the greatest French writers of his day, he received the Nobel Prize for Literature in 1921.

Wilbur Wright who, with his brother Orville, produced the first powered aircraft to fly, was born in 1867.

Charlie Chaplin, who made his name in films as the helpless romantic little tramp, was born on 16 April 1889.

This day was the last, in 1828, for Francisco de Goya the Spanish artist of paintings, drawings and engravings.

It also saw the death, in 1850, of Marie Tussaud, the founder of Madame Tussaud's Waxworks exhibition in London. She learned the art of wax modelling from her uncle and, during the Reign of Terror, in France, had the unpleasant job of making death masks, often of her friends, from heads cut off by the guillotine. She moved to England in 1802.

This day in 1746, saw the death of any hopes of Charles Edward Stuart, 'Bonnie Prince Charlie', of gaining the British throne. He was defeated at the Battle of Culloden.

17 April

Dost thou love life? Then do not squander time, for that's the stuff life is made of.

Good advice offered by a man who made good use of time. Whether they were his own words or those of another we do not know, for Benjamin Franklin loved collecting and making up sayings and proverbs, many of which appeared in *Poor Richard's Almanack,* which he published for about 25 years.

He was the fifteenth child of a poor candlemaker in Boston, USA, but became very famous for his scientific work and inventions, including the lightning conductor (p. 136) and bifocal lenses. He spent eighteen years in England before returning to the United States at the time of the War of Independence. After the war, he helped draw up the constitution of the United States. He died on 17 April 1790.

Also on this day. . . .

Martin Luther was excommunicated in 1521.
The religious community of Taizé was founded in 1949.
Nikita Khrushchev, leader of USSR, was born in 1894.
Sir Leonard Woolley, archaeologist, died in 1960.

18 April

Gone with the Wind, one of the most famous films to be made, had its London premiere on 18 April 1940, at the Ritz Cinema, having had its world premiere in Atlanta, Georgia, four months earlier. In spite of air raids on war-time London, the film ran for four years.

Some people who died on 18 April were . . . .

John Foxe, writer of the *Book of Martyrs,* in 1587.
Judge Jeffreys, of the 'Bloody Assizes', in 1689.
Erasmus Darwin, writer and physicist, in 1802.
Albert Einstein, scientist, in 1955.

This was the date of Paul Revere's ride (1775); the birth of Franz von Suppé, composer (1819); San Francisco earthquake (1906).

Today is Primrose Day, so named because of a wreath of primroses sent by Queen Victoria on the death of Benjamin Disraeli. 'His favourite flower', she wrote, meaning the favourite flower of her late husband, Prince Albert. Some mistakenly thought she meant they were Disraeli's favourite.

He was an unusual man to become a British Prime Minister. Born into an Italian Jewish family, he was baptised a Christian. Elected a Member of Parliament in 1837, he became Prime Minister in 1868, when he said, 'Yes, I have climbed to the top of the greasy pole.' He became Prime Minister for a second time in 1874 and accepted a peerage as Earl of Beaconsfield in 1876. He died on 19 April 1881.

Lord Byron was, for a short time, in the House of Lords. He made his maiden speech in 1812, the year in which his great autobiographical poem *Childe Harold's Pilgrimage* was published. He said afterwards, 'I awoke one morning and found myself famous.' Famous he was. He was the most popular poet in London and thousands of copies of his poems were sold. In 1823, he went to Greece, which was then ruled over by Turks. He wanted Greece to be free.

The mountains look on Marathon —
And Marathon looks on the sea;
And musing there an hour alone,
I dreamed that Greece might still be free.

Byron joined the Greek fighters but fell ill and died, on this day in 1824.

Another leader who dreamed of freedom was Konrad Adenauer. He was twice imprisoned by the Nazis, in 1934 and 1944, but became the first Chancellor of the Federal Republic of Germany, in 1949, helping to build the new Germany. He died on 19 April 1967.

Anthony van Diemen also died on 19 April in 1645. He was the Dutch governor of the East Indies after whom Van Diemen's Land (Tasmania) was named by Abel Tasman. Charles Darwin, whose *On the Origin of Species*, a theory of evolution, caused quite a stir, died on 19 April 1882.

King James II of England wanted to win back the crown he had lost in 1688. From France, to which he had fled, he thought he would invade Ireland, then Scotland and finally England. Landing in Ireland, James took his armies to Londonderry, where he expected the governor to let him into the city. The people of Londonderry, led by Rev. George Walker, had other ideas. They closed the gates of the city.

On 20 April 1689, the king's army surrounded the city and a barrier was set up across the river to prevent food reaching the people. But, if James thought he could starve them into surrender, he was mistaken. Although the people suffered great hardship and several thousand died, they held out for 105 days until a ship carrying supplies broke through the barrier.

This was the birthday, in 1808, of one who wished to regain the power and authority which had been taken from his family. He was Charles Louis Napoleon Bonaparte, nephew of the great Napoleon. He tried to seize power in 1836 and in 1840 but was unsuccessful. Then, after a revolution in 1848, he was elected President of France. Four years later, he declared himself Emperor and ruled as a dictator. His downfall came in 1870, when he made war against Prussia, was captured, deposed and later sent to exile in Britain, where he died.

A few years later, on 20 April 1889, another dictator was born. Adolf Schicklgrüber was the son of a customs official in Austria. Later, under the name of Adolf Hitler, he was to found and lead the National Socialist (Nazi) Party in Germany in 1919. His movement gained in strength until, in 1933, Hitler was appointed Chancellor. A year later he became dictator of Germany and soon he was embarking upon the conquest of neighbouring lands, resulting in World War II and Hitler's eventual defeat and suicide.

It was on 20 April 1653 that Oliver Cromwell became a kind of dictator in England by dismissing the Long Parliament. Of the mace, the symbol of Parliament, he said,

What shall we do with this bauble? There, take it away.

Arthur Young, English farming pioneer, died 20 April 1820.

One of the colourful characters to emerge in World War I was Baron Manfred Von Richthofen, the ace German fighter pilot, who was nicknamed the 'Red Baron' or the 'Red Knight' because of his bright red plane. His squadron was referred to as 'Richthofen's Flying Circus'. To the Germans he was a hero: he shot down no less than 79 British aircraft and one Belgian. But fortune does not normally smile on heroes for ever and the Red Baron met his fate on 21 April 1918, when he was shot down by Captain Roy Brown and killed.

This day, in 1142, saw the end of one who was probably the most controversial teacher of his time and the subject of one of the world's celebrated love stories. Peter Abelard was a canon of Notre Dame, in Paris, where he ran a school. There he fell in love with, and secretly married Héloïse, a niece of Canon Fulbert. They had a son. Fulbert ordered Abelard to be castrated and Héloïse to enter a nunnery. Later Abelard was arrested because of his teachings and his writings were ordered to be burned. Some years later he became abbot of a community of nuns founded by Héloïse. At last he was reconciled to the Church and finally buried alongside his Héloïse.

Another story to capture the imagination of many was *Jane Eyre*, the novel written by Charlotte Brontë. Queen Victoria, in her diary wrote, 'Read to Albert out of that melancholy, interesting book, *Jane Eyre* . . .' Charlotte Brontë, eldest daughter of the rector of Haworth, Yorkshire, was born on 21 April 1816.

Popular with people for many years have been the books written by Mark Twain, — *Tom Sawyer, Huckleberry Finn, The Prince and the Pauper* and others. Mark Twain was the pen name of Samuel Langhorne Clemens, who died on 21 April 1910.

Also. . . .

This is the traditional date for the founding of Rome in 753 BC;
Anselm, Archbishop of Canterbury, died in 1109;
Friedrich Froebel, originator of kindergartens, died in 1782;
Queen Elizabeth II of Great Britain was born in 1926;
The Opening of [a new] Parliament was first televised in 1966;
The Royal Victorian Order, an Order of Chivalry to reward personal service to the sovereign, was instituted 21 April 1896.

'Captain Dick' Trevithick proudly drove his steam carriage along Oxford Street, London, to the amazement and wonder of all who saw him. It was the result of several years of experimenting by a clever young engineer. Richard Trevithick was a Cornishman who looked after the pumping engines used in the mines but who saw a future for engines that moved. But that carriage, built in 1802, could not cope with the bumpy roads.

In 1808, Trevithick was back in London, this time with an engine that ran on rails. He had been experimenting in South Wales with a locomotive and trucks. Now he set up a circular railway at Euston with a small locomotive, called *Catch-me-who-can*, that pulled a passenger coach. Thousands of people paid a shilling for a ride, until one day a rail broke and the coach overturned. Although he played no further part in the development of railways, his work on locomotives was of great importance in their history. He died on 22 April, 1833.

Half a century earlier, on 22 April 1778, James Hargreaves died. He, too was an inventor, whose work was to be of great importance in the Industrial Revolution. He was a poor weaver, who had the idea of a machine which could spin several threads of cotton at the same time. He made several of these machines which he called jennies and sold them to support his large family but local spinners in Blackburn, fearing unemployment, smashed those in his house. Hargreaves moved to Nottingham, where he continued building jennies.

This was the birthday of a man who played an important role in another kind of revolution. Vladimir Ilich Ulyanov was born on 22 April 1870. Under the name of Lenin, he inspired the Bolshevik Revolution in Russia and became the first head of the Soviet state.

Other birthdays on 22 April. . . .

In 1707, Henry Fielding, novelist and playwright.

In 1912, Kathleen Ferrier, popular British contralto singer.

In 1916, Yehudi Menuhin, world-famous violinist.

On 22 April 1794, Edmund Bon of Epsom became the first man in Britain to qualify as a Veterinary Surgeon.

I see you stand like greyhounds in the slips,
Straining upon the start. The game's afoot:
Follow your spirit; and, upon this charge
Cry 'God for Harry! England and Saint George!

Today is St. George's Day, the day of the patron saint of England, of soldiers, knights, archers, armourers, Boy Scouts and others, popularised by the story of his slaying the dragon. In fact little is known about him and, in 1969, his status was reduced by the Roman Catholic Church, when he was linked with other saints to be remembered on 1 January.

But, for most people, 23 April will remain St. George's Day, when his flag with its red cross on a white ground will fly proudly as the symbol of England and St. George.

But who was Harry in the verse above? That was King Henry V and the verse is taken from the play *Henry V* by William Shakespeare, who is renowned as England's greatest playwright. St. George's Day is Shakespeare's day too. He was probably born on 23 April 1564, (he was baptised on 26th); and he died on 23 April 1616.

Born and brought up in Stratford-upon-Avon, he went to London, became a member of a theatre company and wrote many plays, which are performed more often and in more places than ever in the past. Ben Jonson was right when he said that Shakespeare 'was not of our age but for all time'. He retired to Stratford-upon-Avon, where, on 23 April 1932, the Shakespeare Memorial Theatre was opened and where, each year, on 23 April, colourful Shakespeare Birthday Celebrations are held. Flags of many nations fly from decorated poles. Local people and visitors walk in procession to lay wreaths on the grave of the 'Bard of Avon'.

So many words of Shakespeare are familiar to large numbers of people but perhaps these, from *Richard II* are particularly appropriate for St. George's Day:

This royal throne of kings, this sceptered isle,
This earth of majesty, this seat of Mars,
This other Eden, demi-paradise,
This fortress built by Nature for herself
Against infection and the hand of war,
This happy breed of men, this little world,

This precious stone set in the silver sea,
Which serves it in the office of a wall,
Or as a moat defensive to a house,
Against the envy of less happier lands.
This blessed plot, this earth, this realm, this England . . .

England! A land of beauty, green pastures, rocky coasts, moorland and mountain. And for those who like to explore, how better than on foot — perhaps along the Pennine Way, the footpath which covers 250 miles (402 km) from Edale in Derbyshire to Kirk Yetholm in Roxburghshire. It was Britains's first long-distance footpath and it was opened on 23 April 1968.

William Wordsworth captured something of the beauty of England in the words of his poems.

I wandered lonely as a cloud
That floats on high o'er vales and hills,
When all at once I saw a crowd,
A host, of golden daffodils.

Wordsworth, who lived most of his life in the English Lake District, described himself as a 'worshipper of Nature'. In 1843 he was appointed Poet Laureate and he died on 23 April 1850 at Grasmere, Cumbria.

Another with an eye for beauty and colour was Joseph Mallord William Turner, the greatest 19th Century British landscape painter. He was born on 23 April 1775, and began painting as a boy. He was a member of the Royal Academy and became rich but he never married and liked to be alone. When he died he left 300 oil paintings and 20,000 water colours and drawings to the nation. Two of his well-known paintings are *Rain, Steam and Speed* and *The Fighting Téméraire* — a colourful picture of the old warship.

The subject of ships is a reminder that this was also the birthday, in 1697, of the great British admiral, Lord Anson (p. 126).

Long before, on 23 April, England lost one of her weaker kings, Ethelred the Unready. He died in 1016.

A great cheer resounded across the waters of Stockholm on 24 April 1961 as some ancient timber broke the surface of the water. The warship *Vasa* had risen from the dead, having lain on the bottom of the harbour for 333 years. *Vasa* had sunk on 10 August 1628 (p. 206) and remained lost until 1956, when she was discovered by Anders Franzen. There followed the long, slow work of taking every precaution to ensure the raising of the ship. The result of their labours is that *Vasa* now rests securely under cover in the Vasa Museum, visited by many tourists each year as the restoration work continues.

There was nothing attractive or historical about the *Spray*. She was a little 9–ton sloop, 36 feet (11 m) long and a derelict hulk when she was bought by Captain Joshua Slocum, who spent over a year and 554 dollars to make her fit for sea. Having done so, he set sail from Boston, USA, on 24 April 1895, on the first single-handed voyage round the world. It took him nearly 3¼ years to complete the journey.

Robinson Crusoe was not so fortunate on his voyage! Most people are familiar with his adventures after being wrecked on a desert island. *Robinson Crusoe* is the most famous of several books written by Daniel Defoe, who died on 24 April 1731. This day was the birthday, in 1815, of another famous author, Anthony Trollope.

Born on 24 April 1743, was Edmund Cartwright whose wool-combing machine and power loom were important inventions during the 18th Century Industrial Revolution.

Today is St. Mark's Eve, one of the evenings on which young ladies would try to find out about their lovers. One custom was to put nuts on the hearthstone and say:

If you love me, pop and fly;
If not, lie there silently.

In some places people kept the St. Mark's Eve vigil in the church porch between 11 pm and 1 am, expecting to see the ghosts of anyone who would die during the coming year.

I have no more right to the name of a poet than a maker of mousetraps has to that of an engineer.

So wrote William Cowper of himself in a letter to a friend not long after his ballad *The Journey of John Gilpin* was being popularly sung all over London. He was one of the most widely read poets of his day and, whilst living at Olney, Buckinghamshire, where the Revd. John Newton was curate, he wrote some well-known hymns which have helped many people. Cowper himself had many problems including attacks of melancholy and mental illness. He had been in a state of despair for several years when he died on 25 April 1800. Another hymnwriter, John Keble, was born on 25 April 1792.

I was by birth a gentleman, living neither in any considerable height, nor yet in obscurity. I have been called to several employments in the nation, — to serve in parliaments, — and (because I would not be over tedious) I did endeavour to discharge the duty of an honest man in those services, to God, and His people's interest, and of the Commonwealth . . . .

Oliver Cromwell, who was born on 25 April 1599, in Huntingdon, spoke thus of himself to the First Parliament of the Protectorate, in 1654. Elected to Parliament in 1628, he was one of the commanders of the parliamentary army during the Civil War and led the country after the execution of King Charles I until he, himself, died in 1658.

This was the birthday, in 1874, at Bologna, Italy, of Guglielmo Marconi, who studied physics and invented one of the world's most important means of communication, radio telegraphy. Having transmitted signals over short distances, he became the first to send one across the Atlantic (1901). He was awarded a Nobel Prize for Physics in 1909.

Another birthday today is that of Ella Fitzgerald. Born in 1918, she became world famous in the mid-20th Century as a popular jazz, blues and scat singer.

Also on 25 April. . . .

Jacob van Heemskerck, Dutch admiral and explorer, died 1607.
Sir Marc Isambard Brunel, engineer, was born in 1769.
The guillotine was first used, in 1792, in Paris.
Work began, in 1859, on the cutting of the Suez Canal.

'Blind Jack of Knaresborough' was a remarkable man who achieved far more than many a sighted person. Indeed, some of the things he did seem almost unbelievable. Who would imagine a blind man fighting in the army? Or driving a stage-coach? Or building 185 miles (297 km) of good roads and several bridges?

John Metcalf was left blind at the age of six as a result of smallpox but that did not prevent him from climbing trees or learning to play the violin. He fought in the battles of Falkirk and Culloden — and he did a bit of smuggling. It is, however, as a road-builder that he is especially remembered, laying good roads over poor land and tapping the surface with his stick to ensure that they were sound. His methods were adopted by other famous road-builders. John Metcalf retired from this at the age of 70 but had no wish to remain idle. He bought a farm and ran it for twenty-two years until he died on 26 April 1810.

John James Audubon used his eyes to observe the birds around him and to make accurate drawings of them. He was born on 26 April 1785, the illegitimate son of a French naval officer in the West Indies. As a boy, in Paris, he began drawing birds and, when sent to the United States, continued this interest. His business ventures were unsuccessful but his art work prospered. He painted portraits and gave drawing lessons as a livelihood — and he continued to draw birds. These hand-coloured drawings, of all known species of North American birds were published in four volumes of *The Birds of North America*.

A good eye for detail is also needed for the waxwork effigies to be seen in Madame Tussaud's. It was on this day, in 1928, that Madame Tussaud's new building opened in London, to remain one of the tourist attractions of the capital.

A man with an eye for business was Alfred Krupp. Born in Essen on 26 April 1812, he worked in the cast steel factory founded by his father, perfected the means of making rails and railway wheels, manufactured weapons such as field guns and supplied arms to 46 nations.

In 1937, Guernica, Spain, was destroyed by aircraft.

There are times when we sit enthralled as we listen to a great organist, who is able to make the organ speak with so many voices as he opens one bank of stops or adjusts by opening or closing one or two here and there. How does he manage to play the tunes on not just one manual (keyboard) but on several and with his feet as well as his hands? And if we are amazed at the skill of the organist, what of the organ builder?

The greatest organ builder in Britain in the 19th Century was born on 27 April 1821. Henry Willis was not only a clever designer but one who took the greatest care over the craftsmanship that went into the building of them. He was not just an organ builder: he learned to play well and spent most of his life as a church organist. Having gained a good reputation by building the organ for the Great Exhibition in the Crystal Palace, he built or rebuilt about 1,000 organs.

To music of a different kind . . . .

The green grass is bowing,
The morning wind is in it,
'Tis a tune worth thy knowing
Though it change every minute.

. . . . just a thought about the world of nature by the American poet and essayist, Ralph Waldo Emerson, who died on 27 April 1882.

For Edward Whymper, the voice of nature was not in the grass but the call of the mountains. Born on 27 April 1840, he was the first man to climb the Matterhorn in the Alps and spent some time climbing other mountains in the Alps as well as in the Andes and the Rockies. His books about his mountaineering are illustrated with his own engravings.

Also on this day: Ferdinand Magellan, explorer, was killed in 1521; Samuel Morse, inventor of the Morse Code was born in 1791; General Ulysses S. Grant was born in 1822.

On 27 April 1818, the Order of St. Michael and St. George was instituted, normally for loyal service in the British Empire and subsequently the Commonwealth.

When President Charles de Gaulle of France resigned on 28 April 1960, it marked the end of the political career of one of the outstanding and colourful leaders of the 20th Century. He had served with distinction in World War I and was a general in command of a tank division in the early days of World War II. When France was overrun, de Gaulle moved to London, where he took charge of the Free French forces and formed a council to be responsible for French colonies overseas. When the allied forces entered Paris, in 1945, General de Gaulle was amongst the first. Later he retired to his country home.

The years that followed were unsettled ones. There were many changes of government and there was conflict with Algeria, which was one of the French colonies in north Africa. There seemed to be only one leader to whom France could turn — Charles de Gaulle. He was invited to become President and he helped to restore a sound government. He was soon seen to be a leader with a strong personality, a great deal of determination and an insistence that his views should be heeded. His resignation, some eighteen months before his death, followed his failure to win a national referendum.

On this day in 1936, Farouk succeeded his father, King Fuad as king of Egypt at the age of 16. He inherited and continued a state of rivalry between the crown and the popular Wafd Party. There were lots of internal disputes and rivalries; and Farouk was not always wise in his decisions. At last the military leaders lost patience and, led by Gamal Abdul Nasser, they ousted Farouk in 1952. He lived in exile until his death in 1965.

Johann Friedrich Struensee also had problems with others in authority. The difference was that he had more-or-less made himself ruler of Denmark in the early part of the 18th Century. The king was mentally unstable and Struensee, a German doctor, was chosen to accompany him on a tour. He became court physician, dominated the king, abolished the council of state, became the queen's lover, and accepted the title of Count.

Count Struensee introduced many liberal reforms but he angered some officials who conspired against him. He was arrested and later tortured to death on this day in 1772.

This was the birthday, in 1889, of Antonio de Oliveira Salazar. He became Prime Minister of Portugal in 1932. In the following year he proclaimed a new constitution, making himself President and virtual dictator, until his death in 1970, of a police state with press censorship and no room for opposition.

Following a Fascist march on Rome in 1922, Benito Mussolini became the first of Europe's Fascist dictators. In 1935, he set about the conquest of Abyssinia and later overran Albania. After the fall of France in 1940, he aligned with Hitler against the allies. Italy was invaded in 1943. Mussolini was overthrown and imprisoned but later rescued by German parachutists. On 28 April 1945, he tried to escape with his mistress to Switzerland but was captured and shot by his fellow countrymen.

Another leader to be overthrown on 28 April was Captain William Bligh. He was captain of HMS *Bounty*, a ship which had been sent to Tahiti to load breadfruit trees for replanting in the West Indies. In 1789, the ship had sailed as far as Tonga (Friendly Islands) when the master's mate, Fletcher Christian, led a mutiny and seized the ship. Captain Bligh and 18 others were set adrift (p. 135), whilst the *Bounty* was sailed on to Pitcairn Island, the mutineers remaining undiscovered there for many years.

A much more peaceful, yet very adventurous voyage, began on this day in 1947. It was made on a raft made of balsa wood and named *Kon-Tiki* after a legendary Inca god. It was the brainchild of Norwegian scientist Thor Heyerdahl, who wanted to prove the possibility that the ancestors of the Polynesian people could have sailed from South America. His voyage from Peru to the South Pacific Tuamotu Islands took 101 days. *Kon-Tiki* is preserved in an Oslo Musuem.

It was on this day, in 1801, that Anthony Ashley Cooper, later Lord Shaftesbury, was born. Without doubt he was one of the greatest reformers of the 19th Century and is remembered in connexion with many reforms concerning climbing boys and conditions in factories and mines. He did much, in many ways, to help children and the poor.

This was the birthday of two well-known and well-loved British conductors.

Sir Thomas Beecham ('Tommy') was born on 29 April 1879, the son of the millionaire pill and medicine manufacturer. He did not attend a school of music but became a conductor in 1906, then spent his life in encouraging an interest in music in many ways. In 1947, he founded the Royal Philharmonic Orchestra. He is remembered for his many abilities, including conducting without a music score.

Sir Malcolm Sargent, who was born on 29 April 1895, trained as an organist but made his debut as a conductor at a Promenade Concert in 1921. He enjoyed great popularity as a conductor both at home and abroad and is especially remembered by many for his lively conducting at the 'last night of the Proms' in the years prior to his death in 1967.

For many years, Michiel de Ruyter 'called the tune' in a different sense. He was a Dutch sailor who went to sea as a cabin boy but rose to be a captain in the Dutch navy by the age of 28. During the naval wars between the English and the Dutch, he had his defeats but also successes. In 1666, as Admiral-in-chief, he held his own against Monk and Prince Rupert: in the following year he actually sailed up the Medway, where he burned some British ships at Rochester. He had more successes in 1672 and 1673. In 1675, he sailed for the Mediterranean to fight for the Spaniards against the French. In his second battle he was wounded, and he died at Syracuse on 29 April 1676.

Emperor Hirohito of Japan was born on 29 April 1901, the 124th in a direct line of Emperors held to be divine. After the end of World War II, Hirohito renounced his divinity and became a constitutional ruler with a democratic government.

The master of suspense, Sir Alfred Hitchcock, director of many thrilling films (p. 209), died on 29 April 1980.

Events of the day. . . .

Joan of Arc entered Orleans with an advance guard in 1429.
The Germans in Italy surrendered unconditionally in 1945.
Also in 1945 the famous 'Peace' rose was so named.

30 April

This night in Germany is known as Walpurgisnacht, the night that has long been associated with witchcraft and superstition at the beginning of summer, much as some people remember such things at Hallowe'en, the end of summer, just six months later. The ancient beliefs were associated with St. Walburga, whose remains were transferred on this day from Heidenheim to Eichstatt. St. Walburga was a nun from Wimborne, Dorset, who went with St. Boniface to Germany in the 8th Century and later became head of a double monastery, living there until her death. So, by coincidence, an English saint became associated with and gave her name to a night when evil was abroad.

Perhaps it is appropriate that this was the day on which one of the most evil men in Germany in this century came to the end of his life, in 1945. Adolf Hitler, founder of the National Socialist (Nazi) Party, gained complete power and became dictator of Germany in 1933, then turned his attention to neighbouring countries, so sparking off World War II. His 'new order' led to the extermination of Jews and others. By 1945 the war was nearly over. The man who had caused untold suffering or death for millions knew he was defeated. On 29 April, he married his mistress, Eva Braun, and on this next day they committed suicide.

Still in Germany, this was the birthday, in 1777, of Carl Friedrich Gauss, one of the greatest mathematicians to have lived. He also studied electricity and magnetism besides being professor of astronomy and director of the observatory at the University of Gottingen.

This was the birthday, in 1602, of William Lilly. He looked at the stars not as an astronomer but an astrologer, making many predictions, which brought him fame and fortune.

On 30 April 1870, Franz Lehar, composer of operettas such as *The Merry Widow* and of other music, was born. Edouard Manet, French impressionist painter, died in 1883.

The Vietnam War, 1965–1975, ended on this day.

Near beginning of month Draycott-in-the-Clay, Staffordshire: Egg Rolling and Pace-Egg Play.
About the 5th London: John Stow's Quill Pen Ceremony. In St. Andrew Undershaft church, Leadenhall Street, a new quill is placed in the hand of the statue of Stow, the antiquary of London, on or near the anniversary of his death in 1605.
First Sunday after the 6th Tatworth, Somerset: Candle Auction for the annual use of a meadow. Granted to the last to bid before the candle goes out.
Last Sunday London: Tyburn Walk. Annual procession from the site of the old Newgate Prison to the site of Tyburn gallows, the route taken by many who were hanged there.

EASTERTIDE (see pp. 42–4) Also:
Easter Monday Winchelsea, Sussex: Proclamation of Mayor.
Tuesday after Easter Bristol, Avon: Distribution of 'Tuppenny Starvers' — large buns given to choirboys of St. Michael's Church.
Wednesday after Easter Keevil, Wiltshire: Tayler Charity service and distribution of buns.
Thursday after Easter Ratcliff Culey, Leicestershire: Spring setting the lanes — selling grass verges for animal grazing.
Saturday after Easter Bideford, Devon: Manor Court meets annually to hear suggestions for improving the town.

SOME APRIL FAIRS
Easter fairs in various places
23rd (or day either side) Fordington, Dorset: Charter fair with sheep roasting and skittles matches.
Some Spring fairs or May fairs are brought forward to April.

SOME AGRICULTURAL AND OTHER SHOWS
Ayr, National Pig Fair, National Shire Horse Show, National Stallion Show, Spring Potato event, Badminton Horse Trials.

MAY

The name May could have come either from a goddess named Maia or from the word *maiores* (elders), for it was during this month that old people were honoured by the Romans.

For the ancient Celtic people, the first day of May was the first day of summer. It was Beltane, 'Bel's Fire', when bonfires were lit to help the sun regain its strength, when cattle were driven between the flames to purify them and protect them from disease, and when sacrifices to the gods were made by the Druids with prayers for a fruitful year.

In some ways, May is still regarded as the beginning of summer and people enjoy the warmer weather, but a cold spell with frosts is not unusual and an old saying gives warning:

Ne'er cast a clout till May is out.

By this time all the cereal crops should have been planted for it is too late to do so in May. Crops are then liable to be attacked by frit fly:

Who sows in May gets little that way.

Yet, for other 'harvests', May is a good beginning:

A swarm of bees in May
Is worth a load of hay.
A swarm of bees in June
Is worth a silver spoon.
A swarm of bees in July
Isn't worth a fly.

Bees need a long summer in which to store up sufficient food for the winter. Nowadays, bee keepers can compensate with artificial feeding. But the sound of the bees and the song of the birds are just part of the scene which heralds summer and warms the heart to the world around.

In May I go a-walking to hear the linnet sing,
The blackbird and the throstle, a-praising God the King;
It cheers the heart to hear them, to see the leaves unfold,
And the meadows scattered over with buttercups of gold.

There is, indeed, something special about May which singles it out from other months. It begins and ends with holidays, having May Day, though not celebrated festively as once it was, on the first Monday and the Spring Bank Holiday on the last Monday. Other festivals and merry-making fall between.

But the merriest month in all the year
Is the merry month of May
'Robin Hood and the Three Squires'

The sun is set, the spring is gone —
We frolic while 'tis May.
'Ode on the Spring', Thomas Gray

The month of May was come, when every lusty heart
beginneth to blossom, and to bring forth fruit.
'Morte d'Arthur, Sir Thomas Malory

In former years the May festival began early, young men and women making their way to the woods soon after midnight to gather the branches and flowers that were to be used to decorate the village and build the bower for the May Queen. In many places a young tree would be felled so that it could be set up as a Maypole, reminiscent of the tree that stood in the centre of the Celtic fires. On the way back, the young women were sure to bathe their faces in the morning dew believing this would help give a good complexion and protection from certain illnesses.

The greatest honour for any young lady was to be chosen as Queen of the May. She represented Flora, the Roman goddess of flowers, whose festival, Floralia, fell at this time of the year. From her throne, she was able to watch the fun of the Maypole dancing, the antics of the Green Man, the thrusts of the swordsman, archery contests and any other frolics or amusements that were taking place, perhaps followed by an ox roasting or similar feast.

Many of the May Day customs were associated with the death of winter and birth of summer, the encouragement of the spirits that made things grow and the driving out of evil. May Day was always a happy day.

Come, lasses and lads, get leave of your dads
And away to the Maypole hie,
For every he has got him a she,
And the fiddler's standing by.

Dancing around the maypole in days of old was not colourful dancing with ribands as has been seen in more recent times. It was a boisterous, noisy dance, similar in many respects to the Morris Dance and serving the same purpose, to arouse or drive out the spirits of the earth. May is the month when the Morris men are to be seen in many parts of the country as they begin their season of dancing which brings enjoyment to a great many people.

The first of May is Garland Day,
So please remember the garland;
We don't come here but once a year,
So please remember the garland.

This Garland Day verse from Hampshire is typical of those used by children in many parts of the country. They had been out on the previous day to gather flowers for their garlands. These were usually in the form of two crossed hoops to form a cage, which was decorated with flowers and ribbons. Inside was a doll — 'the lady'. Children covered their garlands with muslin until the first donation had been received; then they went from house to house collecting.

Garland Day is still observed in Abbotsbury, Dorset, though on 13 May (May Day in the old calendar). Originally a garland was made for each of the local fishing boats and cast onto the sea as an offering. Now there are no local fishing boats but children still make garlands and, having paraded them round the village, place them in the evening by the war memorial.

In Castleton, Derbyshire, Garland Day came to be transferred at some time to 29 May. It is unusual in that it is the only celebration remaining anywhere in the country in which the pagan May King has survived. The Garland King, with a large bell-shaped garland of flowers on his shoulders is accompanied by the May Queen, Morris dancers and the Town Band. The garland is finally hoisted to the top of the church tower.

March winds and April showers
Bring forth May flowers.

May is a month for flowers — and not just those of field, hedgerow and garden. It is the month in which some of the finest displays of flowers are to be seen. The first of these is the Spalding Flower Parade, held in the tulip-growing area of Lincolnshire on the Saturday nearest to 10 May each year. The parade has some twenty floats with steel frameworks, into which the heads of tulips — the waste product of the bulb-growing industry — are pinned. Accompanying bands help to make this a festive occasion.

Toward the end of May in London is the Chelsea Flower Show. The Great Spring Show, to give it its correct title, is set up in the grounds of the Royal Hospital, Chelsea by the Royal Horticultural Society. The great marquee is filled with flowers of almost every season and includes new varieties of flowers as well as old favourites. There are colourful rock gardens, patios and displays of flower arrangements, the whole being enjoyed each year by nearly a quarter of a million people.

Popular floral displays of a different kind are to be seen during May and in later months. These are the Well Dressings in a number of Derbyshire villages, the first being on Ascension Day, which falls between 30 April and 3 June. The most famous, on this day, are at Tissington, where five wells are dressed.

Each well has a screen or framework filled with soft clay into which flowers, petals, bark, cones, stones, moss and any other natural, but not man-made objects, are pressed, to form a colourful picture, usually on a religious subject. On the day of the well-dressing a procession passes from the church through the village to the wells, where prayers are offered.

The Well Dressing processions resemble the various Rogationtide processions to be found in many parts of the country at this same time of year — the few days before Ascension Day — when prayers are offered for the fruits of the land. Some Rogationtide processions include Beating the Bounds to familiarise people with parish boundaries.

Ten days after Ascension Day, usually late in May or in the first half of June, is the Christian festival of Whitsun, when people recall how the followers of Jesus Christ received the Holy Spirit. The day after the festival, Whit Monday, became a Bank Holiday and an opportunity for people to enjoy themselves in lots of different ways. Whitsun does not always fall at the same time of the month: it is a 'movable feast', being six weeks after Easter. A few years ago, Parliament decided that the Spring Bank Holiday should, instead, always be on the last Monday in May. Many of the local customs once associated with Whit-Monday came to be held instead on the new Spring Holiday.

Some of these customs go back to very ancient times. At the Ram Fair, Kingsteignton, Devon, the carcase of a ram is roasted, cut up and sold. This originated as a pre-Christian sacrifice in thanksgiving for a local spring of water.

A different kind of animal provides the meat at Dunmow, Essex. For some five hundred years or more a flitch of bacon has been awarded to any couple who are able to prove that they have not quarrelled or regretted their marriage for a year and a day. At one time the Dunmow Flitch Trial was taken much more seriously than it is today and few claimants were successful.

A much greater element of chance is found in a contest at St. Ives, Cambridgeshire. A bequest was made in 1675 to provide poor children of the parish with Bibles. The condition was that they were to be diced for in church. At one time the altar became the gaming-table but a century ago a table was used instead. Now the dicing takes place in the Church School to find the six lucky winners.

At Birdlip, Gloucestershire, a large cheese is bowled down the hill to remind people of their rights to graze sheep on that hill. Men and boys chase the cheese, the winner keeping the cheese and getting a small prize.

These are but a few. May is a merry month!

1 May

May Day begins early for some people, as it has done for many centuries. Some of the early birds are the members of the choir of Magdalen College, Oxford, who climb to the top of the tower at 6 am to welcome the sunrise with carols. This is followed by the ringing of bells and Morris dancing in the High.

Elsewhere the crowds also begin to gather for those May Day festivities which have a popular appeal. Notable is Padstow, Cornwall, where huge crowds enjoy the Hobby-horse Festival, joining in the spirit of the day which is summed up in the words of the chorus of the traditional Night Song:

Unite, unite, let us all unite
For summer is acome in today;
And whither we are going, let us all unite
In the merry morning of May.

In many other towns and villages there will be special events and festivities, continuing the traditions and customs of long ago (pp. 79–80).

The people of some other countries have celebrated 1 May in a different way since the Congress of the Second International, meeting in 1889, declared that May Day should be Labour Day. Some celebrate with parades and displays of human achievement.

Long before 1889, this day introduced another display of human achievement. It was on 1 May, 1851, that the Great Exhibition opened in Hyde Park, London. The object of the exhibition was to show the world the kind of goods that were being made in Britain. It was housed in a huge glass building known as the Crystal Palace, which was later moved to a site in South London.

Also on 1 May . . . .
Joseph Addison, writer, was born in 1672.
David Livingstone, explorer, died in 1873.
Antonín Dvořák, composer, died in 1904.

In some places it is customary on this day to hold tall story competitions with a prize for the greatest liar.

On 2 May 1497, John Cabot, a Genoese sailor, left Bristol to sail across the Atlantic and see what lands he could discover for the King of England. His little ship, the *Mathew* had a crew of 18 and took 52 days to cross the ocean before making a landfall at Newfoundland or Nova Scotia on 24 June.

Those who crossed the Atlantic on a voyage which began at Southampton on 2 May 1969, did so in much greater comfort and took only a few days. This was the maiden voyage of the *Queen Elizabeth 2*, the luxury flagship of the Cunard Line. The 67,000 ton liner, with accommodation for over 1,700 passengers, was to spend part of the year crossing between Southampton and New York and the remainder as a cruise liner.

For pleasure and adventure of a different kind, how about a boat on the Thames? Many have enjoyed reading *Three Men in a Boat* by Jerome K. Jerome, whose birthday was 2 May 1859.

Nowadays more people travel by air than ever in the past. The first jet airline service began on this day in 1952. It was the British Overseas Airways Corporation service between London and Johannesburg, South Africa.

A much slower journey was undertaken by those who travelled on the German airship *Hindenburg*, which left Europe on 2 May 1937. Unfortunately it exploded as it approached its destination, killing 33 of those on board and ending regular airship travel between Europe and America (p. 88).

A thought, perhaps, for a famous German airman, born on this day in 1892. He was Baron Manfred von Richthofen, known as the 'Red Baron' from the colour of his aircraft. He was the outstanding German fighter pilot of World War I (p. 64).

A thought, too for one who dreamed long ago of flying machines. Leonardo da Vinci died on 2 May 1519. What would he have thought of the space craft *Pioneer X*, launched on this day in 1972? One year and nine months later it passed the planet Jupiter, sending back information about the planet before travelling on and on outside the solar system.

Also on 2 May . . . .

Catherine the Great of Russia was born in 1729.

Coty is a name that is well-known in many lands to those who are interested in perfumery. The name is that of François Coty, born at Ajaccio, Corsica, on 3 May 1874. He set up a small perfume business which proved very successful. In 1905, he moved his business to Paris and, within a few years, became one of the richest men in France.

Coty was very concerned at the rise of Socialism and Communism and wanted to encourage strong right-wing nationalist ideas. In 1922, he gained control of the conservative Paris newspaper *Le Figaro*. A few years later he founded two other newspapers and, using his wealth from the perfume business, sold them at half the price of their rivals. Naturally, they were popular. Coty used much of his wealth in this way but his views became widely known.

This was also the birthday, in 1469, of a statesman whose political views were to be widely publicised. Niccolo Machiavelli was born of a poor family in Florence but he rose quickly to power and travelled in Europe as a diplomat. In 1513, he was arrested on a charge of conspiracy but, though freed, he withdrew from public life and spent his time in writing. His most famous book was *Il Principe*, ('The Prince'), in which he suggested that all means could be used for establishing and maintaining authority and that even the worst acts of rulers could be justified because rulers were dealing with wicked and treacherous subjects. Because of this, deeds of cunning, deceit or treachery are today referred to as machiavellian.

Margaret Thatcher was never one to mince her words. She had strong political views and she let them be known. It was this that led to her election to the leadership of the British Conservative Party in 1975 and to her becoming the first woman Prime Minister of Britain on 3 May 1979.

On this day, in 1951, the Festival of Britain was declared open by King George VI at a ceremony on the steps of St. Paul's Cathedral in the City of London.

John Speke, British explorer of East Africa, was born on 3 May 1827: Thomas Hood, the London poet, died in 1845.

The most famous of all the horse races run in England is the Derby, an event which has been held on Epsom Downs, Surrey, for over two hundred years. Nowadays it is normally held on the first Wednesday in June (p. 152) but the first Derby was held on 4 May 1780. It takes its name from the twelfth Earl of Derby, who instituted the race.

Derby Day is a colourful and exciting occasion, attended by royalty, nobility, traders, gypsies and countless others who like to bet on the horses or simply enjoy a day at the races. Huge sums of money are won and lost on Derby Day. There, too, are some of the greatest names in racing, for to own or ride the Derby winner is the achievement of the year, or perhaps a lifetime. No horse can win the Derby more than once, as the race is only for three-year olds.

For several days before the Derby, many people scan their papers for news of horses and jockeys and, on Derby Day, the popular newspapers often provide a middle-page spread for their readers. Newspapers aim to provide whatever facilities they think will make people choose to buy that particular paper. So, apart from the news, there are pages for sport, hobbies, interests, fashions and business. Pages of advertisements help pay the costs of producing the newspaper so that it can be sold cheaply. Some papers are in a smaller format than others with more pictures and cartoons. They are known as tabloids or 'popular' newspapers. The first of these to be published was the *Daily Mail*, on 4 May 1896.

President Tito of Jugoslavia died on 4 May 1980. Born Josip Broz, he was one who helped to organise the Communist Party in Jugoslavia. During World War II, he led the partisan forces against the occupying armies and, in 1945, established the Communist government in Jugoslavia.

Born this day in 1825, was Thomas Huxley, scientist and humanist, who agreed with Darwin's theories.

For the record! The tallest building (to date) was completed with its topping out ceremony on 4 May 1973. The Sears Tower, Chicago has 110 storeys and is 1,454 ft (443 m) high.

Today is Europe Day, the anniversary of the day in 1949 when many of the nations of Europe decided to work more closely together by forming the Council of Europe. The members of the Council of Europe encouraged close co-operation amongst member countries in many ways and some later agreed to form the European Economic Community, sometimes called the Common Market. There is a European parliament to which each country sends representatives.

One who had dreams, long before, of a united Europe, but under him as Emperor, was Napoleon Bonaparte. Born in Corsica, he served with distinction in the French army until, after a coup in 1799, he gained control of France. In 1804, he had himself crowned emperor. By this time he had already embarked upon an era of warfare and conquest. He had some successes but his invasion of Russia, in 1812, was a disaster.

Napoleon was defeated in 1814 and exiled to the island of Elba but, in 1815, he returned to France and was again at the helm for the 'Hundred Days'. After his defeat at the Battle of Waterloo by Britain and Prussia, he was again exiled, this time to the lonely Atlantic island of St. Helena and it was there, on 5 May 1821, that he died.

By coincidence it was on this day, in 1659, that St. Helena was first occupied by Captain John Dutton of the British East India Company.

Another who dreamed of a united Europe — or at least of the workers — was Karl Marx. His Communist Manifesto ended 'Workers of the world, unite! You have nothing to lose but your chains . . . ' His policies were adopted in Eastern Europe. Marx, who was born in Germany on 5 May 1818, died in London in 1883 and was buried in Highgate Cemetery.

Also buried in Highgate Cemetery after his death on 5 May 1921, was William Friese-Greene, the inventor of the first practical movie camera.

Sir Gordon Richards, Britain's most sucessful jockey, was born on 5 May 1904. He was champion jockey 26 times between 1925 and 1953 and was the winner of 4,870 races.

Many stamp-collectors like to include a 'Penny Black' in their collection as they were the first stamps to be issued. They were first put on sale at the GPO on 1 May 1840, available for use for the first time on this day. What price a first-day cover for 6 May 1840? Some Penny Blacks are valuable but, in fact, many more were printed than is sometimes imagined — over sixty-eight million of them.

Today's birthdays include:

Maximilien Robespierre, in 1758. He was one of the leaders of the French Revolution and eventually was himself guillotined.

Sigmund Freud, the founder of psychoanalysis, was born in Moravia (now Czechoslovakia) in 1856.

Also born in 1856 was Robert Peary, the American polar explorer, first to reach the North Pole.

Sydney Carter, who gave us many modern hymns including *The Lord of the Dance*, was born in 1915. He turned to singing and song-writing as a result of the post-war English Folk Revival. Apart from hymns and folk songs, he has written poems and programmes for television.

Maria Montessori, the Italian educationalist, died on 6 May 1952. The Montessori system, adopted by many people, is based on the child's creative ability, the desire to learn and the right to be treated as an individual.

An odd-looking boat was launched at Safi on 6 May 1971. It was made of papyrus and named *Ra II*. In it Thor Heyerdahl expected to prove one of his theories about early travel.

It was evening on 6 May 1937, when the airship *Hindenburg* was waiting to moor in America, delayed by thunderstorms. There was an explosion, the airship became a mass of flames and she sank slowly to the ground. Some passengers then jumped out and ran clear of the inferno.

Also in the evening of this day, in 1954, at Oxford, Roger Bannister, paced by Chris Bracher and Chris Chataway, became the first man to run the mile in less than four minutes. His time was 3 minutes 59.4 seconds.

'Heart of oak are our ships; heart of oak are our men . . . . ' In days of old, ships were built of oak . . . and it took a lot of oak trees to build one ship. About 2,500 were needed to build Nelson's flag-ship, HMS *Victory*, which was launched on 7 May 1765.

Another fine ship, but one which ended her days on this day in 1915, was the Cunard liner *Lusitania.* She was torpedoed off the Irish coast and sank quickly. Of 1,959 passengers, 1,198 lost their lives. The sinking of this liner was one of the factors that took the United States into World War I.

Some famous people born on this day . . .

Johannes Brahms, German composer, who wrote music for the orchestra, piano and choirs, was born in 1833.

Peter Ilich Tchaikovsky, Russian composer of orchestral music and renowned for his ballet music, was born in 1840.

Josip Broz, who was to become President Tito of Jugoslavia, was born in 1892.

Robert Browning, one of the great English Victorian poets, was born on 7 May 1812. His dramatic monologues are masterpieces. From one, *Rabbi ben Ezra*, come the well-known words:

> *Grow old along with me!*
> *The best is yet to be,*
> *The last of life, for which the first was made:*
> *Our times are in His hand.*
> *Who saith, 'A whole I planned,*
> *Youth shows but half; trust God; see all nor be afraid!*

Today marks the end of this life's journey for. . . .

James Nasmyth, the Scottish engineer, who died in 1890, was the inventor of the steam hammer. He also built steam locomotives, pumps, presses and other machinery.

George Lansbury, socialist reformer and leader of the British Labour Party from 1931 to 1935, died in 1940.

Sir James Frazer, anthropologist and folklorist, author of *The Golden Bough,* died in 1941.

Alison Uttley, author of children's books, died in 1976.

The first Drury Lane Theatre opened on 7 May 1663.

Jean Henri Dunant, who was born on 8 May 1828, was an eye witness at the Battle of Solferino (24 June 1859), at which there were some 40,000 casualties. He was appalled at the carnage and organised emergency aid for the French and Austrian wounded. Three years later he proposed that all countries should set up emergency services to alleviate suffering in war and peace for all people regardless of nationality or creed.

In 1864, in his home town of Geneva, Switzerland, the Red Cross came into being, its emblem being the Swiss flag in reverse. The first Geneva Convention was held in that year too. Dunant was a founder member of the World Young Men's Christian Association and spent much of his life working for prisoners of war, the abolition of slavery, disarmament and other causes. He was co-winner, in 1901, of the first Nobel Prize for Peace.

Dame Ethel Smyth was a campaigner, too. She was an English composer of orchestral and choral works as well as opera. In 1911, she took up the cause of women's suffrage and was once imprisoned for three months. In 1922, she was created a DBE. She died on 8 May 1944.

Many people have been thankful for the work of Thomas Hancock, who was born on 8 May 1786. Regarded as the founder of the British rubber industry, his chief invention was the masticator by which shredded scraps or rubber could be made into sheets or blocks. He went into partnership with Charles Macintosh, the Scottish chemist, to produce waterproof articles, one of which, the macintosh coat, was to prove a great boon.

This was a day of great rejoicing in 1945. The unconditional surrender of the German armed forces gave victory in Europe to the allies. VE Day marked the end of World War II in Europe after nearly six years of fighting.

In the Far East, it was on this day, in 1942, that the Battle of the Coral Sea ended.

Also on this day . . . .

Hernando de Soto discovered the Mississippi River in 1541.

H. G. Selfridge, founder of Selfridge's in London, died in 1947.

The last London trolleybus ran in 1962.

This was the day, in 1932, when the lights went on in London — in Piccadilly Circus to be precise, where those famous lights were first lit by electricity. It is still one of the attractions for tourists, who enjoy the ever-changing colours of this well-known junction and the neighbouring theatre-land.

One name that may well go up in lights each year is *Peter Pan,* the well-loved pantomime that has been performed regularly since it first appeared in 1904. The play was written by Sir James Barrie, who was born on 9 May 1860. He also wrote *The Admirable Crichton, Dear Brutus* and other works.

This was also the birthday, in 1874, of Lilian Baylis, one of the best known personalities in the English theatre world in the first half of this century. She went with her parents to South Africa but returned to help her aunt manage the Royal Victoria Hall. In 1912, she made of it the 'Old Vic', a centre for Shakespearean productions. In 1931, she took over the derelict Sadlers Wells Theatre and made it a centre for opera and ballet. Her ballet company became, in 1956, the Royal Ballet.

The puppet theatre on the beach is a long way from the London theatre but children love the Punch and Judy Show with all the outlandish escapades of Punch. The show originated in Europe, from whence it came to England in the reign of Charles II, the first performance being on 9 May 1662.

It was also in the reign of Charles II, on 9 May 1671, that a most amazing real-life drama took place. Colonel Thomas Blood attired himself as a priest and, with three companions, entered the Tower of London, overpowered a warder and stole some of the Crown Jewels. Blood was captured but pardoned by the king, freed and given back lands that had been taken from him by Cromwell. No one is quite sure why.

This was the birthday, in 1800, of John Brown, whose 'soul goes marching on' and, in 1873, of Howard Carter, the Egyptologist who discovered the tombs of Hatshepsut, Thutmoze IV and Tutankhamun. It saw the death, in 1688, of Frederick William, the Great Elector, and, in 1805, of dramatist Friedrich von Schiller.

Many people have now circumnavigated the world, some on voyages of exploration, others as solo adventurers. This day, in 1961, saw the completion of a voyage that was different. The US nuclear submarine *Triton* completed a round-the-world voyage of 41,519 miles (66,816 km). The whole voyage was undersea and took 84 days.

Sir Thomas Lipton preferred to do his sailing as a yachtsman. Born in Glasgow on 10 May 1850, of Irish parents who ran a small grocery shop, he went to America for several years but returned to Glasgow to open his own shop. He was so successful that he opened other shops throughout Britain, bought plantations overseas as well as farms and factories in the UK and built up the Lipton grocery empire. As a yachtsman he raced his yachts, each named *Shamrock*, in the America's Cup but failed to win.

In America, 'Stonewall' Jackson died on 10 May 1863. Named 'Stonewall' because of his firm stands, Thomas Jonathan Jackson was a Confederate general in the Civil War and is regarded as one of the greatest tacticians in military history. He was very successful in his campaigns but died eight days after being accidentally shot by one of his own men.

Six years later, also in America, on 10 May 1869, the first railway to cross the continent was completed with the link up at Promontory Point, Utah, of the Central Pacific and Union Pacific Railroads. Governor Stanford of California drove a golden spike into the last railway tie.

This day, in 1857, saw the outbreak of the Indian Mutiny, when Indian soldiers revolted after a rumour that bullets were smeared with cow and pig fat, offensive to both Hindu and Muslim beliefs.

Henry Morton Stanley died on 10 May 1904. He is especially remembered for his search for Dr. Livingstone, whom he found at Ujiji. 'Doctor Livingstone, I presume?'

Some people regarded this day as a turning point in World War II. Neville Chamberlain resigned as Prime Minister on 10 May 1940 and Winston Churchill took the reins.

On 11 May 1553, three little ships set sail from Deptford on the River Thames. Their destination was north of Russia to seek a North-east passage round Europe and Asia to the Pacific. In charge of the expedition was Sir Hugh Willoughby. The ships became separated. Two were driven into the icy wastes off Lapland where all, including Sir Hugh, perished. The third, commanded by Richard Chancellor reached the White Sea, from which Chancellor journeyed to Moscow before returning to England.

Baron Munchhausen was born on 11 May 1720. He, too, went to Russia, where he fought with the Russians against the Turks. After he retired to his estates in Germany, in 1760, he became famous for telling tall stories about his experiences as a soldier, sportsman and hunter. Many people have enjoyed reading *The Adventures of Baron Munchhausen*, first published in 1785. Although these are tall stories of the Munchhausen type, they have little to do with the actual baron.

Two British Prime Ministers ended their lives on 11 May. William Pitt the Elder, Earl of Chatham, was one of the great statesmen of the 18th Century. It was under his leadership that Britain gained a large empire through successes in the Seven Years' War (1756–63). He resigned in 1768 but continued to speak for the American colonists. At last, though ill, he rose to speak in the House of Lords but collapsed. He died on 11 May 1778. Spencer Perceval was Prime Minister from 1809 until 11 May 1812, when he was assassinated by a mentally deranged merchant in the lobby of the House of Commons. The merchant, John Bellingham, was hanged a week later.

This was the birthday in 1888, in Russia, of Israel Baline. He went with his parents to America where, as Irving Berlin, he became famous as a songwriter. He wrote more than 3,000, many being great 'hits'. Still in the world of entertainment, this was the birthday, in 1892, of Dame Margaret Rutherford, who endeared herself to many as the portrayer of eccentric women. Eccentric in his own way was Salvador Dali, the Spanish surrealist artist, who was born on 11 May 1904. This was also the birthday, in 1854, of Ottmar Mergenthaler, inventor of the Linotype machine used in printing.

THE STRIKE IS OVER. Headlines such as this appeared on most of the evening newspapers on 12 May 1926. Such headlines are not uncommon today: we have become familiar with strikes by one group of workers or another. But, in 1926, they marked the end of the General Strike, in which key workers — railwaymen, transport workers, builders, gas and electricity workers and, later, engineers and shipyard workers downed tools in response to a resolution of the Trades Union Congress to support the action of miners.

Much of Britain came to a standstill, but not as much as some would have hoped. There were many volunteer strike-breakers. On 13 May most industries were back to work, but not the miners who continued their strike until the autumn.

On 12 May 1969, voting took place in the borough elections, as is customary at this time of the year. The difference in 1969 was that this was the first election in which 18-year-olds had been able to vote after the age had been lowered from 21.

How pleasant to know Mr. Lear!
Who has written such volumes of stuff!
Some think him ill-tempered and queer
But a few think him pleasant enough.

Edward Lear, author and writer of nonsense poems, wrote this of himself. Today was his birthday in 1812. It was also the birthday, in 1820, of Florence Nightingale, 'The Lady with the Lamp', of Crimean War and nursing fame. Also born on 12 May was Dante Gabriel Rossetti, poet and painter, in 1828.

This was the birthday too, in 1880 of Lincoln Ellsworth, the American explorer, engineer and scientist, who led the first transarctic air crossing in 1926 and the first transantarctic in 1935.

Some who died on 12 May were: Bedrich Smetana, the Czechoslovakian composer, (1884); Jozef Pilsudski, the freedom fighter who helped establish an independent Poland after World War I, (1935); and John Masefield, 15th Poet Laureate, (1967).

The Great Little Tilley made her first stage appearance at the age of four. A year later she did her first male impersonation — and she never looked back. Before she was fourteen she was playing in two different London music halls each evening and, for the next 42 years, until she retired in 1920, Vesta Tilley remained the most celebrated of male impersonators in London, the provinces and the United States. Some of her songs such as *Burlington Bertie* and *Following in Father's Footsteps* became well-known. This was her birthday in 1864.

This was also the birthday, in 1842, of Sir Arthur Sullivan, who composed music of many kinds but is remembered best, by many people, as the partner of W. S. Gilbert in the composition of the 'Gilbert and Sullivan' Savoy operas such as *The Mikado* and *The Pirates of Penzance.*

Also born on 13 May, in 1857, was Sir Ronald Ross, whose investigations into the causes of malaria led to his receiving a Nobel Prize in 1902. Josephine Butler was born on this day, too, in 1828. She was a social reformer who campaigned against the white slave traffic and prostitution.

Fridtjof Nansen, who died on 13 May 1930, was a campaigner, too. In 1922, he received the Nobel Peace Prize for his great work in the repatriation of prisoners and famine relief after World War I. He had previously earned a name for himself as an Arctic explorer, investigating the sea currents and the drift of the ice.

Cyrus Hall McCormick, who died on 13 May 1884, is generally credited with the invention of the mechanical reaper, which he patented in 1834. Some years later, he built a factory in Chicago to manufacture his reapers in large numbers.

John Nash, who died on this day in 1835, gave London some of its most imposing architecture. Under the patronage of the Prince Regent, he developed Regent Street and Regents' Park with its lake, canal, arcades and picturesque groupings of residences. He also rebuilt the Royal Pavillion, Brighton, redesigned St. James's Park and began the rebuilding of Buckingham Palace as a royal palace.

By now the football season has usually come to an end, though there may still be the excitement of international or World Cup matches yet to come. For one footballer, 14 May 1977, marked the end of a long and distinguished career as a player. Bobby Moore spent most of his time playing for West Ham United, many years as captain: then for a short period he moved to Fulham. He played in his first international match for England on 20 May 1962 and he created a British record when he played in his 108th international in 1973. For several years he captained the England team, including the period when England won the World Cup in 1966. The match on 14 May 1977, was an appropriate one at which to retire: it was the 1,000th in which he had played. He is remembered not only for the skill of his play but for the quality and cleanness of his gamesmanship.

Quality is uppermost in the minds of all who have a name to live up to or a trademark that is respected. Most people are happy to buy foods that are marked as one of 'Heinz 57 Varieties'. Henry John Heinz lived in Pittsburgh, USA, where, at an early age, he became interested in selling food. At the age of sixteen he employed several people to cultivate food and deliver to local grocers. The '57 Varieties' slogan was first used in 1896, even though more varieties were already being made. By the time Heinz died, on 14 May 1919, his Company employed over 6,000 people in 25 factories.

Robert Owen, who was born on 14 May 1771, looked for quality of a different sort — a quality of life for people who worked in the mills at the time of the Industrial Revolution. At his New Lanark Mills, he offered better housing, schools and infant care, setting a high standard that was the basis of many social reforms that followed.

It was on this day, in 1796, that Edward Jenner made the first successful vaccination against smallpox.

The Roman Catholic Cathedral of Christ the King, in Liverpool, was consecrated on 14th May 1967. It is a circular building of striking appearance with the altar in the centre.

15 May

On 15 May 1928, a small aeroplane touched down in the middle of nowhere, in the outback of Australia. A doctor clambered out of the 'plane and treated the first patient of the new Royal Flying Doctor Service of Australia.

The Flying Doctor service was the brainchild of John Flynn, a Presbyterian minister, who realised that many people were suffering and dying in out-of-the-way places because they could not get a doctor. Nowadays such people can call the doctor by radio and receive a visit from him or instructions as to what they can do to help themselves.

Pierre Curie, who is remembered for a great contribution to medicine, was born in Paris on 15 May 1859 and became a professor of physics at the Sorbonne. With his wife, Marie, he discovered how to isolate a radioactive element in pitchblende. From this discovery came the use of radioactivity and radium in medicine, which has brought relief to many sufferers.

16 May

How important is a smile? Stella, Lady Reading, once gave up her seat on a bus to an Irish woman, who promptly said in a loud voice, 'It ain't the seat I'm thanking her for, but the smile.'

It made Lady Reading think. If a smile can mean so much to a lonely person, a good many smiles are needed . . . and helping hands, willing feet and warm hearts. So, on 16 May 1938, the Women's Voluntary Service was born. Soon, in wartime, they were caring for soldiers and refugees and doing a host of other jobs. When the war had ended, they were described as 'the army that Hitler forgot'. The WVS — 'Women of Various Sizes' as Lady Reading called them — continued their service in many ways, running clubs, driving ambulances, taking meals on wheels, helping and visiting, chatting and smiling. In 1966, they became the Women's Royal Voluntary Service.

On this day, John Cotman, Norwich artist, was born (1792); and 'Oscars' for film performances were instituted (1929).

What is the cost of a piece of coal? In one sense, perhaps, it is not very much but we have to remember that coal has to be dug out of the ground, often a long way below the surface, and, although nowadays there is modern machinery available, there are still many pits in which miners have to hack away at the coal-face in very uncomfortable conditions. In spite of all the precautions that are taken, there are sometimes accidents in which miners lose their lives.

On 17 May 1965, there was a colliery disaster in Wales in which 31 miners were killed. It was one of several colliery disasters that took place in one ten-week period. On 28 March, 267 had been killed in India; on 1 June, 237 were killed in Japan; and, on 7 June, 128 in Jugoslavia.

So what is the cost of a piece of coal?

On a sunnier note, this was the day, in 1916, when the Summertime Act was passed. Daylight saving became a permanent measure in 1925 and we are now accustomed to putting clocks forward one hour each year about the end of March, putting them back again to Greenwich Mean Time towards the end of October.

Edward Jenner put a little brightness into the lives of many people. He was the Gloucestershire doctor who discovered that people injected with cowpox did not catch smallpox which, in his day, took the lives of about 2,000 a year in London alone. Nowadays most people in Britain are vaccinated against smallpox. Edward Jenner was born on 17 May 1749.

The roses painted by Sandro Botticelli were beautiful. He was masterful in his use of colour, and his paintings, many of them on religious subjects, make him one of the greatest of the Florentine artists of the Renaissance. Botticelli — a nickname meaning 'Little Barrel' — died on 17 May 1510.

Also. . . .

The French composer of *The Sorcerer's Apprentice* and other music, Paul Dukas, died on this day in 1935.

Guildford Cathedral, Surrey, on which building had begun in 1936, was consecrated on 17 May 1961.

The relief of Mafeking on 17 May 1900, after a seven-month seige by the Boers, caused great rejoicing in Britain.

Lionel Lukin, a London coachbuilder, who was born on 18 May 1742, began experimenting on the River Thames with a Norwegian yawl. He made various alterations, using watertight compartments, cork and other lightweight materials which would keep the boat afloat even if it filled with water. He patented his idea in 1785, so giving the world the 'unsinkable' lifeboat which has proved invaluable in rescue work at sea.

Rescue of a different kind was necessary in the years leading up to 18 May 1960, when the Kariba Hydro-Electric Project High Dam on the Zambezi River was opened. Designed to provide electricity for Zambia and Rhodesia (now Zimbabwe), the project involved building a 420 ft (128 m) high dam across the Zambezi, so creating Lake Kariba, a reservoir 175 miles (281 km) long and up to 20 miles (32 km) wide. With so much land being flooded, a great rescue operation was set in motion. 'Operation Noah' involved the movement of thousands of animals to new homes. It was also necessary to resettle some 57,000 Tonga tribesmen whose villages would become submerged.

Tonga is also the name of a kingdom in the South Pacific, otherwise known as the Friendly Islands. On 18th May 1900, it became a British protectorate and remained so for seventy years, when it became an independent kingdom within the Commonwealth. For most of that time the popular ruler was Queen Salote (1918–65).

This was the birthday, in 1920, of another popular leader. Karol Wojtyla, who was the son of a Polish factory worker, became a priest and, in 1978, was elected Pope, taking the name of Pope John Paul II. On his many journeyings he received enthusiastic welcomes by huge crowds of people.

Also born on 18 May. . . .

In 1836, Wilhelm Steinitz, the Austrian Chess master, who held the world championship for a record period from 1866 to 1894.

In 1883, Walter Gropius, the German who greatly influenced modern architecture.

In 1919, Dame Margot Fonteyn, the outstanding English ballerina.

On 19 May 1935, a mechanic in the Royal Air Force, by the name of T. E. Shaw, mounted his motor cycle and sped along the road. He swerved to avoid some children, came off his cycle and died from the injuries he received. As T. E. Shaw no one would remember him today but that was not the name by which he was known in earlier years. He was T. E. Lawrence, better known as 'Lawrence of Arabia', an officer in the British Army who so came to understand the Arabs that he gained their confidence and was able to lead them to victory during the first World War. 'Lawrence of Arabia' was a name honoured and respected by many.

Such a thing could hardly have been said of Charles Montagu, Lord Halifax, who died on this day in 1715. In many ways he was a remarkable man. He was a poor student who was elected a Member of Parliament. At the age of thirty-three he was Chancellor of the Exchequer and a man we might term a financial wizard. He helped establish the Bank of England and set up money systems used by governments ever since.

Lord Halifax became rich and famous. He had a fine house and ate exotic foods. He also became very vain and arrogant, hated by many people for his success, for his politics but most of all for the kind of man he was. When he died there were few who wished to shed a tear.

How different when William Ewart Gladstone died on 19 May 1898! He, too, was a politician and, indeed, Prime Minister for no less than four terms of office. People did not necessarily agree with him but they could not help but respect him as a great speaker and man of the highest character. Affectionately known as the Grand Old Man, he was given the honour of burial among the greatest in Westminster Abbey.

On this day the Church remembers St. Dunstan, Archbishop of Canterbury, deviser of the coronation service, who died on 19 May 988.

Today, in 1536, Queen Anne Boleyn was beheaded; in 1795 James Boswell, the biographer, died; and in 1861 Dame Nellie Melba, the Australian singer, was born.

John Clare died on 20 May 1864, a poor man as he had been all his life. As a boy he had looked after animals on the common and during his life had to be satisfied with what work he could find, including spells as a militiaman, a gardener and a worker in a lime kiln. He also had the habit of stopping work from time to time to write poetry on scraps of paper. Some people recognised his talent and set up a fund to enable him to have a small income. His poems were popular. John Clare may always have been poor but, with poems such as this, he left the world a richer place.

I long for scenes where man has never trod;
A place where woman never smiled or wept;
There to abide with my Creator, God,
And sleep as I in childhood sweetly slept:
Untroubling and untroubled where I lie;
The grass below — above the vaulted sky.

Christopher Columbus found scenes where no European had ever trod but his was far from a peaceful voyage. His crew were near to mutiny as he headed toward America with nothing but the sea around him and the sky above. He died on 20 May 1506, having set the scene for the beginnings of new nations.

In fact today is a day of beginnings. On 20 May 1514, the first Master was appointed to the newly formed Corporation of Trinity House, given a Royal Charter by King Henry VIII to 'train pilots and come to the relief of shipping'. It continues to do this, as well as maintaining buoys and lighthouses around Britain.

On 20 May 1867, the foundation stone was laid of the Royal Albert Hall, London, scene of many fine concerts and festivals.

On this day, in 1913, the first of many colourful Chelsea Flower Shows (p. 81) was staged by the Royal Horticultural Society.

On a less happy note, the first American hydrogen bomb was exploded over Bikini Atoll on 20 May 1956.

It was a beginning for Honoré de Balzac, poet, born in 1799, and for John Stuart Mill, writer and reformer, in 1806.

It was the end for the Marquis de Lafayette, the French noble who helped the American colonists against the British and later became very powerful in France. He died on 20 May 1834.

Travel and transport are highlighted today. On 21 May 1498, three ships under the command of Vasco de Gama anchored off Calicut, India, having made the first voyage to that country round the Cape of Good Hope. Four years later, in 1502, a Spaniard in the service of Portugal, João de Nova discovered the island which was named St. Helena, this being St. Helen's feast day. Some years later, another Spaniard, Hernando de Soto, was exploring the southern part of North America. It was while following the course of the Mississippi that he died on 21 May 1542.

One of the most famous fleets of ships to sail was the Spanish Armada. Today was the birthday, in 1527, of the king who sent the Armada, Philip II of Spain.

The Duke of Bridgewater, who was born on 21 May 1736, was the man who set a new pattern for transport when he commissioned James Brindley to construct the Bridgewater Canal from Worsley to Manchester. In later years, the nearby Manchester Ship Canal, which created a port from an inland town, was opened on 21 May 1894.

Glen Hammond Curtiss was born on 21 May 1878. He began his career by building cycle engines but, after building one for an airship, turned his mind to the development of amphibious aircraft in the United States. His planes were widely used during World War I and afterwards. On 21 May 1927, Charles Lindbergh landed his monoplane *Spirit of St. Louis* in Paris at the end of the first transatlantic flight. Five years later to the day, Amelia Earhart became the first woman to fly the Atlantic solo.

In the world of the arts and music, this was the birthday of Albrecht Dürer (p. 50), in 1471, and of Henri Rousseau, the French primitive painter, in 1844. The poet, Alexander Pope, was born this day, in 1688, and Franz von Suppé, composer of light operas, died on 21 May 1895.

The Marquis of Montrose, Scottish general and supporter of King Charles I, was hanged by his enemies in the market place at Edinburgh on 21 May 1650.

Elizabeth Fry, Quaker prison reformer, was born 21 May 1780.

Flavius Valerius Aurelius Constantinus, best known as Constantine, was the eldest son of Constantius Chlorus, the ruler, under the Roman Emperor Diocletian, of Britain, Gaul and Spain. His mother was Helen (or St. Helena) whom legend says discovered the cross of Jesus Christ. He fought as a soldier before taking the place of his father, who died in 306 A.D.

Constantine was one of several leaders who claimed to be the Roman Emperor. He succeeded in defeating all his rivals in the West. Before the last battle, Constantine is said to have seen a cross in the sky with the words, 'In this sign conquer'. After his victory, Constantine ended three centuries of persecution by allowing the Romans to become Christian. He went on to defeat Licinius, who was the Emperor of the Eastern Empire, and so became the ruler of the whole Roman Empire. He moved his capital to Byzantium, which he renamed Constantinople, and he made Christianity the official religion, being baptised himself shortly before his death on 22 May 337. He is remembered as Constantine the Great.

This was the birthday, in 1907, of one of the greatest British actors of this century, Sir Laurence Olivier. Following his first stage appearance in 1924, he played all the major Shakespearean roles. In 1944, he became one of the directors of the Old Vic Company and, in 1962, director of the National Theatre. He has also directed, produced and acted in several films.

Margaret Rutherford began acting with the Old Vic Company in 1925 and played in many films. She was much loved for her amusing character acting of eccentric women. Dame Margaret Rutherford died on 22 May 1972.

As a child, Wilhelm Richard Wagner was often in the theatre. Later he wrote some outstanding operas but had difficulty in having them produced. So he opened his own theatre at Bayreuth, Bavaria, where a Wagner Festival is still held annually. This was his birthday, in 1813.

Sir Arthur Conan Doyle, creator of Sherlock Holmes, was born on 22 May 1859; Victor Hugo, French author, died in 1885.

Whipsnade Zoo, Bedfordshire, the world's first 'open zoo', was opened on 22 May 1931.

When is a pirate not a pirate? There were times in the past when people were encouraged to be privateers or pirates if they wished to attack and loot enemy ships. Captain William Kidd, in 1696, was given a 30-gun ship by William III to suppress piracy but also to attack the French. He had previously gained a reputation for courage. However, in 1697, he turned pirate, making his way from Madagascar to the West Indies and Boston. There he was arrested and sent to England, where he was tried and hanged on 23 May 1701.

This was the day, in 1960, when the past caught up with Karl Adolf Eichmann. He was a Nazi war criminal, guilty of the death of many Jews, but he escaped to Argentina. Eventually he was traced by a group of Jews and seized on 23 May 1960, then taken to Israel, tried and executed.

Girolamo Savonarola was also executed on this day, in 1498. His crime was that he said what he thought and was not afraid to speak out against rulers or the Church. He was a Dominican friar, who, at one time, was accepted as leader by the people of Florence.

The strongest man upon earth is he who stands most alone.
'An Enemy of the People'

Henrick Ibsen, the Norwegian dramatist who wrote this, as well as poems and plays such as *Peer Gynt,* died on 23 May 1906.

Carl Linne was born in Sweden on this day in 1707. He is known as 'the father of modern botany'. He invented a system for classifying plants and animals, using Latin as a common language. He is usually known by the Latinised form of his name — Carolus Linnaeus.

Kit (Christopher) Carson, American frontiersman, trapper and soldier, a legendary folk hero, died on 23 May 1868.

John D. Rockefeller, American oil magnate, businessman and philanthropist, died on this day, in 1937.

Thomas Hood, English poet, was born on 23 May 1799.

This is the anniversary of the Battle of Ramillies, in 1706, when the Duke of Marlborough defeated the French.

William Lloyd Garrison, who died on 24 May 1879, was a very determined man. He had very strong views about slavery and wanted to see it abolished in the United States. At the age of 25 he joined an abolition movement in Boston and he supported Lincoln during the Civil War. To spread his views, he published *The Liberator*, in the first issue of which, on 1 January 1832, he left his readers in no doubt as to where he stood:

> *I am in earnest — I will not equivocate — I will not excuse — I will not retreat a single inch — and I will be heard!*

John Wesley was also determined to be heard. He was an Anglican clergyman who was not very satisfied with his religion until he had a deep religious experience on 24 May 1738. Then there was no stopping him. He travelled the length and breadth of the country, preaching in the open air because he was no longer welcome in the churches. Often heckled or attacked by mobs, nothing could stop him preaching the Gospel of Jesus Christ.

Wesley's followers became known as Methodists. One of the great Methodist preachers of the 20th Century, Revd. Dr. W. E. Sangster, who held large congregations spellbound in Westminster Central Hall, died on this day in 1960.

What hath God wrought.

The words of a man who determined to be heard in another way. It was the first public message sent in morse code on the electric telegraph by Samuel Morse on 24 May 1834.

Two who made themselves heard, giving a great deal of pleasure to many. Joan Hammond, the talented Australian soprano and opera singer was born on this day in 1912. One of the greatest figures in jazz history, 'Duke' Ellington, pianist, composer and bandleader, died on 24 May 1974.

On this day Queen Victoria was born in 1819 and Jan Christiaan Smuts, South African statesman, in 1870. The 'father of modern astronomy', Nicolaus Copernicus, died on 24 May 1543.

On 24 May 1941, HMS *Hood* was blown to pieces by a direct hit on the main magazine from the *Bismarck*, 13 miles away. Only 3 of the *Hood's* crew of 1,421 survived.

Tom Sayers, who was born in Brighton on 25 May 1826, was one of Britain's most famous pugilists. Weighing only 155 pounds (70 kg) and nicknamed 'Little Wonder' and 'Napoleon of the Prize Ring', he took on many bigger opponents but lost only one fight in his career. In 1860, he was one of the fighters, in America, in the first international heavyweight contest, after which he retired.

A fighter of a different kind was born on 25 May 1879. Max Aitken, a Canadian, settled in Britain and entered politics, serving in the Cabinet during both World Wars. In 1916, he accepted a peerage as Lord Beaverbrook and that year he bought control of the London *Daily Express*. It is as a successful newspaper magnate and journalist that he is chiefly remembered. He fought many crusades to 'keep Britain great' and for private enterprise, winning some and losing others but, as he once wrote,

> *My principle is — take a trick while you can and go on with the game.*

Igor Sikorsky also knew success and failure in a different sphere. Born in Kiev, Russia, on 25 May 1889, he became interested in aircraft design, in 1908, after meeting the Wright brothers and other pioneers. His first attempts to build helicopters failed, so he turned to biplanes. In 1919, he emigrated to the United States where he set up in business. Amongst his achievements were the first four-engined aircraft in the world (1913), the first aircraft to have a toilet (1931), and the first successful helicopter (1939).

How do we measure success? In material things or by other standards? Ralph Waldo Emerson was born on 25 May 1803 and became a very successful poet and writer, recognised in Europe as well as his own country, America. He once wrote:

> *We take care of our health, we lay up our money, we make our roof tight and our clothing sufficient, but who provides wisely that he shall not be wanting in the best property of all — friends?*

On this day the world gained a symbol of friendship when the new Coventry Cathedral was consecrated in 1962. Lost to the world today were Rosa Bonheur, French artist, in 1899, and Gustav Holst, composer, in 1934.

King Charles II landed at Dover on 26 May 1660. Three days later he was welcomed in London. There was great rejoicing as people knew they would again be able to enjoy pleasures that had been banned by the Puritans.

Two years later, on 26 May 1662, Samuel Pepys wrote in his diary, 'Homewards by coach, through Moorefields, where we stood a while, and saw the wrestling.' After Charles II had returned, Pepys rose quickly in the service of the Admiralty, of which he became Secretary in 1672. In 1684, he became President of the Royal Society. From 1660 to 1669 he kept his famous diary, in which he gives vivid pictures of life in his day and of the three great disasters of that time — the plague, the Great Fire of London, and the Dutch attack on the Medway. The diary was written in code. It was on this day, too, in 1703, that he died.

A contemporary of Samuel Pepys was John Churchill, 1st Duke of Marlborough, who was born on 26 May 1650. He was to become one of the greatest soldiers of his day. He was a loyal supporter of 'Dutch Billy' (William of Orange) and later had command of the British Army in the War of the Spanish Succession. His victories at Blenheim, Ramillies and Oudenarde brought him fame and many honours. He was a military genius but also a man who cared for the welfare of his troops.

It was on this day, in 735, that the Venerable Bede died at Jarrow, where he had spent almost the whole of his life. Bede was a great scholar, student and teacher, devoting much of his time to writing. His most valuable work was his *History of the English Church and People*, from which we get most of our early English historical information. He will be remembered on his feast day tomorrow, 27 May.

Alexander Pushkin, who was born in Moscow on 26 May 1799, is regarded by many as Russia's greatest poet, novelist, short-story writer and dramatist. At the height of his success, at the age of 37, he was killed in a duel.

Sir Eugene Goossens, a prominent English 20th Century conductor and composer, was born on 26 May 1893.

We live in a wonderful world in which there is so much to be seen and enjoyed. There are strange and fascinating wild creatures, plants and blossoms both odd and exotic, and natural resources of so many kinds that are available to man. Yet it is only in recent years that people have begun to realise the importance of conservation and the dangers of pollution.

One person to whom we are indebted for this is Rachel Carson, who was born on 27 May 1907. She was deeply interested in all wildlife and worked for the US Fish and Wildlife Service. In 1951 she published *The Sea Around Us*, which won the National Book Award and, in 1962, *Silent Spring*, which startled the world into an awareness of the dangers of pollution.

David Hartman could see nothing of the beauty of the world around. He had become blind at the age of eight. He became accustomed to his world of darkness and to doing things for himself. By the age of 13 he had decided to be a doctor. But who would want a blind doctor? Despite opposition and setbacks, David passed his examinations with flying colours on 27 May 1976 and went on to study psychiatry, particularly related to the emotional problems of the disabled.

One who 'saw' into the future, with a vision of better times, Julia Ward Howe, was born on 27 May 1819. She wrote the verses which have been a source of comfort and inspiration to many, beginning, 'Mine eyes have seen the glory of the coming of the Lord' — the famous Battle Hymn of the Republic.

Into battle of a different kind. In 1941, the signal was sent out to naval ships in the North Atlantic '*Sink the Bismarck*'. She was a powerful German battleship, which had sunk HMS *Hood* and was a danger to allied shipping. On 26 May, she was crippled by a torpedo, then pounded by two battleships for 24 hours before being sunk by torpedoes on 27 May.

Also on 27 May. . . .

John Calvin, religious reformer, died in 1564.
Sir Joseph Swan, inventor, died in 1914.
Jawaharlal Nehru, Prime Minister of India, died in 1964.
The Habeas Corpus Act became law in 1679.

One of the best-known spies of recent times is James Bond, otherwise known as 007. He is not a real spy, but a fictional character invented by Ian Fleming, whose birthday was 28 May 1908. The first of 13 James Bond novels appeared in 1953. Some of them, *From Russia with Love, Dr. No, Goldfinger, Thunderball* and *Diamonds are Forever,* were made into very popular films. James Bond, handsome and clever, with a love of fast cars, beautiful women and gambling, with a knack of escaping out of violent, dangerous and nigh-on impossible situations, provided thrill and excitement for millions of people. Ian Fleming, who died in 1964, saw the sales of his books run into many millions in eleven languages.

Others, who like the thrill of motor cycling, may make their way to the Isle of Man for the TT (Tourist Trophy) race, the toughest and most famous race in the world. The 37-mile race, on the roads of the island, is now twice the length of the first race, which was held on 28th May 1907.

Francis Chichester enjoyed the thrill of doing something out of the ordinary, or facing the challenges of nature. As a young man, he went to New Zealand but returned to England. After obtaining a pilot's licence, he flew a Gipsy Moth biplane solo to Australia. In 1960, he won the first solo transatlantic sailing race in *Gipsy Moth III*. His most famous voyage was his solo voyage round the world in *Gipsy Moth IV*. Leaving Plymouth in August 1966, he sailed to Sydney, Australia, in 107 days. His return, via New Zealand and Cape Horn, took 119 days. The passage of 15,517 miles (24,971) km) was the longest voyage by a small sailing vessel without a port of call. On 28 May 1967, he received a tumultuous welcome at Plymouth before sailing on to Greenwich, where he was knighted Sir Francis Chichester by Queen Elizabeth II, who used the sword of Sir Francis Drake.

Also on 28 May. . . .

In 1089, Lanfranc, Archbishop of Canterbury, died.

William Pitt the Younger, British statesman, was born in 1759.

The authoress, Anne Brontë (Acton Bell), died in 1849.

In 1934, the Dionne girl quintuplets were born in Canada.

The Duke of Windsor, uncrowned King Edward VIII, died in 1972.

Today is Oak Apple Day, not celebrated as widely now as once it was but there are still local celebrations in many parts of England. It is the anniversary of the day, in 1660, when King Charles II rode into London on his 30th birthday to be welcomed by huge crowds of happy people, pleased to have a king once more and to be able to enjoy again those festivals and enjoyments that had been banned under Oliver Cromwell and the Puritans.

Until the early part of the present century, it was customary for people to decorate houses, shops and churches with boughs of oak leaves, for people to wear oak leaves or oak-apples, for horses to have them in their harnesses and even for railway engines to be festooned with greenery. This had nothing to do with the King's return but rather with the story that captured the imagination of so many people of the way in which the king had escaped capture after the Battle of Worcester, nine years earlier, by hiding in an oak tree.

The day had many names, according to the part of the country in which it was being celebrated. Oak Apple Day, Royal Oak Day are names which speak for themselves. It was also Oak and Nettle Day, probably because of the custom of beating with nettles any who did not wear the oak-leaves or oak apple. It was also Shig Shag, or Shick Shack Day, on which some labourers would beg for beer. If refused they shouted:

Shig Shag, penny a rag.
Bang his head in Cromwell's bag
All up in a bundle.

In many places, Oak Apple Day took on some of the May Day customs, such as dancing round the Maypole, which was decorated, of course, with oak leaves.

This day is observed as Founder's Day at the Royal Hospital, Chelsea, where the Chelsea Pensioners celebrate the birthday of their royal founder by decorating his statue, wearing oak leaves, parading and enjoying extra food and beer. Other special celebrations are at the old soldiers' hospital, the Leycester Hospital at Warwick and, of course, in Worcester, where the battle took place in 1651.

On or about this day in Fownhope, Herefordshire, members of the Heart of Oak Friendly Society still parade, carrying wooden staves decorated with oak apples.

Two men had their own special celebration on this day in 1953. They were Edmund Hillary and Tensing Norkey and they were standing on top of Mount Everest, the highest mountain in the world. They celebrated by thumping each other on the back until they were almost breathless. They were, indeed 'on top of the world', the first men to conquer Mount Everest, thanks to a great team of men that had been led by Sir John Hunt.

There didn't seem much to celebrate on the beaches of Dunkirk, France, on 29 May 1940. The tide of battle in World War II had gone in favour of the German armies which swept through France toward the Channel. The British Army retreated to Dunkirk to be taken back to England. There, on the beaches, they were constantly attacked by German aircraft as they waited for the craft to take them off. Troopships, destroyers, landing craft, paddle steamers and an armada of fishing boats and private launches came in quick succession, taking off as many as they could. Some didn't make it: they were destroyed by bombs or gunfire. But the others succeeded in evacuating some 300,000 troops between 29 May and 3 June.

Long before, another small ship had set sail, not to rescue but to explore. Her captain was Bartolomeu Dias, sent by the King of Portugal to find out whether there was a route round the south of Africa to India. Dias reached the Cape of Good Hope and then turned back. Later he sailed in company with Vasco da Gama and then Cabral. It was near the Cape of Good Hope that Dias was lost at sea on 29 May 1500.

Born on this day were Sir Henry Wickham (1846), who took seeds of rubber plants from Brazil and established the rubber industry in the Far East; G. K. Chesterton (1874), writer and poet, author of the *Father Brown* stories; John Fizgerald Kennedy (1917), President of the United States 1960–3.

One of Britain's greatest scientists and chemists was Sir Humphry Davy, a Cornishman who discovered several chemical elements. He was the inventor of the Davy safety lamp for miners. He died on 29 May 1829.

I disapprove of what you say, but I will defend to the death your right to say it.

These words, attributed to Voltaire, sum up the attitudes of the man who is regarded as one of the greatest 18th century authors. Voltaire was opposed to all forms of cruelty, tyranny and bigotry. He took a great interest in any cases of injustice, especially those where religious intolerance was involved. At one time, his writing offended those in authority so much that he was imprisoned in the Bastille and later exiled to England. He did return later to France, where he continued writing books and plays. For the last 24 years of his life he lived in Switzerland but died on one of his trips to Paris, on 30 May 1778.

It was in France, three centuries earlier, that a young woman made her own mark on the history of the world. Joan of Arc, having heard voices which told her to help drive the English out of France, went to see the king. Dressed in a suit of armour and riding a black horse, she led the army to victory at Orleans. Later she was captured by the English, tried on a charge of witchcraft, and burned at the stake in Rouen on 30 May 1431. She was later canonised. Today is the feast day of St. Joan of Arc.

Peter the Great was born on 30 May 1672, the son of Tsar Alexei of Russia. He became Tsar himself in 1682 and set about the task of changing Russia. He built up an army and navy, then went to war with Sweden and Turkey so that he could gain access to the Baltic and Black Seas. He travelled in Europe finding out many things about western civilisation, then took back skilled engineers and craftsmen to Russia. He built a new capital on the Baltic coast, which he named St. Petersburg (now Leningrad). By the time he died, in 1725, Russia was a very different country from the one into which he was born.

On 30 May 1593, there was a fight in a tavern in Deptford, London, in which a man was stabbed and killed. He was Christopher Marlowe, an important Elizabethan poet and dramatist, whose work influenced Shakespeare. Others who died on this day include Peter Paul Rubens, artist, in 1640, and Alexander Pope, poet, in 1744.

30 May 1959: First flight of a hovercraft (SRNI), at Cowes.

In the faces of men and women, I see God.

So wrote Walt Whitman, the American poet, who was born on 31 May 1819 and who really enjoyed meeting and talking with people. Often he would take a ride on a stage coach or a ferry boat, attend a concert or a lecture, so that he could talk with others. He also had a great love for his country, the United States, expressed clearly in *Leaves of Grass*, the collection of his poems which is regarded as one of the world's great literary works.

Today marks two milestones in the world of sport. In 1787, the first cricket match was played at Lords, not on the present site, but the first of many first-class matches played on a London ground bearing this famous name. In 1868, the first cycle race was held. It was in the Parc St. Cloud, Paris, and was won by James Moore, an Englishman who was living in France.

On this day, in 1669, Samuel Pepys made the last entry in his now famous diary. It contains many personal notes but gives a good insight to life in his day. By this day he was no longer able to see properly but wrote:

> *And so I betake myself to that course, which is almost as much as to see myself go into my grave; for which, and all the discomforts that will accompany my being blind, the good God prepare me.*

Today marked the end of the road for. . . .

Franz Josef Haydn, composer, who died on 31 May 1809.
Joseph Grimaldi, the famous clown, who died in 1837.
Many sailors and some fine ships in the Battle of Jutland, the major naval battle of World War I, between the British fleet under Admiral Jellicoe and the German fleet under Admiral Scheer. The battle left Britain supreme on the sea.

Sadly this day saw the end of some other ships. They were the treasure ships of the Roman Emperor, Caligula, built in the 1st Century AD. The lake in which they were found was drained and the huge galleys housed in a museum. On 31 May 1944, during World War II, petrol was poured over the ships, probably by German soldiers, and the whole museum set ablaze. Nothing but ashes remained.

Some May Events and Commemorations

(*see also pp 79–82*)

1st May Day festivals and celebrations in many places.
Padstow, Cornwall: Hobby-horse festival.
Berwick-on-Tweed, Northumberland: Riding the Bounds.
First Saturday Knutsford, Cheshire: Royal May Day. Decorated pavements; May Queen; Maypole, Morris and Country Dancing.
First Sunday Bridport, Dorset: Flower Sunday. Spring flowers, taken to church by children, are sent to old people in London.
8th (or nearest Saturday) Helston, Cornwall: Furry Dance. Dancing in streets and in and out of houses.
Wednesday before Ascension Day Whitby, North Yorks: Planting the Penny Hedge — stakes and branches at water's edge.
Rogationtide In many places: Rogation processions and Beating the Bounds. Some are at other times in the month.
Southampton, Whitby and elsewhere: Blessing the Sea.
Ascension Day In various places: Beating the Bounds.
Tissington, Derbyshire and Bisley, Gloucestershire: Well Dressings.
About 20th High Wycombe, Buckinghamshire: Weighing the Mayor. Retiring and new mayors are both weighed.
Nearest Sunday to 21st Meriden, West Midlands: Cyclists' Memorial Service at Cyclists' War Memorial, unveiled 21 May 1921.
21st Tower of London: Ceremony of Lilies and Roses. Flowers laid on slab commemorating murder of King Henry VI.
26th or near Hastings, Sussex: Blessing the Sea. Procession.
End of month Sileby, Leicestershire: Orange distribution.
In various places: Mayoring ceremonies.
29th Wishford, Wiltshire: Grovely Forest Rights procession.
Whitsuntide (or on Spring Bank Holiday) In many places: Hay strewing, Parish Walks, dancing, sports and other events.

SOME MAY FAIRS
In various places: May fairs, hiring fairs or Whitsun fairs.
12th Stow-on-the-Wold, Gloucestershire: Horse fair.

SOME AGRICULTURAL AND OTHER SHOWS
Denbighshire and Flintshire, Devon, Hertfordshire, Montgomery, Newark and Nottinghamshire, North Somerset, Oxfordshire, Royal Dublin, Royal Jersey, Royal Ulster, Shropshire and West Midlands, Staffordshire County, Surrey County.

JUNE

June

It is thought that June was named either after the goddess Juno or from *Iuniores* (young people) since this was the month in which young people were highlighted. The Anglo-Saxon sixth and seventh months were 'Litha' ('Moon').

Month of leaves,
Month of roses;
Gardens full
Of dainty posies;
Skies of blue,
Hedgerows gay,
Meadows sweet
With new-mown hay.

Flowery banks,
A-drone with bees,
Dreaming cattle
Under trees:
Song-birds pipe
A merry tune —
This is summer,
This is June.

Irene F. Pawsey

By June the warmer weather and the fine days have come, giving a general air of contentment:

A calm June puts the farmer in tune.

Crops are growing well, and so are the weeds, thistles having a reputation for growing prolifically:

Cut your thistles before St. John: (24 June)
You will have two instead of one.

By the end of the month the weather may have changed:

Before St. John's Day for rain we pray;
After that we get it anyway.

But

A good leak in June sets all in tune.

Midsummer

St. John's Day, 24 June, is Midsummer Day, at one time a very important festival but nowadays celebrated less in Britain than in some other countries.

The origins of the Midsummer festival are very, very old, and related to the strength of the sun. The summer solstice, the longest day, is 21 June and the winter solstice, the shortest day is 21 December. Both were regarded by various ancient peoples as the beginning or change of the year.

In the early days of the Christian Church, many of the old festivals were Christianised. So the Midwinter festival on 25 December was used to celebrate the birth of Jesus Christ and became Christmas. But what of the Midsummer festival? According to the Bible story, John the Baptist was six months older than Jesus and so it was decided that 24 June should be the festival of the Nativity of John the Bapist.

John once said of Jesus, 'He must increase, and I must decrease.' And that is just what the sun does at the time of their respective festivals. It begins to increase in strength after Midwinter and to decrease after Midsummer.

In ancient times people believed that they needed to help the sun on both of these occasions and, to do so, they lit huge bonfires. At one time, Midsummer Eve bonfires were built on hills and in open spaces in many parts of the country. After the fires had been lit, people would dance around the fires, always in a sunwise direction. Some would jump through the flames to gain good fortune. Then, as the flames died away, animals were driven through the embers to protect them from evil spirits.

Bonfires were just one way of helping the sun. In some places barrels of tar were set alight, perhaps mounted on poles, fire balls were swung and blazing wheels were rolled down the hillsides, reminiscent of similar midwinter ceremonies.

Most of these customs have now disappeared, though they remain here and there. Some of them are held a little later at the beginning of July because, before the calendar was changed in 1752, 5 July was Midsummer Day and the bonfires were lit on 4 July, which then was Midsummer Eve.

The old custom of lighting bonfires on St. John's Eve, was revived in the 1920s in Cornwall by the Federation of Old Cornwall Societies. The bonfire built by the Redruth OCS on Carn Brea is usually the first of the chain of fires to be lit. At each of the fires the lighting ceremony is conducted by a Master of Ceremonies using the old Cornish language. After the fire has been lit, flowers and herbs are cast into the flames.

In the past, St. John's Day was not only associated with the sun and fires but with magic and witchcraft. Here and there, relics of the old beliefs remain. At St. Clear, near Liskeard in Cornwall the Midsummer Eve bonfire includes the ceremony of Banishing the Witches. Apart from the oak sickle, flowers and herbs that are cast into the fire to combat witchcraft, the bonfire is topped with a witch's hat and broom — a good indication to any witch to keep away.

There were quite a lot of plants and flowers which were once believed to have anti-witching or magical properties. The one especially associated with St. John's Eve was St. John's wort. Its small golden flowers were regarded as a symbol of the sun, whilst the red on the leaves was a reminder of the blood of St. John the Baptist.

On the eve of St. John, wreaths of St. John's wort were hung on the cattle to drive away evil spirits. Sprays of the plant were also fixed above the doors of cattle sheds. Houses were likewise decorated with St. John's wort, fennel, lilies and other plants that would help or protect.

Midsummer Eve was also the time for gathering fernseed. This is almost invisible and, consequently, was thought to give the gatherer the ability to become invisible as well as to find hidden treasure and to command any living man or beast.

To gather fernseed was difficult and dangerous. It had to be gathered at midnight; it must not be touched by hand but brushed off with a forked hazel stick onto a pewter plate; and the gatherer was liable to be destroyed by demons as he worked. There were few who had the courage to try.

The magical aspect of Midsummer Eve was also thought to help young ladies to discover whom they were going to marry. This was 'Maidens' Night' and there were various methods open to a young lady. She might like to go out that evening into a churchyard or garden, where she should throw hempseed over her shoulder, reciting at the same time.

Hempseed I set; hempseed I sow:
The man that is my true love
Come after me and mow.

Perhaps it might be easier for her to arrange her shoes carefully before going to bed.

Hoping this night my true love to see,
I place my shoes in the form of a T.

One of the methods was clearly only for those who were able to be patient. The young lady was to walk backwards into the garden and pluck a rose, which should then be sewn up in a bag and placed in a bottom drawer until Christmas Day. Then she should take it from the bag and wear it in her bosom when she attended church. If any young man should ask her for the rose — or take it from her without asking — he would one day become her husband.

Crowds of people travel each year to be at Stonehenge, in Wiltshire, before dawn on Midsummer Day so that they can watch the ceremony that will take place.

Stonehenge is probably 4,000 years old and was built during different periods. One feature of this ancient temple is the Hele Stone (Sun Stone). On the Summer Solstice, 21 June, the rays of the sun shine over the Hele Stone onto the altar. Probably in the Iron Age this altar was used by the Druids for sacrifice. Nowadays a dawn ceremony is held by a group of modern Druids. After an overnight vigil, the Druids, in their white robes and scarlet hoods, and carrying symbolic banners, process amongst the monoliths and beneath the great trilithons to the altar, where a service is held. In recent years, the ceremony has been transferred from 21 June to dawn on Midsummer Day.

Also on St. John's Day, a sermon is preached from a pulpit in a quadrangle at Magdalen College, Oxford. It serves as a reminder that the college, founded in 1458, was built on a site formerly occupied by a Hospital of St. John the Baptist.

About this time, on the last Saturday in June, is the very impressive Pilgrimage to Glastonbury, Somerset. Thousands of Anglicans, many of them carrying banners, gather round St. John's Church in the High Street near the Holy Thorn. From there they process to the ruins of Glastonbury Abbey, where an open-air service is held.

At various times during June, in many parts of the country, processions wend their way to parish churches for annual rush, hay, or grass strewing ceremonies. They are reminders of former days when rushes or hay were strewn on the earthen floors of the churches. Some places where such services are held are Borrowden, Braunstone and Langham in Leicestershire, Wingrave in Buckinghamshire, Warcop in Cumbria and Pavenham in Bedfordshire. Similar services are held elsewhere during July and August.

Well dressings (p. 81) may be seen at some time during June at the Derbyshire villages of Wirksworth, Ashford in the Water, Tideswell, Youlgrave and Hope. Morris men and other folk dancers provide colour of a different kind and are a popular form of entertainment.

But for lots of people, June is a month in which to enjoy their favourite outdoor activities and, for many anglers, it starts a new year: the coarse fishing season opens on 16 June.

God grant me the serenity to accept the things I cannot change, the courage to change the things I can, and the wisdom to distinguish the one from the other.

Reinhold Niebuhr, who expressed these feelings, died on 1 June 1971. He was one of the most important American 20th Century theologians, and had a considerable influence upon the American protestant churches as well as upon United States politics.

This was the birthday, in 1801, of another American, who was to have an impact on American religion. He was Brigham Young who, in 1844, became the second president of the Mormon Church. In the face of mob violence, he led the Mormons from Nauvoo, Illinois, to Utah, where he selected a site for the settlement which grew into Salt Lake City, the centre of the Mormon religion to this day.

Also from America comes the great success story of one who had the courage to change what she could. Helen Keller, blind, deaf and dumb, with help and encouragement, overcame her handicap in a way that was to be an example to many others, becoming a world-famous figure whose life was spent in helping others. That life ended on 1 June 1968.

In 1794, this was the 'Glorious First of June', the name given to a naval battle fought between a British fleet of 26 ships commanded by Earl Howe and a French fleet of the same size under de Joyeuse. Technically it was a British victory but the French had succeeded in their aim to draw the British away from a huge French convoy of 130 merchant ships carrying grain from America.

Also on 1 June . . . .

Henry Francis Lyte, hymnwriter (*Abide with me*), born 1793.
Sir James Clark Ross discovered the Magnetic Pole in 1834.
John Masefield, 15th Poet Laureate and novelist, born 1878.
London poet and playwright, John Drinkwater, born 1882.
Sir Frank Whittle, inventor of the jet engine, born 1907.
Sir Hugh Walpole, novelist and dramatist, died 1941.
In 1950, the first BEA passenger helicopter flight.

Silent? ah, he is silent! He can keep silence well. That man's silence is wonderful to listen to.

These words from *Under the Greenwood Tree* are by Thomas Hardy, who was born in Dorset on 2 June 1840, and became a great novelist and poet. He wrote mostly about South-west England, or 'Wessex', making good use of his knowledge of local dialects and customs. From his pen came such masterpieces as *The Mayor of Casterbridge, Tess of the d'Urbervilles. Far from the Madding Crowd. . . .*

No doubt there were many who wished they could have been far from the crowds in Paris on 2 June 1793, for this was the day when the Reign of Terror began. The Jacobins, led by Robespierre were responsible for sending many nobles and political leaders to the guillotine.

It was a different kind of reign that was celebrated throughout the world on 2 June 1953, when the coronation took place of Queen Elizabeth II. This was the first coronation to be televised and people in many places were able to enjoy, in the comfort of their own homes, the pageantry and procession, the ceremonial and the music, which all help to make an unforgettable occasion.

Patriotic music played on great occasions may well include the *Pomp and Circumstance* marches by Sir Edward Elgar. This was his birthday in 1857. Elgar was the son of an organist and music dealer. He began composing at an early age and went on to write some fine orchestral works and oratorios. His is an important name in the history of English music.

John Travers Cornwell died on 2 June 1916, from wounds he had received at the Battle of Jutland. He was only sixteen but had shown 'a splendid instance of devotion to duty' for which he was awarded the Victoria Cross.

This day also saw the death, in 1882, of one of the greatest guerilla leaders in modern history. Giuseppe Garibaldi, with an army of only 1,000, had outstanding success in an attempt to gain unity and independence for Italy.

Watch some archaelogists at work on an ancient site and you will see how carefully the earth is removed and notes made as to the location of fragments of pottery or other remnants of the ancient times. The methods used were inspired by Sir William Matthew Flinders Petrie, who was born near London on 3 June 1853. He became very interested in ancient monuments and buildings, making a study of Stonehenge and publishing his findings in 1880. That was the year in which he turned his attention to the excavation of the Great Pyramid and many sites in Egypt and Palestine. When he suggested that the dates of these places could be determined by studying the potsherds, other archaeologists disagreed but this method has now become fully accepted. Flinders Petrie, who returned to Egypt year after year to excavate, was recognised as a leading Egyptologist and author on archaeology. He was knighted in 1923 and died in Jerusalem in 1942.

The careful studies made by William Harvey were concerned with the human body. Harvey, who was a physician at St. Bartholomew's Hospital, London, and a royal physician, was the man who discovered how blood circulated, having the heart as a pump. He died on 3 June 1657.

Johann Strauss, the Younger, set the hearts a-beating and the feet a-dancing with his Viennese waltzes. Known as 'The Waltz King', he composed over 400 waltzes besides operettas and other music. He conducted his own orchestra, with which he toured Europe and visited America. His famous waltzes capture the spirit of romantic 19th Century Vienna, where he died on 3 June 1899.

Another composer to die on 3 June, in 1875, was Georges Bizet. He came from a musical family and composed various works before his greatest, the opera *Carmen*, completed only shortly before his death.

This day also saw the death, in 1963, of Pope John XXIII, one of the most popular popes in history. Four years later, in 1967, Arthur Ransome died. He is remembered for his children's books, including *Old Peter's Russian Tales* and *Swallows and Amazons*.

This day, in 1798, saw the death of one of the world's most famous romantic lovers, Giovanni Casanova. Born in Venice in 1725, he had many different occupations as abbé, secretary, violinist, soldier, adventurer, alchemist, spy and others too. Imprisoned in 1755, he made a daring escape, then travelled Europe meeting the most important people of his day and being introduced to the top society, with whom he enjoyed great popularity until he found it necessary to 'disappear' usually because of his affairs with women. His memoirs, published some years after his death, tell of his many love affairs. Still today the name 'Casanova' is applied to any man who is a 'lady-killer'.

The King's horse Anmer became a lady-killer on 4 June 1913. Those were the days when Suffragettes were very active as they endeavoured to get votes for women, using many means to draw attention to their cause. People watching the Derby at Epsom were horrified to see Emily Davidson throw herself in front of the King's horse. She was killed.

Another death on 4 June became a historical event. In 1844, some Icelandic fishermen landed on the island of Eldey to catch and kill Great Auks. Once there had been many thousands of these birds, the penguins of the north, but they were easy to catch and good to eat. The two Great Auks killed on this day were the last in the world. People can see stuffed specimens in museums but no one will ever again see a live Great Auk.

'Farmer George' was born on 4 June 1738. That may seem a disrespectful title for a British king but George III was a popular monarch and his interest in farming was one of the important factors in the agricultural revolution of his day. He not only had a model farm at Windsor, but he wrote pamphlets on farming under the name of Ralph Robinson. Toward the end of his life he became blind and insane, the result of a rare and painful disease.

The first white Australian 'settlers' went ashore on 4 June 1629. They were mutineers, marooned there by the Dutch Captain Pelsaert. No one knows what happened to them.

5 June

This was the day the balloon went up. On 5 June 1783, Joseph and Etienne Montgolfier gave the first public demonstration of a hot-air balloon, at Annonay, Languedoc, France. Their balloon, made from cloth and paper, had an opening at the bottom, held open by a wooden frame. The balloon was filled with hot air from a fire on the ground, and then needed eight men to hold it down. When released, the unmanned balloon stayed in the air for ten minutes before drifting gently to the ground. It was the first of many flights which were to develop into the sport of ballooning and the commercial dirigible, or steerable, airship.

This was the day, in 1967, when the balloon went up in a different sense. Tension had existed between Israel and the neighbouring Arab States from the time the independent state of Israel had been established in 1948. Matters came to a head in May 1967, when Israel, Egypt, Syria and Jordan began talk of war. On 5 June, Israeli planes attacked Arab airfields, defeated their armies and invaded Arab territories. The war lasted only six days but its consequences lasted many years.

One result of the Six Day War was that the Suez Canal was closed, and remained so for eight years, being reopened on the anniversary of the outbreak of war, 5 June 1975.

A British army officer who first made a name for himself in the Middle East was Earl Kitchener, who became Secretary of State for War at the beginning of World War I, and whose face appeared on large numbers of recruiting posters with the words 'Your Country needs You! On 5 June 1916, the cruiser on which he was travelling to Russia hit a mine off Orkney and Kitchener was drowned.

This was the birthday of two well-known economists. Adam Smith, born on 5 June 1723, is regarded as the founder of modern economics and his book *The Wealth of Nations* a landmark in political economy. John Maynard Keynes, born this day in 1883, is considered one of the most influential economists of all time. His great book, *General Theory of Employment, Interest and Money*, published in 1936, had far-reaching effects.

Thomas Chippendale, furniture designer, was baptised in 1718.

Jeremy Bentham sits in University College, London, with his right hand on his walking stick and his head on the floor between his feet. That may seem an unusual position in which to be but it is, in fact, only the mortal remains of Jeremy Bentham, who died on 6 June 1835. Before he died he stated in his will that his body should be used for scientific purposes. Eventually his skeleton was padded, his own clothes put on it and a wax head added. The head between the feet is his own head, which has been preserved. And there he sits, day after day, in his glass case.

Or does he? There are many who have reported having seen or heard Jeremy's ghost in the college. Some say it is because he is very unhappy at what was done to his body. It is a pity, especially as he always wanted people to be happy. He believed that the object of all individual and government action should be 'the greatest happiness of the greatest number'. His followers were responsible for some of the important reforms which helped make life a little easier for a lot of people.

Lord Anson, Baron of Soberton, died on 6 June 1762, after catching a severe cold. Born at Shugborough, Staffordshire, he entered the Royal Navy at an early age to begin what was to be a distinguished career, in which eventually he became Admiral, Member of Parliament and First Lord of the Admirality.

His most famous voyage was to take him round the world and return with treasure worth £500,000. This voyage in the *Centurion* ranks as one of the most outstanding voyages of history. As Commander-in-Chief of a small fleet, his instructions were to 'annoy the Spaniards', or, in other words, to destroy their ships and perhaps even capture the Manila treasure galleon. That he succeeded at all is remarkable. His ships were crewed largely by invalids. He had to do battle with the stormy Cape Horn, the might of Spain and the trickery of the Chinese. His ships were battered and his crews suffered from hunger and disease. Anson faced all of these with courage, and with the finest qualities of leadership. Moreover, his humane treatment of prisoners had far-reaching effects.

He returned in June 1744, not only rich but applauded by the country he served so well for the whole of his life.

The journey undertaken by King Henry VIII of England was only a short one but one that has also gone down in history because of the splendour and magnificence of the occasion that followed. On 6 June 1520, at Guisnes, he met King Francis I of France to see whether they could make an alliance against Charles V, the Holy Roman Emperor.

Both kings were aged less than thirty and each was anxious to outdo the other in the richness of his retinue. Fountains of wine played in front of a temporary palace erected for the reception and no less than 2,800 tents were used. A Tree of Nobility was set up on which the shields of contesting knights were hung. The trunk was of cloth of gold, the leaves were of green silk with flowers and fruits of silver and gold. The colourful tabards of the heralds and the spectacle of a week's tournaments all helped to give this occasion the name of Field of the Cloth of Gold.

On 6 June 1944, another large body of men crossed the Channel to France. There was no magnificence about this occasion. It was D-Day and hundreds of craft made for the beaches of Normandy to land troops for the invasion of Europe which began the closing stages of World War II.

This is a good day for birthdays and is shared by a number of well-known people.

Diego de Velasquez, the Spanish painter, born at Seville in 1599, painted many fine portraits.

The American artist, John Trumbull, painted portraits and scenes from American history. He was born in 1756.

Alexander Pushkin, Russian poet and novelist — *Boris Godounov*, *Eugene Onegin* and other works — was born in 1799.

Sir John Stainer, born 1840, organist of St. Paul's Cathedral, composed much sacred music including *The Crucifixion*.

Robert Falcon Scott, explorer, was born in 1868. He died in Antarctica after reaching the South Pole in 1912.

Dame Ninette de Valois, the Irish-born ballerina and choreographer, was born in 1898. In 1931, she founded the Sadler's Wells Ballet School, which became the Royal Ballet.

Aram Khachaturian, the Armenian composer of the famous *Sabre Dance* and *Spartacus*, was born in 1903.

One of the greatest names in the history of Scotland is that of King Robert I, Robert the Bruce, the great hero who fought for the independence of his country from England. After unsuccessful risings, he was forced into hiding but his great success came at the Battle of Bannockburn (p. 145), when his army routed the English army that was three times as large. On 7 June 1329, Bruce died of leprosy at Cardross Castle, Firth of Clyde. His heart was being carried to Jerusalem but Douglas, the bearer, was killed and the heart returned to Scotland, where it was placed in Melrose Abbey. His body was interred in Dunfermline Abbey.

A Scotsman much more popular with the English was John Rennie, whose birthday this was in 1761. After working for Boulton and Watt, he set up in business in London as a civil engineer, gaining a reputation as a bridge builder. He designed three Thames bridges, the old Southwark, Waterloo and London Bridges, besides many others in England and Scotland. He also designed or improved docks and harbours, built canals and drained fenland. His son, also named John, a civil engineer like his father, completed London Bridge.

Knud Rasmussen was interested in bridging a few gaps. He was born on 7 June 1879, at Jacobshavn, Greenland, of Danish and Eskimo parents. He believed that the Eskimos and the North American Indians were all descendants of people who had migrated across the Bering Strait from Asia. To prove his theory he directed several expeditions to Greenland and the Bering Strait.

This was the birthday, in 1848, of Eugene Gauguin, the French post-Impressionist painter. Born in Paris, the son of a journalist and a Peruvian Creole mother, he developed his own style of art, related particularly to primitive peoples and their art forms. The latter part of his life was spent in Tahiti and the Marquesas, whose inhabitants feature largely in his best-known paintings.

Also born today: Beau Brummel, leader of fashion (p. 36), in 1778 and Sir James Simpson, pioneer of anaesthetics, in 1811. Dorothy Parker, U.S. poet and journalist, died in 1967.

Two great engineers and lighthouse-builders were born on 8 June. 1724 saw the birth of John Smeaton, the Yorkshireman who became a mathematical instrument maker and made studies of the workings of windmills and water-wheels. His best known memorial is the lighthouse he designed, the third Eddystone lighthouse, which stood on those rocks for over 120 years before being re-erected on Plymouth Hoe. Amongst his other engineering works were the Forth and Clyde Canal and Ramsgate Harbour.

Half a century later, on 8 June 1772, Robert Stevenson was born in Glasgow. In 1796, he succeeded his father as engineer of the Lighthouse Board and, during the 47 years he held this office, he designed or built 23 Scottish lighthouses including the famous Bell Rock. He also invented a system of intermittent or flashing lights. His expertise was much wider than this, however, and he acted as a consulting engineer for harbours, canals, railways, roads and bridges.

The planning and designing of Sir Joseph Paxton was different. He was a gardener employed by the Duke of Devonshire and was responsible for the replanning of the Duke's estate at Chatsworth, Derbyshire. Later he designed the Crystal Palace for the Great Exhibition of 1851. Paxton died on this day in 1865.

This day also saw the death, in 1979, of Norman Hartnell, royal dress designer for 49 years. One of his finest designs was the coronation gown for Queen Elizabeth II, with emblems of the Commonwealth all stitched by hand and taking 3000 hours to complete.

Some others who died on 8 June. . . .
- Muhammad, Prophet and founder of Islam, in 632.
- Edward, the Black Prince, in 1376.
- Sarah Siddons, British actress (p. 163), in 1831.
- George Sand, French writer, in 1876.
- Gerard Manley Hopkins, London poet, in 1889.

Today's birthdays. . . .
- Robert Schumann, French composer, in 1810.
- Sir John Millais, English painter, in 1829.

Oliver Twist has asked for more!

These few words are sufficient to conjure up in the minds of many people a familiar picture of one of the well-known characters created by Charles Dickens. With such others as David Copperfield, Ebenezer Scrooge, Martin Chuzzlewit, Pip and Mr. Pickwick, Oliver Twist is ensured of a permanent place in English literature.

During the 19th Century, it was not only Oliver Twist who asked for more. People were clamouring for the next episode of whatever Dickens happened to be writing. His own experiences of poverty and hardship led to his attempts, through his writings, to highlight the social problems of his day — and he succeeded.

He died on 9 June 1870. Two days later, Queen Victoria wrote in her diary; 'He is a very great loss. He had a large loving mind and the strongest sympathy with the poorer classes. He felt sure a better feeling, and much greater union of classes', would take place in time. And I pray earnestly it may.' Charles Dickens, was laid to rest in Westminster Abbey.

Far away, on the West of Scotland is another abbey, not as ornate as Westminster Abbey but an important centre of Christianity and a place of pilgrimage. There, on the tiny island of Iona, off the coast of Mull, St. Columba founded a monastery, in 563, a centre from which he was to carry the Christian gospel throughout Scotland and from which others were to travel to Northumbria. St. Columba died there on 9 June 597 and this day is kept by the Church as his feast day.

This day also marked an important step forward in the English Church, for it was on 9 June 1549, that the *Book of Common Prayer* was first issued throughout the Church of England — 'Common' because it was in English, a language common to priests and people instead of Latin, used for all church worship prior to this.

This was the first day for . . . .

George Stephenson, 'Father of the Railways', born in 1781.
Cole Porter, popular American song-writer, born in 1892.
The London Symphony Orchestra, opening concert in 1904.
Gatwick Airport, opened in 1958.
. . . and the last day for actress Dame Sybil Thorndike, 1976.

10 June

One of the outstanding Holy Roman Emperors was Friedrich I, also known as 'Barbarossa' (Red beard). He was renowned as a fighter and very capable as an administrator. By various means he achieved peace in both Germany and Italy. He ruled from 1152 until 10 June 1190, the day on which he drowned whilst on the 3rd Crusade. Legend tells that this popular ruler sleeps beneath a mountain in Germany from whence he will return at the time of that country's greatest need.

Greatly respected and loved in Scotland was Queen Margaret, a Hungarian princess who went to England but, after the Norman Conquest, fled to Scotland, where she married Malcolm Canmore, the Scottish king. She did much to civilise Scotland and influenced the Celtic Church. She died in 1093 and was canonised in 1251. Various dates have been kept as her feast day, but it was finally established as 10 June.

A descendent of the Scottish royal line of kings, James Francis Edward Stuart, was born on 10 June 1688. The son of James II, who lost his throne that very year, he claimed the British Crown on his father's death in 1701. Known as the 'Old Pretender', he made an unsuccessful attempt to gain the crown in the Jacobite rebellion of 1715.

This was the birthday, in 1921, of Prince Philip of Greece, who was created Duke of Edinburgh as a result of his marriage to Princess Elizabeth, later Queen Elizabeth II. The Duke of Edinburgh has been a popular consort to the queen with a reputation for occasional outspokenness and for the encouragement of many activities, particularly concerning young people, sport and industry.

Two of today's deaths. . . .
- Frederick Delius, the English composer, died in 1934.
- Spencer Tracy, rugged American film actor, died in 1967.

Events of 10 June. . . .
- The first Oxford v Cambridge boat race was held in 1829.
- The Crystal Palace, re-erected at Sydenham, was opened in 1854.
- The Berlin/Rome Axis was formed by Hitler and Mussolini, 1940.
- Lidice, Czechoslovakia, was destroyed by Germans in 1942.

Barnaby bright, Barnaby bright,
The longest day and the shortest night

This little verse serves as a reminder that, before the calendar was changed in 1752, 11 June was the longest day. It was a day when decorations were put up and when priests, clerks and choristers may have worn garlands.

St. Barnabas was a companion of St. Paul on his journeyings. He had come from Cyprus and he returned to that island, where it is generally believed that, having established the Christian Church, he was put to death for his beliefs. He is often depicted in art carrying a hay rake — a reminder to those long ago that this day marked the beginning of hay-making.

By St. Barnabas put scythe to grass.

Such rustic pursuits serve as a reminder of some of the pictures of Constable. The Hay-Wain is perhaps the best known of the many familiar paintings of the Essex/Suffolk countryside, known to many people as 'Constable country'. John Constable was born on 11 June 1776.

Sir John Franklin died on 11 June 1847, far away from his native English countryside, in the icy wastes of the north of Canada.

At the age of 14 he had entered the Royal Navy and he served in the Battle of Trafalgar. Having taken part in an expedition, in 1818, which tried to reach the North Pole, his appetite was whetted for polar exploration and especially seeking a North-west passage. His ships *Erebus* and *Terror* were last seen in July 1845. It was not until 1859 that a search party found the skeletons of the crews and a log book telling how the ships had been crushed in the ice. Franklin had proved that there was a North-west passage but that it would need special ships to navigate it.

One of today's best known explorers, particularly of the undersea world, is Jacques-Yves Cousteau, born on 11 June 1910.

One discovery from under the sea was oil — North Sea oil, first pumped ashore from Britain's oilfields on 11 June 1975.

This is a day of 'firsts'. It was on 12 June 1667, that the first blood transfusion was given. It was in Montpelier, France, and was performed by Jean-Baptiste Denys. It was a small but significant beginning to the system of blood donors, blood banks and world-wide co-operation which we know today.

Also in France, on 12 June 1895, in Paris, there was the first public showing of a newsreel film. It was the work of the Lumiére brothers, Auguste and Louis, who patented a cinematographic screen and stereoscopic projection.

Bryan Allen decided to take a trip to France on 12 June 1979, not crossing the Channel in the way that most people do but in a specially designed aircraft. It was called *Gossamer Albatross*; it weighed only 55 pounds (24.9 kg) in spite of having a wing span of 96 feet (29¼ m); but, most important of all, it had no engine. All the way to Cape Griz Nez, for nearly three hours the pilot had to pedal to drive the propellor. It was hard work but it was worth it. Not only did he become the first man to cross the Channel in a man-powered machine, but his American team received the prize of £100,000, offered to the first man to achieve this feat.

On this day in 1837 the first practical electric telegraph was patented. Designed by William Cooke and Charles Wheatstone, it operated between Chalk Farm and Euston, in London, and had moving needles which pointed in turn to letters of the alphabet, so spelling out the messages.

This was the first day Londoners could use the new Rotherhithe Tunnel under the Thames. It was opened on 12 June 1908.

It was the first day for Charles Kingsley, clergyman, author, poet and social reformer. His birthday was 12 June 1819. Born this day in 1851 was Sir Oliver Lodge, the physicist whose investigations of electric waves helped develop the radio.

Also today; in 1842, Dr. Arnold of Rugby (p. 134) died; in 1667, Dutch warships attacked English ships in the Medway; in 1748, a total eclipse of the sun in Europe with great storms.

One of the best-known names in the history of the world is that of Alexander the Great, who lived in the 4th Century BC. The son of King Philip of Macedonia, he inherited and surpassed his father's great military and political abilities. He set out to quell the risings that followed Philip's assassination, then travelled eastwards and to the south, conquering the mighty Persians and subduing Syria, Egypt and all the lands as far as the river Indus.

Many are the tales that are told of Alexander and his great horse, Bucephalus. Alexander was a leader in every sense of the word, fighting alongside his men. In one Indian city he was speared and thought by his men to be dead. To prove otherwise, he had himself propped up in a boat so that he could wave to them, then mounted his horse to ride a short distance. Wherever he went he left reminders of Greece and new cities he built, a number of them bearing the name Alexandria.

He had to return home, after his soldiers had clearly had enough travelling, only to find many problems of tyranny and corruption. Having restored order and quelled a rebellion, he made plans for further journeyings and conquest. It was not to be. He took ill, probably with malaria. As the generals filed past his death bed on 13 June 323 BC, one whispered, 'Who will be your successor?'

Alexander smiled weakly as he replied softly, 'The best!'

This was the birthday, in 1795, of one of the best and most famous of headmasters, Dr. Thomas Arnold of Rugby School. He introduced changes which were adopted by other schools too. Dr. Arnold expected high standards from his pupils. Once he said to them,

> *What we must look for here is, first, religious and moral principles; secondly gentlemanly conduct; thirdly, intellectual ability.*

Described by some as the greatest poet of his time, William Butler Yeats was born in Dublin on 13 June 1865. He was awarded the Nobel Prize for Literature in 1923.

Paavo Nurmi, the 'Phantom Finn', the best-known athlete of his day (p. 176) was born on 13 June 1897.

The Boxer Rising, in China, began on 13 June 1900.

One of the greatest voyages undertaken in a small boat ended on 14 June 1789, when eighteen men, led by Captain Bligh, stumbled ashore at Timor after a voyage of 3,618 miles (5,822 km) that had taken 48 days. The voyage had begun after Fletcher Christian had mutinied and taken control of HMS *Bounty*. Captain Bligh, and those who wished to go with him — his clerk, the botanist, eight officers and eight of the crew — were set adrift in a 23 ft (7 m) open boat with provisions for only a few days, no charts and no firearms. Having been attacked by natives on Tofua, the first island where they landed, Bligh realised that Timor was the nearest civilised port. It was a hard voyage in an overloaded boat, open to all weathers. Somehow Bligh managed to keep his crew alive as well as navigate with remarkable accuracy.

It was a much pleasanter journey by boat for *Three Men in a Boat*, a leisurely, yet eventful, time on the Thames. The author, Jerome K. Jerome, who died on 14 June 1927, had been a clerk and a teacher before writing this very successful humorous book. He then wrote several other novels and plays, as well as editing magazines. No doubt he enjoyed his work, as did one of his characters in the boat.

> *I like work: it fascinates me. I can sit and look at it for hours. I love to keep it by me: the idea of getting rid of it nearly breaks my heart.*

Harriet Beecher, who was born on this day in 1811, was a worker too. In 1836, she married the Revd. C. E. Stowe and later worked for the abolition of slavery. Her book, *Uncle Tom's Cabin*, made Harriet Beecher Stowe famous.

G. K. Chesterton, London born journalist, author, critic and short story writer, died on 14 June 1936. Ten years later on this day John Logie Baird, inventor of television, died. Two birthdays today, of very different people — Burl Ives, American actor and singer in 1909, and 'Che' Guevara, revolutionary, in 1928. It was victory on this day in 1645 for Cromwell and his New Model Army over the Royalists at the Battle of Naseby.

Today is celebrated as Flag Day in the United States — the anniversary of the adoption of the 'Stars and Stripes' in 1777.

This is an important day in British history, for it was on 15 June 1215, that the barons, advised by Stephen Langton, Archbishop of Canterbury, all wanting fair treatment, met King John at Runnymede, near Windsor and insisted that he place his seal on the Magna Carta.

In 1381, it was not the nobles but the peasants who were angry, protesting against a new tax. Led by Wat Tyler, a large number marched to London, destroyed John of Gaunt's palace and the Temple, which was the headquarters of lawyers, and killed a number of people. King Richard II met the rebels one day at Mile End and the next day at Smithfield. On the second day, 15 June, William Walworth, the Lord Mayor of London, struck down Wat Tyler with his sword and later killed him. The Peasants' Revolt was over.

On 15 June: Edward, the Black Prince, was born in 1330; and Edvard Greig, Norwegian composer, in 1843. In 1982, the Falkland Islands war ended after 72 days occupation by Argentina.

It was on 15 June 1752, that Benjamin Franklin demonstrated electricity in lightning. He flew a kite during a thunderstorm. When the kite was struck by lightning, the electricity ran down the wet string and made a spark on a key near the ground. Franklin put this knowledge to good use when he invented the lightning conductor to safeguard tall buildings.

This was the day of the first fatal air crash. On 15 June 1785, M. de Rozier took fire and hydrogen in a balloon from Boulogne in an attempt to cross the Channel, but the balloon caught fire and crashed, killing Rozier and his companion.

A more successful flight was completed on 15 June 1919, when (Sir) John Alcock and Arthur Brown made the first non-stop flight across the Atlantic from St. John's, Newfoundland, to Clifden in Ireland, taking 15 hours 57 minutes to do so.

Charles Goodyear was granted a patent on 15 June 1844, for the vulcanisation of rubber. Just as well, perhaps, for you may need your 'wellies' after today (St. Vitus's Day).

If St. Vitus Day be rainy weather
It will rain for thirty days together.

On this day, in 1963, the first woman to travel in space began a series of 48 orbits of the world in the Russian space craft *Vostok 6*. She was Valentina Tereshkova, a 26-year-old and the last cosmonaut of the six *Vostok* missions begun by Yuri Gagarin in 1961. Five months later, Valentina married Andrian Nikolayev, the *Vostok 3* cosmonaut and, in due course, had a healthy baby, proving that neither of them had suffered any radiation effects whilst in space.

It was on 16 June 1977, that Wernher von Braun died. He was the German engineer who experimented with rockets and was largely responsible for the V2 rockets used by Germany towards the end of World War II. After the war he went to the United States, where he became a US citizen and played a major role in the American space programme.

This day also saw the death, in 1930, of the American inventor Elmer Ambrose Sperry. Amongst his inventions were a new kind of dynamo, arc-light and searchlight but perhaps most important was the gyroscopic compass, based on the toy gyro top. This compass gives an accurate indication of the true north and has proved a boon to navigators.

Two soldiers may be recalled today. The most famous is John Churchill, 1st Duke of Marlborough, national hero, victor of the Battles of Blenheim, Ramillies and Oudenarde, who died on 16 June 1722. The other is George Heathfield, who, having served in various parts of the world, was sent as Governor of Gibraltar in 1775. On 16 June 1779, Gibraltar was besieged and Heathfield successfully defended the Rock against attacks by the Spaniards and French for nearly four years. In recognition of this remarkable achievement, he was given the title of Baron Heathfield of Gibraltar.

Also on 16 June . . . .

Stan Laurel, the thin one of the Laurel and Hardy slapstick comedy films, was born in 1890.

Peter Lee, Durham miners' leader and County Councillor, after whom the new town of Peterlee was named, died in 1935.

The Ford Motor Company, which was to spread to many countries, was founded in Detroit, USA, in 1903.

What could one do with £30,000? John Wesley gave it away. It was money received from his many writings but John Wesley did not want it for himself. He was content to live on £28 per year. Born on 17 June 1703, he became leader, at Oxford, of a group who were nicknamed The Holy Club, or Methodists — a name which was to be adopted by his many followers. Apart from his varied literary works, he kept his *Journal*, which records an eventful ministry in which he preached 40,000 sermons and travelled some 250,000 miles (402,325 km), mainly on horseback. The effects of his preaching were very extensive.

One of the early Methodists was Selina, Countess of Huntingdon, who built or bought many chapels which were linked, under the leadership of George Whitefield, in 'The Countess of Huntingdon's Connexion'. She died in London on 17 June 1791.

'We have in England a particular bashfulness in everything that regards religion.' So wrote Joseph Addison in *The Spectator*, the magazine to which he was a leading contributor. The son of a clergyman, he became a poet, dramatist and statesman. As he died on 17 June 1719, he said, 'See in what peace a Christian can die.'

Edward Burne-Jones went to Oxford as a divinity student but, striking up a friendship with William Morris, a fellow student, he decided instead to become an artist, working on stained glass, tapestry and book illustration as well as painting. Sir Edward Burne-Jones died on 17 June 1898.

This was the birthday . . . .

In 1239, of Edward I, King of England, 'Hammer of the Scots'.

In 1818, of the French composer of operas, Charles Gounod.

In 1882, of Igor Stravinsky, Russian composer. He is especially remembered for some of his fine ballet music.

Isambard Kingdom Brunel's great ship *Great Eastern* sailed on her maiden voyage on 17 June 1860, for New York, a voyage which took eleven days.

Americans remember one of the decisive battles of the American War of Independence, Bunker Hill, fought on 17 June 1775.

This day, in 1815, was one of the important days in the history of Europe, for it was the day which finally put an end to the power and ambitions of Napoleon, Emperor of France, with his defeat at the Battle of Waterloo. The smaller British army, under the command of Arthur Wellesley, later to become Duke of Wellington, successfully held out against the crack regiments of Napoleon until the arrival of the Prussian army, under Marshal Blucher. Napoleon, who, at various times, had set his sights on the control of much of Europe, was later exiled to St. Helena.

Later last century, people of Britain were introduced to an unusual land called Erewhon, in which there were many strange laws and customs. Where was it? If you read the name backwards, it almost spells 'Nowhere'. It was not a real land but one invented by Samuel Butler for his book *Erewhon*. Yet people who read the book felt very uncomfortable because in it they could recognise their own world. Later, Samuel Butler wrote *Way of all Flesh*, a book in which his thoughts on some aspects of family and religious attitudes were freely expressed. It was published after his death on 18 June 1902. Some words from the book seem very true of Samuel Butler.

> *Every man's work, whether it be literature or music or pictures or architecture or anything else, is always a portrait of himself.*

This was true of the writings of William Cobbett. He died on 18 June 1835, the year in which Samuel Butler was born. He was a popular journalist, who tried to preserve rural England after the Industrial Revolution. He wrote against the corruption of his day and had to flee to America in 1817 but returned two years later to fight for the rights of labourers.

The writings and prayers of Michel Quoist, born on 18 June 1918, undoubtedly portray a down-to-earth priest, who is well aware of the problems of today's world and seeks to help people to find a meaning for life and a relationship with God.

On this day, in 1928, Amelia Earhart became the first woman to fly the Atlantic — as a passenger. To justify the renown, she made a solo flight across the ocean four years later.

If Cleopatra's nose had been shorter, the whole face of the earth would have changed.

It is an interesting thought — but is it historical? Mathematical? Philosophical? It could certainly have been mathematical or philosophical, for it is one of the thoughts of Blaise Pascal, who was born on 19 June 1623, at Clermont-Ferrand, France. He was a brilliant mathematician and physicist, who astounded people with his knowledge at an early age and invented the first digital calculator, the syringe and the hydraulic press. He was also a religious thinker and philosopher, who spent much of his later life in research and in good works. He wrote, 'If you want people to think well of you, do not speak well of yourself.'

Quietly helping people in need was one of the joys of Charles Haddon Spurgeon, the great Baptist preacher, whose preaching was such that his congregations could be numbered in thousands — more than 10,000 in the Surrey Gardens Music Hall and up to 6,000 in the new Metropolitan Tabernacle. His sermons fill more than 50 volumes. He was born on 19 June 1834.

This was also the birthday, in 1566, of King James I of Great Britain and, in 1861, of Earl Haig, Commander-in-Chief of the British forces in World War I. It was the birthday of the Metropolitan Police too, for it was on 19 June 1829, that they were established by Act of Parliament.

This day also marked the beginning of passenger air travel. The dirigible (steerable) airship, *Deutschland*, was launched on 19 June 1910. It was designed by Ferdinand, Graf von Zeppelin and was the first of many German Zeppelins, which were to dominate the airship scene for a quarter of a century.

An important waterway, the 61 mile (98 km) Kiel Canal, linking the North and Baltic Seas, was opened on 19 June 1895.

Today marked the end for. . . .

Sir Joseph Banks, explorer and naturalist, who died in 1820.
Sir James Barrie, novelist and dramatist, who died in 1937.
The Emperor Maximilian of Mexico, who was executed in 1867.

The Victorian era of British history, which was to last for 64 years, began on 20 June 1837, when Princess Victoria was awakened early and told of the death of her uncle, the king. At the age of eighteen she had become Queen Victoria. She had been brought up with the knowledge that one day she would be queen and she was helped by having some very capable ministers in the government, who were able to advise her well.

The coronation was held a year after her accession, on 28 June 1838, in Westminster Abbey. Nearly two years later, she married Prince Albert of Saxe-Coburg-Gotha, with whom she lived very happily until his death in 1861. Her grief lasted for the rest of her life, much of which was spent at Osborne House on the Isle of Wight or at Balmoral, Scotland. Great celebrations took place at the time of her golden jubilee in 1887 and diamond jubilee ten years later. She died in 1901.

Queen Victoria gave her name to the Victoria Cross, a decoration awarded 'For Valour' — acts of bravery in action against an enemy. Created in 1856, it was awarded for actions that had already taken place. The first award was in respect of an incident on 20 June 1854, when Lieutenant Charles Lucas, of HMS *Hecla*, saved the lives of others by picking up and throwing overboard a live bomb which exploded immediately.

It was on this day, in 1960, that a sheep's coat became a man's coat in just 6 hours and 10 minutes. At a Pitlochry tweed mill, two sheep were shorn, the wool was spun, and passed through many processes to make the woollen cloth from which the tailor cut and completed the coat.

Speed of a different kind was highlighted on 20 June 1927, when greyhound racing was first held at the White City Stadium in London.

Jacques Offenbach was born on 20 June 1819. He composed many operettas and is remembered for his lively music for the can-can as well as melodies such as the Barcarolle.

This was a black day, in 1756, when 146 English prisoners were locked in the Black Hole of Calcutta. By the next morning only 23 had not suffocated.

This is the day, except in Leap Years, of the Summer Solstice — one day, in ancient times, when huge bonfires were lit to encourage the sun to keep its strength. These Beltane fires took their name from the Celtic Bel (Sun God) and Tan or Tean (fire).

John Smith died on this day in 1631. He might have died 25 years earlier had it not been for the pleas of the Red Indian princess, Pocahontas, as he was about to be put to death by members of her tribe (p. 27). In 1608, Smith was elected president of the colony of Virginia but soon returned to England.

Inigo Jones also died on this day, 21 June 1652. Born in London, he became the first of the great British architects, designing such buildings as the Whitehall banqueting hall, the Queen's house at Greenwich and Marlborough Chapel, as well as planning areas such as Covent Garden and Lincoln's Inn Fields.

'Turnip' Townshend died on 21 June 1738. Charles, Viscount Townshend, was an English statesman, who held several high offices of state and was party to international agreements. In 1720, he retired to his Norfolk estate, where he took a great interest in farming, particularly the rotation of crops, using turnips as one crop in a four-year rotation. It was his constant advice to other farmers to 'grow turnips' that gave him his nickname.

Friedrich Froebel, the German educationalist, also died on 21 June in 1852. His ideas for kindergarten schools and his methods of education became widely adopted. Another 21 June death was that of Nikolai Rimsky-Korsakov, the Russian composer, in 1908.

The German Grand Fleet also 'died' on 21 June 1919. At the end of World War I, most of the warships of the German navy were taken to Scapa Flow, Orkney, where they lay at anchor for a long time, whilst governments argued as to what should be done with them. On this day, the whole fleet sank. Their commander, Admiral von Reuter, had given orders that they should be scuttled. The sea-cocks were opened and the mighty men-of-war went to the bottom of the sea.

On 21 June 1948, the first long playing micro-groove record was launched by CBS Research Laboratories in the USA — heralding the 'death' of the 78 rpm record.

There is something strange about the happenings of the afternoon of 22 June 1893. Two lines of warships were steaming on a parallel course in the Mediterranean off North Africa under the command of Admiral Sir George Tryon. For some reason, the admiral gave the order for the ships to turn towards each other. The leading battleship of one line, HMS *Camperdown* ran straight into the admiral's battleship, HMS *Victoria*, which was leading the other line.

Within thirteen minutes the *Victoria* sank. The admiral was last seen on the bridge with his arms folded, saying, 'It's all my fault.' He and 357 others were drowned.

Even more strange is that his wife, Lady Tryon, was giving a party in her London home. Some of the guests saw the admiral walk through the house and told Lady Tryon how pleased they were to see Sir George. But Sir George was not there: it was at that very time that his ship was sinking. Had those guests at the party seen his ghost?

This was the day on which the River Thames seemed to be on fire in 1861. Fire broke out in a warehouse in Tooley Street, near London Bridge and spread to other buildings in which oil, tallow, and inflammable substances were stored. These poured onto the surface of the river. The spectacular blaze caused great damage and the death of London's Chief Fire Officer, James Braidwood.

On 22 June 1805, Giuseppe Mazzini was born. Anxious to make the states of Italy into one united country, he was exiled for his revolutionary activities but later returned.

A very powerful man in Africa last century was Muhammad Ahmad Ibn As-sayyid 'Abd Allah. He called himself al-Mahdi ('the right-guided one'), and made himself master of the Sudan and surrounding lands between 1881 and his death on 22 June 1885.

Also on 22 June. . . .

The Queen Elizabeth Prayer Book was issued in 1559.
H. Rider Haggard, novelist, was born in 1856.
Sir Julian Huxley, biologist, was born in 1887.
Sir John Hunt, Everest expedition leader, was born in 1910.
Judy Garland, stage and film actress, died in 1969.

This is Midsummer Eve, a day on which people in the past engaged in all sorts of strange activities (p. 118). Many of these, and the customs associated with other days, would have been long since forgotten had it not been for the work of people who found out about such things and carefully recorded them. Such a man was Cecil Sharp, who was mainly concerned with folk songs and dances and whose work led to the formation of the English Folk Dance and Song Society. He died on 23 June 1924, but his work kept alive much that was of value.

Brought back to life in 1970 was the old steamship *Great Britain*. Designed by Isambard Kingdom Brunel, she was the first Atlantic liner to be built of iron and have screw propulsion. At the time of her launching, in 1843, she was the largest ship to be built — 3,270 tons and 322 ft (98 m) long. In 1884, she was damaged when rounding Cape Horn, taken to the Falkland Islands and used as a hulk. Nearly a century later, she was given temporary repairs and towed to Bristol, where she arrived on 23 June 1970. Put into a drydock, she has been restored as a valuable piece of maritime history.

Keeping alive was one of the problems faced by the settlers who went to make new homes in America. Many were attacked and killed by Indians who resented the newcomers. But in one place it was different. On 23 June 1683, William Penn signed a treaty of friendship with the Indians so that Pennsylvania became a place of peace.

Hudson River, Hudson Strait, Hudson Bay — perpetual memorials to a great explorer who sought a route to the East via the north of Canada. Having explored Hudson Bay, Hudson, in the *Discovery*, headed for home only to be stopped by ice. The crew mutinied. On 23 June 1611, Hudson, his son and some sick members of the crew were put into a small open boat and cast adrift. At the last moment the ship's carpenter jumped into the boat rather than desert his captain. They were never seen again.

This day in 1757 saw the victory of Robert Clive over a much larger Indian army at the Battle of Plassey.

Today is Midsummer Day, the feast of the Nativity of St. John the Baptist, a day for the observance of many ancient customs (pp. 117–20). It is also the day on which the Liverymen of the Guilds of the City of London meet to elect two Sheriffs and other officers to serve for a year.

This day in 1314 proved to be one of the most decisive days in the history of Scotland for it was on 24 June of that year that Robert the Bruce utterly defeated the English armies of Edward II at Bannockburn, near Stirling. The armies had gathered on the previous day and there had been a few skirmishes. The English army was a formidable one of perhaps 25,000 men. The Scots had probably less than one third of that number, but they had a leader who could take advantage of the situation. The English were badly organised, hemmed into an area too small for them to manoeuvre and attacked by Scottish spearmen. Soon hundreds of English nobles and knights lay dead, to say nothing of thousands of humbler men. The King of England fled with a small bodyguard. Once out of danger, one knight, Sir Giles d'Argentine turned back 'I am not of custom to fly,' he said, 'Nor shall I do so now. God keep you!'

Another who had to raise a large army was Lord Kitchener. Born on 24 June 1850, he served in the army in the Middle East, Sudan, India and elsewhere. When World War I broke out, he was appointed Secretary of State for War. From posters all over the country, his stern eyes and pointing finger proclaimed 'Your country needs YOU'. They brought in two million volunteers. But even that was not enough.

On 24 June 1497, John Cabot landed on the coast of North America, probably Newfoundland or Nova Scotia. He had been sent out by King Henry VII to 'seek and discover' and the king gave him £10 on his return. Cabot sailed again the following year but was never seen again. Sir John Ross also sailed to Canada, in the 19th Century, to seek a North-west passage. He was born on 24 June 1777.

Sir William Penney, atomic scientist, was born on 24 June 1909. He was raised to the peerage as Baron Penney in 1967.

Anthony Woodville, 2nd Earl Rivers, brother-in-law of King Edward IV, was a Yorkist leader and supporter of the King during the Wars of the Roses. He became captain-general of the forces and helped defeat Warwick ('the Kingmaker') at the Battle of Barnet. After the death of Edward, Earl Rivers was put to death by King Richard III on 25 June 1483.

General George Custer met a violent end on 25 June 1876. A US Cavalry commander, he distinguished himself in the American Civil War and later fought against hostile Indians. On this day he led 264 men into battle against the Sioux by the Little Big Horn river in Montana. They all perished in what has become known as 'Custer's Last Stand'.

One of the most respected leaders of the 20th Century was born on 25 June 1900. Earl Mountbatten of Burma distinguished himself as an officer in the Royal Navy, became a supreme commander in World War II and was the last Viceroy of India, guiding India and Pakistan to independence in 1947. He met an untimely end in 1979 (p. 223) when his boat was blown up by IRA terrorists off the Irish coast.

This was also the birthday, in India, in 1903, of Eric Blair, who later served in the police in Burma. When he began writing, he did so under the name of George Orwell. Amongst his books *Animal Farm* was a satire on Communism, whilst *Nineteen Eighty-Four* was a thought-provoking look into the future at a scientifically perfected servile state.

It was the spread of Communism on the one hand and the desire for freedom on the other that led to the outbreak of the Korean War on 25 June 1950, when Communist North Korea invaded South Korea. The war lasted until 1953.

Captain Cook sailed on his last voyage on this day in 1776. He was killed by natives in Hawaii nearly three years later after a quarrel.

Sir William Fothergill Cooke, who worked with Sir Charles Wheatstone to make the electric telegraph, died on 25 June 1879.

On 26 June 1897, great warships of many nations were lined up in the Spithead, off Portsmouth, for a great Naval Review to celebrate the Jubilee of Queen Victoria. Officials were shocked when a small ship, the *Turbinia,* steamed at full-speed between the lines, outpacing the warship sent to stop her. It was Charles Parsons' way of demonstrating that the turbine engine which he had invented was better than those used by the men-of-war.

This is a day shared by other men and women of achievement. It was the birthday, in 1824, of William Thompson, the Scottish mathematician and physicist who made researches into the transmission of electric currents in submarine cables as well as developing various kinds of electrical instrument. He was created Baron Kelvin in 1892.

Samuel Crompton died on this day in 1827. He was one of the pioneers of the industrial revolution in the textile industry and inventor of a spinning machine known as a 'mule'.

On this day, in 1890, William Friese-Greene gave the first public showing of the cine-film. The great pioneer of the film industry also experimented with colour and 3-D films but died almost penniless.

In 1846, this was a day of achievement for Richard Cobden and John Bright, who had campaigned against the Corn Laws. On this day the Corn Laws were repealed.

In North America, on 26 June 1959, the great new waterway, the St. Lawrence Seaway, was opened, enabling ocean ships to reach the Great Lakes of Canada and the United States of America.

Gilbert White achieved fame as a naturalist with his charming book, *Natural History and Antiquities of Selborne.* He died on 26 June 1793.

Lady Olave Baden-Powell, leader of the Girl Guide movement, died this day in 1977.

Francisco Pizarro, conquistador of the Incas in the name of Spain, was assassinated on 26 June 1541.

This day saw, in 1857, the massacre at Kānpur (Cawnpore), India and, in 1945, the signing of the United Nations Charter at San Francisco.

My name shall live in the memory of man, when the titles of the Northumberlands are extinct and forgotten.

Thus prophesied James Smithson, who died on 27 June 1829. Smithson was an illegitimate son of the Duke of Northumberland and he had very strong feelings about this, hence his desire to be remembered above that family.

After being educated at Oxford, he studied science and became one of the finest chemists in Europe. He died in Italy, childless at the age of 64. Within a few years, his whole estate had gone to the United States of America 'to found at Washington, under the name of the Smithsonian Institution, an establishment for the increase and diffusion of knowledge among men'.

So, in 1846, the United States Congress used Smithson's 105 bags of gold sovereigns, worth about £280,000 to set up the Institution.

Today some 20 million people a year visit the Smithsonian, an impressive group of exhibition halls and grounds in the centre of the capital city of the United States and which form the finest museum in the world. And what can they see? There are the National Museums of History, Natural History, Air and Space and other exhibition halls. Nearby are the National Portrait Gallery and the National Zoological Park. There one can see the first aircraft and sewing machine, twelve million postage stamps and the world's longest beard (5⅓ m).

Besides all this, the Smithsonian is the centre of scientific research and promoter of projects in almost every sphere of science and scholarship. It is supported by the government and by gifts from all over the world. James Smithson could surely never have dreamed what his bags of gold would mean to the world.

Helen Keller also had a special gift for the world, though this might have seemed hard to believe at one time. She was born on 27 June 1880 but, as a result of an illness before the age of two, she was left blind and deaf. But, thanks to a good teacher and her own determination, she was able to develop her talents and use them for others, giving encouragement to handicapped people in many lands.

Everything is good when it leaves the Creator's hands, everything degenerates in the hands of man.

So wrote Jean-Jacques Rousseau in his book *Emile*, a book on education which was later to influence great educationalists such as Froebel and Pestalozzi. Some of his thoughts on government and religion were not so well received. Born in Geneva on 28 June 1712, he was a great thinker and writer. His masterpiece *Contrat Social* (Social Contract) began *'Man is born free; and everywhere he is in chains.'* With its slogan, 'Liberty, Equality, Fraternity' it gave inspiration to the French Revolutionaries.

Lord Raglan was a soldier who had served as secretary to the Duke of Wellington during the Napoleonic Wars. When Britain went to war in the Crimea in 1854, Lord Raglan was British Commander-in-Chief. He has often been criticised for his handling of the war but this may be unjust as the whole war was badly managed. Taken seriously ill at Sebastopol, Raglan died there on 28 June 1855. Raglan sleeves, a type that came into use about 1855, took their name from Lord Raglan.

More about fighting! As the Archduke Ferdinand of Austria and his wife pulled up in their car in Sarajevo on 28 June 1914, a student pulled out a gun and shot them both dead. It was the spark that was needed to start a war that had been brewing for some time. World War I lasted for four years and cost the lives of millions. The Treaty of Versailles, which officially ended the war a long time after the armistice, was signed on this day in 1919.

Two royal occasions today. On 28 June 1491, one of the best-known kings of England was born. Henry VIII reigned from 1509 to 1547 and is remembered for having six wives, as well as for changes concerning the Church and monasteries. This day, in 1838, saw the Coronation of Queen Victoria, who was to reign until 1901, the longest reign of any British ruler. In 1840, she married Prince Albert of Saxe-Coburg.

This was the day, in 1859, when the first Dog Show was held — in the Town Hall at Newcastle-upon-Tyne.

This is the feast day of St. Peter, the Galilean fisherman who became an apostle of Jesus Christ and leader of the early Church. He established his see at Antioch before moving to Rome, where he was put to death in the time of Nero. He was the first 'Pope' (though that title was not used until three centuries later) and the great basilica in Rome bears his name.

The last emperor of the Aztecs of Mexico was Montezuma II, who had the misfortune to be emperor at the time when the Spanish conquistador, Cortes, claimed Mexico in the name of Spain. Some of the Aztecs believed that the white-bearded Cortes was the white-bearded god Quetzalcoatl. Montezuma was not fooled. He invited Cortes into his capital, Tenochtitlan, but, realising this to be a trap, Cortes turned the tables, holding Montezuma hostage. From the walls of the city, Montezuma appealed to his people but was assailed with a barrage of stones and arrows, receiving wounds from which he died a few days later, on or about 29 June 1520.

The object of explorers in the years before Cortes had been to find a route to the Indies, the spice islands. America was in the way! For the next 400 years those sailing westwards had to sail round the treacherous Cape Horn. If only there were a way through the centre of America! On 29 June 1858, the man was born who was to construct such a waterway — the Panama Canal. George Washington Goethals, an army officer and military engineer, undertook a task at which others had failed. When the Canal was opened, in 1914, Goethals was appointed the first governor of the Canal Zone.

Ignacy Paderewski was an internationally recognised Polish pianist and composer. He was also a staunch patriot and helped establish an independent Poland in 1919. He resumed his musical career in 1921 and died on 29 June 1941.

Also on 29 June. . .

In 1855, the *Daily Telegraph* was first published.
In 1871, the Trade Union Act legalised the unions.
In 1905, the Automobile Association was formed.

In Hitler's Germany of 1934 this was the 'Night of the Long Knives' in which the dictator 'removed' all who were in opposition to him or his methods. There had been internal struggles in the Nazi party since it came to power in January 1933 and Hitler was a desperate man. During the night of 29–30 June, the black-uniformed SS guards arrested many leaders, took them to barrack squares and shot them. Others were killed in their homes. At least 282 died in the early hours of 30 June. There were no trials. They were branded as traitors — and dead men cannot argue, nor can they disclose facts that others wish to remain suppressed. Hitler had advanced himself: civilised Germany had moved another step backward.

The opposite happened in England on 30 June 1688. In the reign of King James II, seven bishops were imprisoned in the Tower of London because they had declared a document issued by the king to be illegal. In spite of all attempts by the king to obtain a verdict against them on this day, the verdict was 'Not guilty'. Justice had been done.

Mention of the Tower of London serves as a reminder that Tower Bridge, which spans the Thames close by, was opened on 30 June 1894, by the Prince of Wales. It has Gothic towers with twin bascules which can be raised to allow ships to pass through a 250 ft (76 m) gap. High walkways were provided for the use of pedestrians when the bridge was open but these were never popular and were closed to the public in 1909. Nowadays, with few ships entering the Pool of London, the bridge is seldom opened.

One man who did not mind crossing the water at a great height was Blondin (Jean-Francois Gravelet), the French tightrope walker. On 30 June 1859, he made the first of his crossings of Niagara Falls on a 1,100 ft (335 m) tightrope 160 ft (48.7 m) above the water. Each of his crossings was a different 'spectacular' including being blindfolded, pushing a wheelbarrow and once stopping half-way to make and eat an omelette.

Elizabeth Barrett Browning, English poet, died this day in 1861.

Some June Events and Commemorations

(see also pp. 117–20)

First Wednesday (usually) Epsom, Surrey: Derby Day (p. 86).
First Thursday Neston, Cheshire: Ladies' Walking Day. Procession to church for a service, to market cross for a hymn, then tea.
Thursday of week 6th–12th Lanark, Scotland; Lanimer Day. Processions; Lanimer Queen; Beating the Bounds; sports.
Thursday of first full week Hawick and Selkirk: Riding the Marches. Horseback processions commemorating the Battle of Flodden in 1513.
First week Bideford, Devon: Beating the Clock Race. Racing across the bridge between eight strokes of town clock bell.
Second Saturday London: Trooping the Colour.
20th or near Abingdon, Berkshire: Electing the Mayor of Ock Street. Ancient festivity with election and dancing.
About 23rd Various Beltane and Midsummer bonfires.
Thursday nearest 28th Bury St. Edmunds, Suffolk: Cakes and Ale Ceremony — distribution to almshouse residents.
Last Sunday or nearest to 29th Hay, grass or rush strewing — Braunstone, Leicestershire; Langham, Leicestershire; Wingrave, Buckinghamshire; Pavenham, Bedfordshire; Farnborough, Kent.
During the month Plymouth, Devon: Fyshinge Feast.
Southend-on-Sea, Essex: Sailing Barge races.
Windsor, Berkshire: Garter Service in St. George's Chapel.
Ashford-in-the-Water, Hope, Tideswell, Wirksworth and Youlgreave in Derbyshire: Well Dressings.
End of the month (or July) Warrington, Lancashire: Walking Day. Procession of children; church services, recreations. Walking Days are held in some other northern towns too.

SOME JUNE FAIRS
In various places: Midsummer fairs
Appleby, Cumbria: New Fair — horses.
Bromsgove, Worcestershire: Horse fair and Court Leet.
Bradford, West Yorks: Fairs on 8th and 29th, each for 3 days.
Flash, Staffordshire: Teapot Fair.

SOME AGRICULTURAL AND OTHER SHOWS
Essex County, Leicestershire, Lincolnshire, Royal Bath and West, Southern Counties, Royal Cornwall, Royal Highland, South of England, Suffolk, Three Counties (Worcestershire), Break Crops, National Hackney Show.

JULY

July was originally known by the Romans as Quintilis, the fifth month, but it was renamed Julius in honour of Julius Caesar, the great Roman leader. In Anglo-Saxon England, this month, with June, was referred to as Litha ('moon'), but also sometimes as Maedmonath, the month when the meadows were in bloom.

There are plenty of wild flowers to be seen in July in meadow and hedgerow, whilst on the moorlands the heather is in full bloom.

Hot July brings cooling showers,
Apricots and gilly flowers.

Sara Coleridge

In the northern hemisphere, July is normally the hottest month of the year, often with long dry periods.

Then came July, boiling like fire
That all his garments he had cast away.

Edmund Spenser

The summer looks out from her brazen tower,
Through the flashing bars of July.

Frances Thompson

Naturally, there are some old weather sayings about July, which are probably fair comment but not necessarily to be relied upon.

If the first of July be rainy weather,
It will rain, more or less, for four weeks together.

And from Scotland (4th of July is St. Martin Bullion's feast day)

Bullion's Day, gif ye be fair
For one hale month 'twill rain nae mair.

The periods of hot sunshine throughout July and early August are known as the Dog Days, so named by the ancient Egyptians, Greeks and Romans, who believed that Sirius, the dog star, which at this time of the year rises at the same time as the sun, gave the sun extra heat and so caused the long spell of hot weather. Dog Days are actually 3 July to 11 August.

Dog Days, plenty of fruit if bright and clear;
But if there's rain our hopes are vain.

Agricultural Shows

During the summer months, agricultural shows are held in many parts of Britain, most of them attracting large crowds of people from a wide area.

The major show of the year is the Royal International Agricultural Show, usually known briefly as the Royal Show. It is the major event in the calendar of the Royal Agricultural Society of England, which was founded in 1840, and is held at the National Agricultural Centre, Stoneleigh, Warwickshire for four days in July — the Monday to Thursday which includes the first Tuesday of July.

At the Royal Show, there is something to interest anyone who is concerned with agriculture — the finest livestock, machinery of all kinds, and specialised sections on arable crops, forestry, horticulture, food, finance, research and overseas farming. It usually attracts about 200,000 visitors, who can see over 7,000 of the finest animals and over 1,200 exhibitions.

Although July is a popular month for the county shows, they range from May to September (see pages 114, 152, 190, 228 and, in *Autumn and Winter Days*, p. 38).

One attraction at the show is the judging of the finest animals. Cows and bulls are paraded round the enclosure, whilst other animals are judged in the pens. Local farmers vie with each other for the awards and there is usually friendly rivalry as to who can collect the most.

For the farmer, the county show is the opportunity to obtain all the information that he needs to help him with his work, to seek the advice of the experts and to talk with others who may share the same problems. For the visitor who has no connexion with farming, there is much to be admired and enjoyed. For all, there is the additional entertainment given by servicemen, police and others, who put on colourful or exciting displays.

There are other specialist shows and competitions too, at various times of the year, such as pig or poultry fairs, sheepdog trials, ploughing competitions and horse shows. Many people, too enjoy a visit to one of the steam rallies that are held in many places at this time of year to see the old steam traction engines, rollers and machines now beautifully restored.

Wakes and Fairs

The latter half of July sees the beginning of the Wake Weeks, which are kept in many northern towns and observed as the time when all industry stops for the annual holiday weeks (see p. 194). Popular weeks have been the last in July and the first in August, which included the Bank Holiday Monday, formerly the first Monday in August.

In some places fairs and other activities are held at this time. Some of the fairs originated as Lammas Fairs (see p. 196) but were kept at the end of July instead of on Lammas Day itself.

The Wakes originated as celebrations on the day of the patron saint of the church and it was customary in some places to celebrate this day in other ways too. During this month there are certain rush bearing or hay-strewing ceremonies (see p. 120). Well dressings (see p. 120) also take place in July in some villages.

Pilgrimages

July is the month when various pilgrimages are undertaken. For hundreds of years people have gone on pilgrimages to shrines or holy places. For Chaucer's Canterbury Pilgrims it was to the shrine of Thomas à Becket. Many pilgrimages were made to the Shrine of Our Lady at Walsingham, Norfolk. It is to Walsingham that one of the big July pilgrimages is made, on the first Thursday. Other pilgrimages are also made to Walsingham by both Roman Catholics and Anglicans to their respective shrines.

Some of the pilgrimages commemorate local happenings. On the Thursday and Saturday nearest to 12 July, pilgrims assemble at the railway bridge at Grindleford, Derbyshire and walk to Padley chapel, remembering two Roman Catholic priests who were found hiding in the chapel in 1588 and then put to death. The pilgrims celebrate Mass in the chapel.

In Hastings, since 1897, there has been an annual pilgrimage on the last Sunday in July from the church of St. Mary Star-of-the-Sea to the ruins of the chapel of Our Lady in the castle.

In Bristol, on the Thursday nearest to 25 July, there is an annual pilgrimage to St. Ann's Well.

These are but a few of many pilgrimages made by groups large or small for differing reasons.

This is the birthday of Canada. By the British North America Act of 1867, the provinces north of the 49th parallel across North America were united as one country, to which were joined the Hudson's Bay Company territories in 1870, British Columbia in 1871 and other territories later. In 1926, Canada became a fully independent member of the British Commonwealth, having its own parliament but still retaining the British sovereign as head of state. This day is kept each year as a day of commemoration.

This day has been a 'first' in a number of ways, of which the following are a few:

The Westminster Assembly, of Presbyterians called by the English Long Parliament to reform the Church of England, held the first of its 1,163 sessions on 1 July 1643.

Charles Darwin first published a pamphlet on this day, in 1858, expounding his views on evolution.

In 1801, the first Thames steamboat sailed; and, in 1933, London's transport services were taken over by the London Passenger Transport Board.

The first variety 'Command Performance' was held in 1912; and the first colour television programme in Britain was transmitted on BBC2 on 1 July 1967.

Future problems for Britain had their roots on this day in 1920, when the British civil administration of Palestine began.

Wales gained a new Prince of Wales in 1969, when Prince Charles was invested at Caernarvon Castle.

Some of today's births and deaths . . . .

Charles Goodyear, inventor of rubber vulcanisation, died 1860.
Louis Bleriot, French pioneer aviator, was born in 1872.
Harriet Beecher Stowe, author of *Uncle Tom's Cabin*, died 1896.
Seretse Khama, President of Botswana (p. 170), born 1921.

Battles fought on 1 July. . . .

The Battle of the Boyne, in Ireland, in 1690.
The Battle of Gettysburg, US Civil War, began in 1863.
The Battle of the Somme, World War I, began in 1916.

On 1 July 1946, an atomic bomb was exploded under water at Bikini Atoll near old warships to observe its effect.

If it rains on St. Mary's Day it will rain for a month.

That may or may not be right. Many of these old weather predictions are generalisations. There are other kinds of prediction, often published in the form of an almanack, which may uncannily come to pass. We are familiar, too, with the horoscopes prepared by astrologers and published in newspapers or periodicals.

One of the most famous predictors in history was the French astrologer, Michel de Notredame, usually known in the Latin style of Nostradamus. Besides being an astrologer, he was a doctor of medicine and set himself up as a prophet in 1547. He published his predictions under the title of *Centuries*. There were two collections of rhymed quatrains, which were not easily understood. Looking back on history, one can read into them many events which did, in fact, happen. Nostradamus certainly gained for himself a very high reputation during his lifetime, which ended on 2 July 1566.

One might not have predicted at his birth on 2 July 1489, what would become of Thomas Cranmer but one did not need to be a prophet in later years to realise that the man who became Archbishop of Canterbury in days of religious intolerance and persecution would find it impossible to steer clear of trouble. He went to the stake in 1556.

Oliver Cromwell was a man who demanded loyalty. Before the Battle of Marston Moor on 2 July 1644, he addressed his troops,

The State, in choosing men to serve it, takes no notice of their opinions. If they be willing faithfully to serve it, that satisfies.

In the battle which followed they won a decisive victory over the Royalist army under Prince Rupert.

Another army went into battle on 2 July 1865. It was the first meeting of 'The Christian Mission', which was to become 'The Salvation Army', whose soldiers would fight against the evils of the world under the banner of Jesus Christ.

On this day: Christoph Gluck, composer, was born in 1714; Sir Robert Peel, statesman, died in 1850; and President James Garfield (USA) was shot in 1881, — he died 80 days later.

On 3 July 1938, a seven-coach train, pulled by the bright blue streamlined steam locomotive *Mallard*, thundered down Stoke Bank between Grantham, Lincolnshire and Peterborough, Cambridgeshire. Over a 440 yd (402 m) distance, it achieved a speed of 126 mph (202 km/h), the highest speed for a steam locomotive and a record which stands to this day.

This is an age of speed, of rush and bustle. William H. Davies, who was born in Newport, Gwent, on 3 July 1871, always seemed to be on the move. Many times he crossed the Atlantic in cattle boats; he tramped through the United States; and he lost a foot whilst trying to jump a train heading for the Klondyde in Canada. In England he became a pedlar and street singer. He was also a poet who wrote simple verse with an eye to nature . . . and the need to stop and open our eyes.

What is this life if, full of care,
We have no time to stand and stare?

Perhaps we delight in the little things we see. Or maybe we are overwhelmed as we look at the night sky and contemplate the vastness of the universe. Modern astronomers have learned much with huge telescopes such as the one at Mount Palomar Observatory, California, with its 200 inch (5 m) reflecting mirror. It was first used on 3 July 1948.

We may like to stand and stare at the work of man, the exquisite designs, the beauties of art or the handiwork of the craftsman. This was the birthday, in 1728, of Robert Adam, the Scottish architect who designed many fine houses, their interior decorations and the furniture to go in them.

Samuel de Champlain was standing on the deck of his ship, staring at the land as he moved slowly up-river. Then he saw what he was looking for — an ideal place to build a settlement. So, on 3 July 1608, Quebec was founded.

Also founded on 3 July 1854, was the Bible Lands Society, which does much to help people in those lands.

Joel Chandler Harris, author of *Uncle Remus*, died 3 July 1908.

The 'Fourth of July', or Independence Day, is the greatest national holiday in the United States of America. It celebrates the adoption of the Declaration of Independence on 4 July 1776, by which the former British colonies in America, following the War of Independence, formally broke all ties with Britain and laid the foundations for the present United States.

It is celebrated today with great festivity, parades, picnics, pageants, barbecues, fireworks displays and other means of enjoyment, probably more enthusiastically in smaller towns than in the big cities but everywhere with a great deal of patriotism and the displaying of the Stars and Stripes.

It is interesting that four American presidents have personal associations with Independence Day:

John Adams, 2nd President (1797–1801), died on 4 July 1826;
Thomas Jefferson, 3rd President (1801-9), died on 4 July 1826;
James Monroe, 5th President (1817–25), died on 4 July 1831;
Calvin Coolidge, 30th President (1925–9), born on 4 July 1872.

Because of the patriotic nature of the day, a number of important national projects have been started on 4 July. In 1817, it was the digging of the Erie Canal; in 1828, it was the first railway in the country, the Baltimore and Ohio Railroad; and, in 1850, the cornerstone was laid of the Washington Monument.

Another American project to begin on 4 July, but one which was to be of great importance to the whole world, was the construction of the Panama Canal, cutting through the centre of the continent and linking the Atlantic and Pacific oceans so that ships no longer had to make the treacherous and dangerous passage round Cape Horn.

The site chosen for the canal was the isthmus of Panama, which is the territory of the Republic of Panama. By a treaty signed in 1903, the United States was allowed the right to administer a strip of land 10 miles (16 km) wide, which contained the canal and was known as the Panama Canal Zone. The canal itself is 51 miles (82 km) long.

The American novelist and short-story writer, Nathaniel Hawthorne, was born on 4 July, 1804.

When Alec Rose wanted to travel round the world, he had no wish to use the Panama Canal. He was one of those who decided to sail single-handed round the world via South Africa and later Cape Horn. It was on this day, in 1968, in his *Lively Lady*, that he returned to his home port, Portsmouth.

One of the most spectacular rescues of modern times took place on 4 July 1976. The story had begun on 27 June, when an Air France 'plane was hijacked, the purpose being to force Israel and other nations to release 53 Palestinian terrorists then in gaol. The 'plane was flown to Entebbe Airport, Uganda, where the passengers were transferred as hostages to a disused passenger terminal. Some were later released, leaving 106 Israeli hostages. The President of Uganda, Idi Amin, was clearly being helpful to the hijackers.

The Israeli government had no intention of giving in to the hijackers' demands. Using four huge cargo 'planes, one command-and-communications 'plane and one hospital 'plane, an Israeli commando unit landed at Entebbe, rescued most of the hostages, destroyed the Ugandan fighter 'planes that could have pursued them and took to the air again. Eight hours later they were safe on Israeli soil.

Rescue of another sort — this time in London. Thomas Barnardo, who was born in Dublin on this day in 1845, was training in London to be a medical missionary. In the East End of London he discovered many children living rough, having no homes or families. So he began the work that was to develop into Dr. Barnado's Homes.

Also in London, it was on 4 July 1829, that the first London omnibus ran. G. Shillibeer, a coachbuilder, borrowed the idea from Paris, where omnibuses began running in 1827. This first London omnibus, known as a 'Shillibeer', plied between Paddington and the Bank for a fare of one shilling. It was a great success and it was not long before there were other omnibuses running in London.

Also on this day. . . .

William Byrd, organist and composer, died in 1623.

Giuseppe Garibaldi, Italian military leader, was born in 1807.

George Borrow, who was born on 5 July 1803, was the son of a professional soldier, so part of his early life was spent in travelling from place to place. This gave him opportunity to learn other languages.

He did not enjoy the best of health and decided that an open air life would be beneficial. He went on long journeyings through rural England and later in Spain, where he worked for a Bible Society. As he journeyed, he had many opportunities to meet with gypsies and to understand their way of life. His books *Lavengro* and *The Romany Rye* were about the gypsies and the open-air life which was so sweet. From *Lavengro*:

> *There's night and day, brother, both sweet things; sun, moon, and stars, brother, all sweet things; there's likewise a wind on the heath. Life is very sweet, brother; who would wish to die?*

The answer to that question is, 'very few'. Life is sweet and so is good health to enjoy it to the full. Nowadays many people owe life and health to the National Health Service, which came into being in Britain on 5 July 1948.

Often in the past people who did not enjoy good health would go abroad to seek a climate that might be better. Cecil Rhodes was one. He was born on 5 July 1853 and suffered from tuberculosis as a youth. In 1870, he went to South Africa, where one of his brothers grew cotton. He became supervisor of a diamond mine and later took control. Within a short time he had gained control of more mines in Kimberley, entered politics, and gained for Britain all the land once known as Rhodesia, which was named after him (p. 32).

Sir Thomas Stamford Raffles was the son of a sea captain and was born at sea off Jamaica in 1781. He is best remembered for the purchase of an island off Malaya from the Sultan of Johore, which gave Britain a trading base for the East Indies. The island, Singapore, was to become one of the most important ports in the world. He was a sick man when he returned to England in 1824 but founded the London Zoological Society and London Zoo before he died on 5 July 1826.

The world has become much smaller since the time of Raffles. Air travel has made it easy to reach far away places. People plan exotic holidays with the help of brochures from travel agents. The travel agency business could be said to have started on this day, for it was on 5 July 1841, that Thomas Cook ran his first train excursion, between Leicester and Loughborough.

People on holiday like to make the most of the sea and the sun in their beach shorts or bikinis. It was on this day, in 1946, that the first bikini was worn . . . and many people thought it disgusting. Times change.

An agent of another kind was Phineas T. Barnum, born on 5 July 1810. He began his career as a showman, when he exhibited Joice Heth, who claimed to have been George Washington's nurse. He became manager of a midget, whom he called 'General Tom Thumb'. He arranged a triumphant tour for Jenny Lind, whom he called 'The Swedish Nightingale'. He exhibited Jumbo, a huge elephant from the London Zoo.

In 1871, Barnum opened his circus, which became known as 'The Greatest Show on Earth'. After going into partnership with James Bailey, it became The Barnum and Bailey Circus. Barnum also entered politics but he is chiefly remembered as the greatest showman of his time. He used many gimmicks and publicity stunts and was not averse to a little exaggeration or deception. As he once said, 'There's a sucker born every minute.'

This day was also the birthday, in 1755, of Sarah Siddons. She was the eldest of twelve children and went on tour with her father's strolling players. In 1775, she appeared at Drury Lane but was a failure. On her second appearance, in 1782, she was an outstanding success, remaining at Drury Lane until 1803, when she moved to Covent Garden. She has been described as the greatest English tragic actress.

Today the flags will have been fluttering from the avenue of flagpoles at St. John's on the Isle of Man, where people have assembled round Tynwald Hill, as they have for the past eleven hundred years, to hear read out all the laws that have been passed during the year.

Today we may remember people who had strong beliefs and were prepared to stand firm or fight for them. Jan Hus, a priest in Prague from 1402, became one of the first reformers to question some practices of the Roman Catholic Church. He was forbidden to preach and was excommunicated in 1411. Three years later, in spite of a promise of safe conduct, he was arrested, convicted of heresy and, on 6 July 1415, burned at the stake.

Sir Thomas More was on the other side of the fence. He held high office as Chancellor of England and was a Roman Catholic who could not agree with the changes that were taking place. He refused to accept that the authority of King Henry VIII was higher than that of the Church. He was arrested, found guilty of treason and sentenced to death. On 6 July 1535, he was beheaded on Tower Hill. On this same date, in 1935, he was canonised and today is the feast day of St. Thomas More.

The Duke of Monmouth, an illegitimate son of King Charles II of England, claimed that he should have been king when his father died, instead of the Duke of York, who became James II. A few months later, Monmouth landed in Dorset with a few followers, hoping to gain many more. He was unsuccessful. His followers were routed at the Battle of Sedgemoor on 6 July 1685: Monmouth himself was captured and, nine days later, beheaded.

'I have not yet begun to fight!' This was the reply of John Paul Jones, commanding the French East Indiaman *Bonhomme Richard,* when called upon to surrender in the early stages of a gun battle with British warships. He won a great victory. Jones, a Scotsman, born on 6 July 1747, saw service on ships of the United States and, later, of Europe. His grave at Annapolis, Maryland, became a national shrine.

Louis 'Satchmo' Armstrong died on this day in 1971. Born in New Orleans, the black American trumpeter rose to fame in the 1920s, becoming one of the greatest, best-loved and most colourful characters in the world of jazz.

The last London tram ran on 6 July 1952.

The English Channel has, for many years, offered a challenge to people as a means of proving stamina, ingenuity or invention. On 7 July 1981, the first solar-powered flight was achieved by Stephen Ptacek, taking 5½ hours to make the crossing in his 'plane *Solar Challenger*.

On 7 July 1967, that intrepid adventurer, Sir Francis Chichester, was knighted at Greenwich following his solo circumnavigation of the world (p. 109). He was 'dubbed' by Queen Elizabeth II, using the sword previously used by Queen Elizabeth I when she knighted an earlier, though not solo, circumnavigator, Sir Francis Drake. Chichester's yacht, *Gypsy Moth IV*, was later given a museum berth there close to the famous old clipper ship *Cutty Sark*.

King Edward I of England, who died on this day in 1307, was an adventurer of a different kind, anxious to extend his influence. Nicknamed 'Hammer of the Scots', he led campaigns against the Scots, the French and the Welsh, having earlier fought in the Crusades.

The crusade fought by the Revd. Thomas Stephenson was of a different kind, to help ragged, hungry, homeless children. On 7 July 1869, he opened, in Lambeth, London, the first home of what was to become the National Children's Home, which, today, proudly claims to have an ever-open door for any children who are in need.

The creators of two well-loved fictional characters died on this day. Many children throughout the world have enjoyed reading *Heidi*, the work of the Swiss Johanna Spyri, who died in 1901. Sir Arthur Conan Doyle, whose death was in 1930, gave the world that very famous detective, Sherlock Holmes.

This was the birthday, in 1922, of Pierre Cardin, creator of elegant clothing fashions for men and women, recognised as one of the leading clothing designers of the mid 20th Century.

On the subject of neatness and tidiness, the Litter Act was passed in Britain on 7 July 1959.

On 8 July, a strange character appears in the streets of South Queensferry, by the Forth Bridge in Scotland. He is the Burry Man, dressed in a garment covered with thistle and teazel burrs and having a head dress of flowers that conceals his face. It is possible that he commemorates the escape from the English of King Malcolm III, who so disguised himself, but we cannot be sure. The Burry Man is believed to bring good luck but, traditionally, must be unrecognised.

A number of Scotsmen are recognised on this day for their contribution to history.

John Ker, who died in prison in 1726, was a Cameronian who worked with the Jacobites but was really a Government spy.

Sir Henry Raeburn, one of Scotland's greatest portrait painters, died this day in 1823.

Born in 1882, Sir John Anderson, later Viscount Waverley, was the British administrator and politician after whom, whilst Minister of Home Security 1939–40, the Anderson air-raid shelter was named.

The last heavyweight fight under the London Prize Ring rules was held on 8 July 1889, when John L. Sullivan knocked out Jake Kilrain in this 75-round bareknuckle fight. Sullivan, a popular, blustering fighter, known as 'The Great John L.' and 'The Boston Strong Boy', earned over a million dollars from his fighting.

That was peanuts compared with the fortune amassed — and given away — by John D. Rockefeller, who was born on 8 July 1839 and almost monopolised the United States oil industry. He and his son, between them, gave over 3,000,000,000 dollars for philanthropic purposes.

Percy Grainger, who was born in Melbourne, Australia, on 8 July 1882, enriched the world in a different way with his collection and notation of English folk songs and the establishment of a museum of Australian music at Melbourne.

Also on 8 July. . . . Vasco da Gama sailed on his voyage to India (1497); Christiaan Huygens, Dutch astronomer and physicist, died (1695); Percy Bysshe Shelley, English poet, died (1822); and Ferdinand, Graf von Zeppelin, was born (1838).

You could not stand five minutes with that man beneath a shed while it rained, but you must be convinced you had been standing with the greatest man you had ever yet seen.

These words of Samuel Johnson are a great tribute to Edmund Burke, the great 18th Century statesman and writer. Born in Dublin, he became a Member of Parliament, where he had great influence in reducing royal power in the House of Commons. He also sought better treatment for the American colonists and for Roman Catholics.

Burke believed in individual liberty within an ordered pattern but that changes should be gradual. He was appalled by the events of the French Revolution a few years before his death on 9 July 1797. In his *Reflections on the Revolution in France* he wrote:

Because half a dozen grasshoppers under a fern make the field ring with their importunate chink . . . do not imagine that those who make the noise are the only inhabitants of the field.

Another who wished to limit royal powers, and was not afraid to speak out, also died on this day, in 1228. He was Stephen Langton, who had been appointed Archbishop of Canterbury by the Pope against the wishes of King John. He helped the barons with the wording of the Magna Carta and was with them at Runnymede when the charter was sealed in 1215.

Edward Heath, who was Prime Minister of Britain from 1970 to 1974, was born on 9 July 1916. He had been elected a Conservative Member of Parliament in 1950 and held several key posts before becoming Prime Minister. He wanted to see Britain more closely linked with Europe and successfully negotiated for Britain's entry into the European Economic Community (Common Market). Ted Heath is known, too, as a sailor, spending much of his leisure time in racing his *Morning Cloud* — a name held by several yachts.

We live in a 'throw away' age. One who helped start it, in 1903, by inventing razor blades, instead of razors that had to be sharpened, was King Camp Gillette. He died on 9 July 1932.

10 July

One of the most impressive reminders in Britain of the Roman occupation is Hadrian's Wall. Guarding the northern frontier against the warlike tribes, it was built from the Tyne to the Solway Firth, a distance of 73½ miles (118 km). Its construction was ordered by the Emperor Hadrian, who spent half his reign in travelling around his empire, strengthening defences and ordering the construction of monuments. Hadrian, who died on 10 July 138, is also remembered as a poet and man of culture.

Captain Frederick Marryat was born on this day in 1792. After service in the navy, he turned to writing. Of his children's books, *The Children of the New Forest* (1847) is a classic.

Also on 10 July. . . .
  John Calvin, protestant reformer, was born in 1509.
  George Stubbs, British artist (p. 220), died in 1806.
  Toyohiko Kagawa, Japanese Christian reformer, was born 1888.
  Joe Davis, snooker champion (p. 59), died in 1978.
  First communications satellite, *Telstar*, was launched in 1962.

11 July

This was the birthday, in 1274, of Robert the Bruce of Scotland, who claimed the crown in 1306 but was immediately driven into hiding by the English. He won a decisive victory at Bannockburn (p. 145) and others subsequently, establishing himself without doubt as king.

Born this day, in 1826, was John Fowler, agricultural engineer and inventor of the steam-hauled plough.

Also on this day. . . .
  Joseph Lalande, French astronomer, was born in 1732.
  John Quincy Adams, US diplomat and president, born 1767.
  George Gershwin, American popular composer, died 1937.
  Sir Arthur Evans, archaeologist of Crete, died 1941.
  John Churchill, Duke of Marlborough, won a great victory in the Battle of Oudenarde, in 1708.

This is the day when the members of the Irish protestant Grand Orange Lodges take to the streets of the larger towns of Ulster, with marches, bands, pageants, carnivals and processions intended to show the strength of Protestantism and opposition to Roman Catholicism.

These celebrations date from 1690–1, when the Catholic James II, who had lost the English crown, attempted a return via Ireland supported by the French. On 1 July 1690, William III of England (William of Orange) defeated James's army in the Battle of the Boyne. In the following year, on 12 July, in the Battle of Aughrim, the French general was killed and the army routed. Hence the choice of this date to celebrate both victories.

One who refused to take sides in religious controversy was Desiderius Erasmus, a great scholar and traveller in Europe in the days of the Reformation. He was quite prepared to make fun of things he believed wrong in the Church but wished his learning to be available to anyone. He sought truth and stood firmly by his beliefs until his death on 12 July 1536.

Thomas Guthrie was a Scottish churchman who was ready to speak out for what he believed. He helped to establish the Free Church in Scotland and used his gifts of oratory to encourage temperance, compulsory education, the founding of Ragged Schools and other social reforms. This was his birthday in 1803.

Some other 12 July birthdays. . . .

Julius Caesar, one of the greatest generals of the ancient world and perhaps the best known Roman (p. 21), in 100 BC.

George Eastman, photographic pioneer, inventor of roll films, maker of cheap cameras and founder of Kodak (p. 20), in 1854.

Kirsten Flagstad, Norwegian Wagnerian soprano and the first director of the Royal Norwegian Opera, in 1895.

Also in 1895, Oscar Hammerstein II, lyricist for several composers, musical comedy author and theatrical producer (p. 219).

On 12 July 1910, the Hon. Charles Stewart Rolls, partner of Henry Royce (Rolls-Royce) became the first Englishman to die in an air crash. He was piloting an aeroplane at Bournemouth.

Few of the leaders of the new nations of Africa have led lives that have been free of problems. Seretse Khama of Bechuanaland, later Botswana, was no exception. Born at Serowe, Bechuanaland, and nephew of the chief regent of the Bamangwato people, he was educated in his own country and then at Oxford. Whilst in England, he married an English woman. Soon, however, he was in dispute with the British government over his claim to the chieftainship of the Bamangwato and was banned from his country.

Having renounced his claim, Seretse was allowed to return in 1956. He became active in politics, was restored to the chieftainship in 1963, became prime minister of Bechuanaland in 1965 and was knighted. When Bechuanaland became the independent country of Botswana in 1966, Sir Seretse Khama became its President. He died on 13 July 1980.

This day, in 1793, saw the death of the French Revolutionary leader, Jean Paul Marat, murdered in his bath by Charlotte Corday (p. 174). He was probably the most unpopular of the revolutionaries. His infamous paper *L'ami du peuple* stirred up hatred but made him popular with the rabble of Paris. Twice he had to flee to London and once was forced to hide in the sewers of Paris, where he contracted the disease from which he was dying at the time of his assassination.

This was the birthday, in 1859, of one of the leaders of socialism in Britain, Sidney Webb. Together with his wife, Beatrice, he wrote *The History of Trade Unionism* and other books, made important contributions to education, including founding the London School of Economics, and started a new journal *The New Statesman*. Theirs was a partnership dedicated to the cause of socialism.

It was on this day, in 1793, that John Clare, the poet (p. 101), was born and, five years later, that Wordsworth wrote his *Lines composed a few miles above Tintern Abbey*.

On 13 July 1919, the airship R34 landed in England, having flown across the Atlantic in both directions — the first transatlantic airship flight.

Bastille Day has been a national holiday in France since 1880 and is celebrated with parades, merrymaking, dancing in the streets and fireworks. It commemorates the storming of the Bastille, the formidable Paris fortress, in the early days of the French Revolution by a mob of Parisians on the morning of 14 July 1789.

Originally part of the Paris fortifications, it became the state prison in which important persons could be held and was seen by many as a symbol of royal tyranny. When the mob arrived at the Bastille, they demanded that the governor, the Marquis de Launay should release the arms and munitions kept there. When he refused, the Bastille was stormed, captured and destroyed. So today is kept as a symbol of the deliverance from the evil days of the *ancien regime.*

Emmeline Pankhurst was a revolutionary of a different kind, taking Britain by storm as a leader of the Suffragettes, who took extreme measures to obtain votes for women. Like other Suffragettes, she was imprisoned for her actions and went on hunger strike. After a campaign lasting 40 years, women were given equal voting rights with men in 1928, a few weeks before Mrs Pankhurst's death on 14 July.

'Iron-mad Wilkinson' died on 14 July 1808. Known also as 'the great Staffordshire ironmaster', John Wilkinson built the first iron furnace at Bilston when he was 20. He also constructed a very accurate machine for boring the cylinders for Watt's engines; he worked with Abraham Darby to build a bridge across the Severn; he astounded people by building an iron barge; he cast all the ironwork for the Paris waterworks; and he made heavy guns for the British government. He was buried in a coffin he had designed himself — made of iron, of course.

About the same time, Friedrich Krupp established an iron foundry at Essen. His son, Alfred developed it, by means of the Bessemer process, to form the great German steel empire (p. 70). Alfred died on 14 July 1887.

Gertrude Bell, who was born on this day in 1868, was the granddaughter of iron-smelting industrialist, Sir Isaac Lowthian Bell. Gertrude made a name for herself as a traveller and political officer in the Middle East.

St. Swithun's Day, if thou dost rain,
For forty days it will remain:
St. Swithun's Day, if thou be fair,
For forty days 'twill rain na mair.

This is a popular belief, though meteorological records do no more than suggest that this period is subject to unsettled weather.

St Swithun, whose feast day this is, was a Saxon Bishop of Winchester who died in 862 AD. A humble man, he asked that he should be buried outside his church and this wish was granted. There is an old story that, when he was canonised about a century later, it was decided to take his remains, as a mark of respect, into the cathedral. As the men were about to do so, on 15 July 971, a terrible storm broke out, which lasted for forty days and was seen by some as a clear indication that the saint was very displeased.

There was an old country belief that the rain which fell on St. Swithun's Day christened the apples. Hence the saying:

Till St. Swithun's Day be past
The apples be not fit to taste.

Such data would not satisfy the Royal Society! The Royal Society of London for the Improvement of Natural Knowledge, to give it its full title, received its royal charter on 15 July 1662. It is one of the oldest scientific societies in Europe.

Inigo Jones was born on 15 July 1573. He designed several important buildings in London and is recognised as the one who introduced the English classical style of architecture.

This was the birthday, in 1606, of the greatest of all Dutch painters, Rembrandt van Rijn. At an early age, he gained a reputation as a portrait painter. He became quite rich and owned a fine house but, later in life, his fortunes changed. He left about 600 paintings and 300 etchings.

Also on this day. . . .
Jerusalem was captured by the Crusaders in 1099.
The Duke of Monmouth, rebel, was beheaded in 1685.

The ambition of many artists is to have a painting hung in the Royal Academy and to have the distinction of being able to put the letters R.A. after their names. The Royal Academy was founded in 1768 and its first President was one of the greatest artists of the time, Sir Joshua Reynolds. Born on 16 July 1723, he painted many fine portraits and encouraged others, recognising that effort was needed by all:

> *If you have great talents, industry will improve them: if you have but moderate abilities, industry will supply their deficiency.*

Another artist born on this day, in 1796, was Jean-Baptiste-Camille Corot, the French painter who drew and sketched from nature and is especially noted for his landscapes. The silvery woodland scenes he painted from the 1860s onwards were popular and a source of inspiration to other painters. He spent most of his life living in Paris.

Works of art of a different kind came from the pottery of Josiah Spode at Stoke-on-Trent. There were three Josiah Spodes. The first founded the pottery, producing blue and white earthenware. His son perfected the means of combining hard-paste porcelain, made from china clay and china stone, with bone ash to make bone china. He also designed blue and gold tableware in the oriental style. When he died on 16 July 1827, his son, also Josiah Spode, inherited the business. He died only two years later, but the name Spode on the pottery chimney in Stoke serves as a memorial to three Josiah Spodes.

Two great Norwegians shared today as their birthday. Roald Amundsen, polar explorer and first to reach the South Pole, was born in 1872. He also flew over the North Pole and eventually lost his life whilst trying to rescue Nobile after an airship crash at Spitzbergen. Trygve Lie, born in 1896, was the first Secretary general of the United Nations Organisation. He tried to mediate for peace in several areas.

Hilaire Belloc, poet and writer (p. 185), died on 16 July 1953.

On this day in 622 AD, the Muslim era began.

This day, in 1981, marked the official opening by Queen Elizabeth II of the new Humber Estuary Bridge. It had already been in use for a while, having been structurally completed a year before this. It has the longest bridge span in the world — 4,626 ft (1,410 m) between the towers. The total length of the bridge, which links Lincolnshire with South Yorkshire, is 1.37 miles (2,220 m).

There was a special link-up on 17 July 1975. A Russian spacecraft had been launched two days previously and an American one a few hours later. Way above the Atlantic Ocean, the two craft linked together in space, the Russian and American astronauts exchanged gifts, and for two days carried out experiments together. Not only was it an amazing achievement, but it showed that the two super powers were able to bridge their differences and work together.

There was little chance of co-operation in France in the days of the French Revolution. Those who did not agree with the revolutionaries were likely to end up at the guillotine, as Charlotte Corday did on 17 July 1793 — though her case was a little unusual to say the least. Born of a noble family, she was educated in a convent but became very sympathetic towards a political group known as the Girondists. Determined to support them, she went to Paris, where she sought an interview with the revolutionary leader, Jean-Paul Marat.

On 13 July, she was admitted to his presence. He was in his bath, where he spent several hours a day because of a skin complaint. She named several opponents of the regime who were in Normandy and Marat said they would be guillotined, whereupon Charlotte drew a knife from out of her clothing and stabbed him through the heart. She was arrested on the spot and later sentenced to death by the guillotine.

Also on this day. . . .

Isaac Watts, hymn writer, was born in 1674.

Adam Smith, social philosopher and economist, died in 1790.

James Cagney, 'tough' American film star, was born in 1899.

The first issue of *Punch*, the magazine famous for cartoons and caricatures, satire and humour, appeared on 17 July 1841.

One of the most famous cricketers of all time was born on 18 July 1848. He was W. G. Grace, the doctor who became a legend in his time and certainly the most famous cricketer in Victorian England. He played first-class cricket for 43 years, scored 54,896 runs, made 126 centuries and took 2,876 wickets. C. P. Snow wrote of him; 'Grace was the star cricketer and one of the greatest of all Victorian heroes. He played as an amateur, and amateurs were not supposed to be paid. That did not prevent Grace making large sums of money out of the game. He was a cheat, on and off the cricket field. . .'. Nevertheless, people enjoyed his cricket, which was entertaining and skilful, often on very rough pitches. The Nottinghamshire bowler, J.G. Shaw, said; 'I puts the ball where I likes, and that beggar, he puts it where he likes.'

Godfrey of Bouillion, who died on 18 July 1100, was one of the most famous crusaders. Leader of the First Crusade, he was offered the crown as king of Jerusalem after the holy city had been captured from the Muslims in July 1099. He accepted the crown but refused the title and would not wear the crown where Christ had worn a crown of thorns. Instead, he was called 'advocate of the Holy Sepulchre'. His reign, which lasted but a year, showed him to be a weak ruler, but he has gone down in history as the 'perfect Christian Knight, the peerless hero of the whole crusading epic' — and what better reputation could there be than that?

How different is the reputation of Vidkun Quisling, who was born on 18 July 1887. He was a Norwegian army officer who urged Hitler to occupy Norway and, when the Germans had invaded, declared himself head of the government. At the end of the war, he was tried for war crimes and for treason, was found guilty and executed. His name — 'Quisling' — became synonymous for 'traitor'.

Also on 18 July. . . .

John Paul Jones, naval hero of the United States, died in 1792.

William Makepeace Thackeray, novelist, was born in 1811.

Jane Austen, novelist, died in 1817.

John Glenn, first US astronaut to orbit the earth, born in 1921.

On 19 July 1952, the 15th Olympiad, Olympic Games, opened at Helsinki, Finland. At the opening ceremony, the Olympic flame was carried proudly into the stadium by the great Finnish athlete, Paavo Nurmi, who was once the best-known athlete in the world. Nicknamed 'the Phantom Finn', he ran with a stop-watch in his hand so that he could check his timing. In the 1920s he gained six gold medals in three Olympic Games; he set no less than twenty world records for running; and he held the world record for the mile run (4 mins 10.4 secs) for eight years.

No world records will be made as a result of races held on 19 July each year at Piddinghoe, Sussex — but the children enjoy the races — and the tea, known as Little Edith's Treat, in memory of Edith Croft, who died there, aged 3 months, in 1868.

For people in many parts of the world, the name Wimbledon means one thing — lawn tennis — for Wimbledon is the head-quarters of the All England Club and Wimbledon is the popular name for the All England Lawn Tennis Championships, in which tennis players from many parts of the world compete each summer. It was on 19 July 1877, that the first of the championships was held and won by Spencer Gore.

People who prefer driving rather than more energetic pursuits may like to know that the first parking meters were installed on 19 July 1935, in Oklahoma City, USA.

On 19 July 1904, the building began of the new Anglican Cathedral in Liverpool. It was consecrated on the same day in 1924. This day, in 1869, saw the completion of the Wolf Rock Lighthouse off the Isles of Scilly.

Samuel Colt was born on 19 July 1814. He was the inventor of the Colt revolver, the famous six-shooter. He also invented a submarine battery.

Also on 19 July. . . .

Matthew Flinders, the navigator who sailed round Australia and charted the coast, died in 1814.

Edgar Degas, French painter and sculptor, was born in 1834.

This day witnessed two landmarks in space travel. The first was the arrival of men on the moon on 20 July 1969. Four days after leaving Cape Kennedy (Cape Canaveral), the Command Module *Columbia* reached the moon. Michael Collins remained therein, whilst Neil Armstrong and Edwin Aldrin entered the lunar module *Eagle* and descended to the moon. They landed on the Sea of Tranquility at 4.17 pm US Eastern Daylight time and stepped onto the moon at 10.56 pm (21 July British Time qv). Armstrong commented; 'That's one small step for man, one giant leap for mankind.'

Seven years later to the day, on 20 July 1976, the unmanned lander from the US *Viking I* made the first soft landing on Mars. That had been a much longer journey, taking 310 days from blast off at Cape Canaveral. The lander was able to scoop up samples of soil, analyse them and radio the results to earth. The radio signals confirming the safe landing took 19 minutes to reach the earth. They were followed by television pictures.

To think that radio telegraphy was unknown eighty years before this! The first successful radio telegraphy experiments were conducted by Guglielmo Marconi in 1896–7. In 1899, he sent a message across the English Channel and, in 1901, amazed the world with his first transatlantic message. What would Marconi himself have thought about a message from Mars? Marconi died on 20 July 1937.

Some of today's birthdays. . . .

In 1304, Petrarch (Francesco Petrarca), the Italian poet, who led the revival of learning in Italy. When the custom of presenting a poet with a laurel crown was revived in 1341, Petrarch was the first to be so honoured.

In 1860, Margaret MacMillan, educational pioneer and first president of the Nursery School Association.

In 1919, Sir Edmund Hillary, the New Zealander who became the first man to reach the summit of Everest and later explored Antarctica.

This day also saw, in 1944, the unsuccessful attempt to assassinate Hitler and, in 1974, the Turkish invasion of Cyprus which divided that country.

When Daniel Lambert died on 21 July 1809, he left a gap that no one could fill, for he was the fattest man on record in England. When he died, at Stamford, Lincolnshire, he weighed 52¾ stone (335 kg), measured 112 inches (284 cm) round the body and 37 inches (93 cm) round his leg.

Nothing Daniel could do through sport or dieting could prevent his rapid growth. He weighed 32 stone (203 kg) at the age of 23. As he could not control his growth, he decided to use it to his advantage. When he was 25, he had a special carriage built to take him to London, where he exhibited himself. From there he toured the country — a travelling freak show.

Not surprisingly, his weight affected his heart and he died at the age of 39. His coffin was made with wheels so that it could be pushed to the church.

For the record, there was one heavier man recorded in England. William Campbell, who died in 1878, was a little heavier and taller but not so fat!

For sheer size of achievement nothing could be greater than that of 21 July 1969, when Neil Armstrong, command pilot of the *Apollo XI* mission, became the first man to set foot on the moon, an achievement made possible by the efforts of vast numbers of people (p. 177).

This was also the day, in 1960, when the world saw the election of the first woman as Prime Minister. She was Mrs. Bandaranaike of Sri Lanka.

Also on this day. . . .

Robert Burns, the Scottish poet, died in 1796.
Dame Ellen Terry, English actress, died in 1928.
The Tate Gallery, London art gallery, opened in 1897.

At the Battle of Shrewsbury, on 21 July 1403, Sir Henry Percy was killed. The eldest son of the Earl of Northumberland, he was nicknamed 'Hotspur' by the Scots because of the efficient way in which he patrolled the border lands. Later, Hotspur rebelled against King Henry IV and this led to the battle in which he was slain. He is one of the leading characters in Shakespeare's *Henry IV*.

Sir, you have tasted two whole worms; you have hissed all my mystery lectures and have been caught fighting a liar in the quad; you will leave by the next town drain.

This is one of the sayings attributed to the Revd. William Spooner, who was a learned Anglican clergyman and warden of New College, Oxford. He was a nervous man, who often made mistakes in his speaking so that initial letters or syllables became transposed, so giving a humorous effect. Such sayings are now known as 'spoonerisms' after this reverend gentleman and are often used deliberately for amusement. This day, in 1844, was the birthday of the Revd. William Spooner.

There was nothing humorous about the speech made on 22 July 1875, in the House of Commons, by Samuel Plimsoll. He had wanted laws passed to prevent ships from being overloaded because many sank and their crews were drowned. He was so angry when Members of Parliament voted against the law that he called them villains and shook his fist. But there were many people who agreed with him and, in the following year, a law was passed. Ships had to be inspected to see whether they were seaworthy and to have a Load Line, or Plimsoll Line painted on the side to show the maximum load they were allowed to carry.

Half a century earlier, on 22 July 1822, another Act of Parliament had been passed. It was the first law to give protection against cruelty to animals. Known as Martin's Act, it was named after the Member of Parliament who had introduced it, Richard Martin, who was also one of the founders of the Royal Society for the Prevention of Cruelty to animals.

Also on this date, with thoughts for the well-being of people in many parts of the world, the World Health Organisation was set up in 1946.

On 22 July 1847, the Mormons entered Salt Lake City.

It was on this day, in 1934, in Chicago, that 'Public Enemy Number One' met his end. John Dillinger, escaped bank robber and killer, was gunned down by 27 FBI agents.

Ulysses S. Grant was one of the outstanding soldiers of his day. Trained at the US Military Academy at West Point, he began a career in the army but resigned in 1854. Seven years later, when the American Civil War broke out, he returned to be a leader of the Federal (Northern) Army. He was so successful that he was placed in command of all the Union forces in 1864 and led them to victory in 1865.

Four years later, in 1869, General Ulysses S. Grant was elected 18th president of the United States and served for two terms of office until 1877. He is remembered for his determination, his support for amnesty for the confederate leaders and for the protection of civil rights for negroes. He died on 23 July 1885.

Philippe Pétain was also a soldier, who became a national hero of France after his victory at the Battle of Verdun during World War I. In 1918 he was made a marshal of France and later given many military honours.

In 1939 France was again at war with Germany and was overrun in the following year. Marshal Pétain, at the age of 84, was named as premier of France and had to arrange an armistice with the Nazi German leaders. Then, until 1944, he was the head of the Vichy Government which governed that part of France not occupied by the Germans. After the war the one time hero was regarded as a traitor, tried and sentenced to death but the sentence was changed to one of life imprisonment and it was as a prisoner that he died on 23 July 1951.

When the German armies overran France the British army had to get out quickly. They made their way to the beaches at Dunkirk, where they were taken off in hundreds of naval and civilian craft. Today was the birthday, in 1883, of the man responsible for the successful evacuation from Dunkirk, Field Marshal Sir Alan Brooke, later Viscount Alanbrooke.

Another leader, born on this day in 1892, was Haile Selassie, Emperor of Ethiopia from 1930 until forced into exile in 1936 by the Italians, and from 1941 until deposed by a military coup d'état in 1974.

The English poet, Coventry Patmore, was born on 23 July 1823.

Who has not thrilled to the story of the *Count of Monte Cristo* or the adventures of *The Three Musketeers*? These are two books from the prolific writings of Alexandre Dumas (Dumas Pére), who was born on 24 July 1802. One of the most popular French authors of the 19th Century, he was forced into writing more and more because of his extravagant tastes.

There was nothing fictional about the successes, early in the 19th Century in South America of Simon Bolivar. Born into an aristocratic Venezuelan family, on 24 July 1783, he became a revolutionary soldier-statesman, determined to free his country from Spanish rule. After several attempts, he achieved this in 1821. What he could do for his own country, he determined also to do for others. In a short time, he had liberated six, had one of them renamed Bolivia in his honour, and was president of several of them at the same time.

Two other of today's birthdays . . . .
In 1725, John Newton, preacher and hymn writer.
In 1898, Amelia Earhart, celebrated American air woman.
And three deaths . . . .
In 1842, John Sell Cotman, water-colour artist — a landscape painter of the Norwich school.
In 1883, Captain Matthew Webb, the first man to swim the English Channel (August 1875), was drowned whilst attempting to swim the Niagara Falls.
In 1981, Peter Sellers, popular British actor.

It was on 24 July 1704, that a British naval force, under Admiral Sir George Rooke, captured Gibraltar from Spain. The Rock, which was ceded to Britain by the Treaty of Utrecht, in 1713, became a strategic military and naval base during the next two-and-a-half centuries.

This day in 1851 was a bright day for the house owner. Window Tax was repealed. The tax had first been levied in 1696 to cover the cost of replacing damaged coins. House owners were taxed according to the number of windows — so many windows were bricked in to avoid the tax.

Please to remember the Grotto,
It's only once a year.
Father's gone to sea,
Mother's gone to fetch him home,
So please remember me!

This and similar rhymes, or pleas such as 'A penny for the Grotto', were once commonly heard in London on St. James's Day, 25 July, and on days leading up to old St. James's Day, which was 5 August. Children called out as they sat beside the little grottoes they had made mainly from shells but using whatever materials were at hand, such as glass or pottery.

The reason for the shells was that the scallop shell was the emblem of St. James the Great. He was one of the Galilean fishermen who became a disciple of Jesus Christ and later took Christianity to Spain. Legend says that, after he had been put to death by Herod Agrippa, his remains were taken to Spain for burial. The site, Santiago de Compostella became the most important place of pilgrimage for Christians after Jerusalem. In the Middle Ages, thousands went there and returned wearing the scallop-shell emblem.

Many travellers today wear an emblem or medallion of a different sort — a St. Christopher. This is his day too. Little is known of him but various legends are told, including one of the way in which he carried Christ over some water. He has long been regarded as the patron saint of travellers. Many a traveller has worn a St. Christopher, a cross or similar talisman to try to ensure a safe journey or divine protection.

In *The Rime of the Ancient Mariner* we read of a ship that was followed by an albatross, regarded by sailors as a good omen. The Ancient Mariner shot the albatross and trouble began. The wind dropped and they were becalmed beneath a blazing sun with no water to drink. The Ancient Mariner was blamed.

Instead of the cross, the albatross
About my neck was hung.

It is one of the great narrative poems of Samuel Taylor Coleridge, who died on 25 July 1834.

Louis Bleriot was a very courageous man. He needed to be to attempt to cross the Channel from France to England in the fragile aircraft that he had designed, especially as he had already crashed several times in similar aircraft.

But he made it! On 25 July 1909, he became the first man to fly the Channel, earning himself a prize of £1,000 for so doing. It was probably easier taking off than it was landing, for Bleriot crash-landed his 'plane on Castle Hill, Dover, smashing part of the front of the 'plane as he did so.

It was exactly fifty years later, on 25 July 1959, that the Channel was first crossed by hovercraft.

Another 'first' today was an important stage in the development of railways. We tend to think of the beginning of railways as the day when the Stockton-Darlington railway opened in 1825, with passenger coaches pulled by George Stephenson's *Locomotion*. It was eleven years before that, on 25 July 1814, that George Stephenson had given the first successful demonstration of a steam locomotive, with his *Blucher*, on a colliery tramway.

The story of steam engines goes back much earlier than that. These were not locomotives but engines for pumping water out of the mines. The credit for the first steam engine goes to Thomas Savery. The use of this engine was first recorded on this day, 25 July 1698.

When it rains, we may put on a 'mac' or 'macintosh'. It takes its name from Charles Macintosh, who invented the first waterproof clothing. He died on 25 July 1843.

The Earl of Balfour, Prime Minister from 1902 to 1905, was born on 25 July 1848. He is remembered for the Balfour Declaration, in 1917, pledging support for a Jewish national home in Palestine.

Dr James Barry, an army surgeon who was outspoken on the subject of soldiers' conditions and who had fought three duels, died on 25 July 1865. Only then was it discovered that 'he' was a woman.

Today is St. Anne's Day, kept in honour of one of whose life nothing is known. It is the name traditionally given to the mother of the Blessed Virgin Mary. There are many churches and holy wells dedicated to her in Britain. In fact lots of holy wells are dedicated either to St. Anne or St. Bridget (Bride) and the reason may well go back to ancient times. Two of the Celtic goddesses were Anu and Brigantia, to whom offerings may have been made at holy wells. Early Christian teachers often Christianised old customs when they were unable to abolish them. Who better to replace Anu and Brigantia than Anne and Bridget? So, on or about today, there will be little ceremonies at wells in a number of places.

Today was the birthday, in 1875, of Carl Jung. He did not plumb the depths to find water: he plumbed deep into the subconscious mind to find out why people acted in certain ways. Psychologists today owe much to his work and writings.

A good study for a psychologist might be Pygmalion, the King of Cyprus who fell in love with a statue of Aphrodite. The more modern *Pygmalion* tells of a Professor Henry Higgins, who falls in love with his Cockney student, Eliza Doolittle. The play, first performed in 1913, was adapted to make the successful musical *My Fair Lady*. *Pygmalion* was one of the plays of George Bernard Shaw. Born in Dublin on 26 July 1856, he was to become one of the greatest British playwrights, often expressing through his plays his strong desires for social reform. In 1925, he was awarded the Nobel Prize for Literature.

This day was also the birthday of two other great writers. André Maurois, born in 1885, was a French biographer and novelist, whose many books were held in high esteem both in France and in Britain. Aldous Huxley, the British novelist was born in 1894.

George Borrow, the writer about gypsy life, died on 26 July 1881. No doubt he and the others could look back on life's achievements and say, as in Borrow's *Lavengro*,

> *Youth will be served, every dog has his day, and mine has been a fine one.*

Child! do not throw this book about;
Refrain from the unholy pleasure
Of cutting all the pictures out!
Preserve it as your chiefest treasure.

These profound words of advice are offered as a dedication in *The Bad Child's Book of Beasts* by Hilaire Belloc, whose birthday was 27 July 1870. This, and his *Cautionary Tales,* have remained popular with children. He was also a historian and writer of a number of books. French by birth, he moved to England and became a British subject in 1902.

A very deep thinker died on 27 July 1844. Many people regard John Dalton as one of the greatest of scientists. As a young man he enjoyed studying mathematics and physics. He made a life-long study of meteorology; he collected butterflies; he made a study of colour-blindness, from which he himself suffered; he studied gases and gave us Dalton's Law; and he put forward atomic theories which were of great value in the study of science. John Dalton enjoyed his work. He was a kindly, though reserved, man who 'never found time to marry'.

Another to whom we are indebted for his theories was Sir Flinders Petrie, who also died on this day, in 1942. He was an archaeologist, who taught methods of excavation and the means of dating the pots and other implements that were found.

Two 'firsts' today. In 1696, the Bank of England was granted its charter. In 1866, the first permanent Atlantic Telegraph cable was completed, laid by the *Great Eastern.*

This day saw two Scottish battles. In 1054, Macbeth, made famous by Shakespeare, fought Siward at Dunsinane and had to retreat. In 1689, Scots fighting in support of James II won a battle in the Pass of Killiecrankie but their leader, John Graham of Claverhouse, Viscount Dundee ('Bonnie Dundee') died after being hit by a musket ball.

The Korean War armistice was signed on 27 July 1953.

Boiled, baked, sauté, chipped, mashed . . . What would we do without our potatoes? We accept them as part of the traditional wholesome English diet, yet they are English by adoption. They were first introduced to Great Britain from Colombia, on 28 July 1586, by Sir Thomas Herriot.

Beatrix Potter was first introduced to Britain on 28 July 1866, when she was born in London of rich Lancashire parents. As a child she was lonely and spent a lot of her time in sketching and painting in water colours. When she began writing her popular children's books, she illustrated them with very lifelike water colours of her lovable little animals.

The well-loved music of Johann Sebastian Bach was introduced to Britain from Germany, where the great composer lived, and where he died on 28 July 1750. He held some very important positions as organist and musical director. He composed some orchestral music, notably the Brandenburg Concertos, and also an enormous amount of sacred music, including over 200 cantatas. Some of his best loved music is that which he composed for the organ, of which he was a master.

So to organs of a different kind. William James Mayo died on 28 July 1939. He was a surgeon, specialising in surgery of the abdomen, kidney and pelvis. His nephew, Charles William Mayo, was born on 28 July 1898 and died on 28 July 1968. He, too, was a skilful surgeon who, with other members of the Mayo family, worked a group practice at the Mayo Clinic in Rochester, Minnesota, USA.

It was not the surgeon's knife that operated on two leaders of the French Revolution on 28 July 1794. Maximilien Robespierre and Louis Saint-Just were extremists of the Revolution, playing leading roles in the Reign of Terror, in which many nobles and political leaders were executed. At last they were overthrown and went themselves to the guillotine.

Scotland also had its head chopped off on 28 July 1790. On this day, the Forth and Clyde Canal was opened. It created a waterway that completely crossed southern Scotland.

About midnight on 28–29 July 1588, six fire ships were launched into the harbour at Calais, where the Spanish Armada lay at anchor after a week of fighting up the English Channel. To avoid the fire ships, the Spaniards cut their anchors loose, set sail and fled in disarray. The English attacked again during the day and the Spaniards were finally routed, only a sudden change of wind enabling some of them to escape.

Perhaps both sides would have benefitted from a weather forecast, had one been available. Nowadays we often refer to weather forecasts in newspapers or on the radio or television before we make plans as to what we may do. It was on this day, in 1949, that the BBC gave its first weather forecast on television.

Before making a journey, we may also consult a timetable. This day, in 1801, was the birthday, in Salford, of George Bradshaw, who published the first timetables for canal boats and railways. In time *Bradshaw's* was to become a name synonymous with railway timetables.

This was the birthday, in 1887, of Sigmund Romberg, one of the most successful composers of operettas in America and of some very well-loved songs. It was the birthday, in 1883, of Benito Mussolini, who decided to call the tune in Italy and became its dictator. Three years later, Robert Schuman, French politician and Prime Minister was born.

Robert Schumann, the German composer, died on 29 July 1856; leaving behind many songs and music for the piano.

William Wilberforce also died on this day, in 1833. He was a well-known politician and philanthropist, who spent the greater part of his life working to abolish the slave trade and then slavery itself. The Slavery Abolition Act was passed by parliament one month after Wilberforce's death.

This was the last day for Vincent van Gogh, a talented Dutch painter but an unhappy and unbalanced man. One night he cut off one of his ears and delivered it to a house; later he spent time in an asylum; but he still painted. His last painting was *Cornfield with Flight of Two Birds*. It was in that place that he shot himself on 29 July 1890.

The first World Cup Final for Association Football was played on 30 July 1930, in Montivideo, Uruguay, when Uruguay beat Argentina by four goals to two. The competition was instituted by the Federation Internationale de Football Association (FIFA) and the cup was the Jules Rimet Trophy, named after the Frenchman who proposed the competition. It is normally held every fourth year.

For England the World Cup year was 1966, when, on 30 July, England beat West Germany in the final, in which Geoff Hurst scored three goals, a record for the World Cup. The team was captained by his fellow West Ham player, Bobby Moore.

This day was the birthday of another Moore who was to achieve world-wide fame. Henry Moore was born at Castleford, Yorkshire, on 30 July 1898. He made his name as an artist and sculptor. During World War II, he was an official war artist and his wartime drawings became well-known. But it was his particular style of modern sculpture which gave him an international reputation and his sculptures adorn cities on both sides of the Atlantic Ocean.

This was also the birthday of Henry Ford, in 1863. He was not so concerned with the single work of art but with mass-production. His famous Model T car, of which 15 million were sold, was the first of many models of car to bear the name 'Ford'.

The curfew tolls the knell of parting day,
The lowing herd winds slowly o'er the lea,
The ploughman homeward plods his weary way,
And leaves the world to darkness and to me.

These well-known lines begin the *Elegy Written in a Country Churchyard* by Thomas Gray. He died on 30 July 1771, and was buried in the churchyard at Stoke Poges, Buckinghamshire, the setting for his poem.

These also died on 30 July. . . .
William Penn, Quaker leader, founder of Pennsylvania, in 1718.
Otto von Bismarck, German 'Iron Chancellor', in 1898.
Umberto Nobile, Italian polar aviator, in 1978.

John Ericsson was born in Sweden on 31 July 1803. He became interested in engineering. When he was 23, he moved to England, where he built a locomotive for the competition at Rainhill, Lancashire, which was won by George Stephenson's *Rocket*. He then turned his attention to naval engineering. He made many suggestions for improved warships, and he patented the screw propellor.

In 1839, he emigrated again, this time to America, where he settled in New York, later becoming a United States citizen. It was he who designed the *Monitor*, a revolutionary type of warship with a revolving gun turret. Later he developed a torpedo and worked on the possibility of solar-powered motors.

Sir Francis Younghusband travelled in the opposite direction. He was born in India and became an army officer and an explorer of Asia. His expeditions across the Gobi desert and to remote parts of central Asia provided a lot of useful knowledge of the geography of those parts. In 1902, he took an expedition to Tibet and opened up that country to the western world. He was a deeply religious man, who wrote several books and, in 1936, founded the World Congress of Faiths. He died on 31 July 1942.

This is the Feast Day of St. Ignatius Loyola, who died on 31 July 1556. He turned to religion after reading religious books whilst convalescing after a battle injury. He became one of the leading figures in the 16th Century Roman Catholic Reformation and founded the Society of Jesus, or Jesuits. A prayer of this soldier-saint, the General of his order, is one of the best-known prayers:

> *Teach us, good Lord, to serve thee as thou deservest; to give and not to count the cost; to fight and not to heed the wounds; to toil and not to seek for rest; to labour and not to ask for any reward save that of knowing that we do thy will.*

Franz Liszt was a religious man, too, and was an abbé in the Roman Catholic Church, but is best known as a musician, a Hungarian pianist and composer of lively music. He began learning the piano at the age of five and grew to be one of the world's greatest pianists. He wrote many pieces of music for the piano and some for the orchestra. He died at Bayrouth, now in West Germany, on 31 July 1886.

Some July Events and Commemorations

(*see also pp 155–6*)

Between 5th and 15th Peel, Isle of Man: Viking Festival. Landing of 'Vikings' from long boats; battle with Celts; election of a king; torchlight procession; fireworks.
First Saturday Rochester, Kent: Admiralty Court. Procession to a decorated barge moored off the pier.
Ambleside and Musgrave, Cumbria: Rush Bearing.
First Sunday Alport Castle, Derbyshire: Love Feast at which worshippers testify to their beliefs.
Thursday after July 4th London: Vintners' Procession.
11th Appleton, Cheshire: Bawming (Adorning) the Thorn. Garlands carried in procession and placed on the Thorn bush.
Tuesday and Wednesday after 19th Honiton, Devon: Hot Penny Ceremony. Hot pennies scattered at opening of fair.
Two weeks beginning second Saturday Keswick, Cumbria: Keswick Convention — religious meetings in huge marquee.
Last Monday Swan Upping (marking) on River Thames.
Towards end of month Haworth, Yorkshire: Rushbearing.
Burbage, Derbyshire: Clipping (Encircling) the Church.
3rd Saturday Durham: Miners' Gala. March, service and fair.
Sometime in month Ashburton, Devon: Ale tasting.
Folkestone, Kent: Blessing the Sea.
Tollesbury, Essex: Giant Gooseberry Pie distributed.
Buxton and Marsh Lane near Eckington, Derbyshire; and Dore, Yorkshire: Well dressing.

SOME JULY FAIRS

Friday and Saturday after first Sunday Charlbury, Oxon: Charlbury Club — a relic of Wychwood Forest Fair.
Second week Holsworthy, Devon: St. Peter's Fair.
14th Ebernoe, Sussex: Horse Fair.
Third Monday Helston, Cornwall: Gooseberry Fair.
25th Findon, Sussex: Lamb Fair.

SOME AGRICULTURAL AND OTHER SHOWS

Abergavenny and Border Counties, Border Union, Cumberland, East of England (Peterborough), Great Yorkshire, Kent, Royal Show, Isle of Wight, Royal Norfolk, Royal Welsh, St. Helens, Tendring Hundred (Essex), Game Fair, International Horse Show.

AUGUST

August

Originally Sextilis, the sixth month, this was renamed Augustus in honour of Augustus Caesar, the first Roman Emperor.

For the Anglo-Saxons this was Weodmonath, the month of weeds. And one does not need to be a gardener to appreciate the reason for this.

August is not only the month for weeds but a month when many flowers are adding colour to garden, field and hedgerow.

On the first drowsy heat of August noon
Comes the plumed goldenrod with flaunting train
And lifts her yellow head along the way.

Judd

The brilliant poppy flaunts her head
Amidst the ripening grain,
And adds her voice to swell the song
That August's here again.

Winslow

Those fields of ripening grain are a reminder that harvest is near. Indeed, before the month is out, the countryside will echo to the roar of the combine harvesters as they move across the fields gobbling up the grain. It is a different world from that of the time of Shakespeare, when all was harvested by hand and the Bard could write of 'You sun-burned sicklemen, of August weary.'

For the farmer, warm, dry August days are welcome.

Dry August and warm doth harvest no harm.

Thomas Tusser

The main weather predictions this month are concerned with St. Bartholomew's Day, 24 August.

As at St. Bartholomew's Day,
So will all the autumn stay.

If the twenty-fourth of August be fair and clear,
Then hope for a prosperous autumn that year.

On the farm, August is a working month as the farmers busy themselves with the harvesting. For many other people it is always the holiday month as many of the schools are closed for the main holiday at the end of the educational year.

August for the people and their favourite islands.
Daily the steamers sidle up to meet
The effusive welcome of the pier.

'August for the people', W. H. Auden

Nowadays it is the accepted custom for people to go away for their holidays, to the seaside, the country or abroad. Holidays in the past were more often spread through the year as people celebrated saints' days by attending church then having the rest of the day free to enjoy themselves. Some holidays, such as Christmas, were longer. The word holiday comes from 'holy day'. These days added up to some eight weeks in the year. A couple of hundred years ago, the Bank of England closed for 33 saints' days and other festivals.

But times changed as industry and commerce increased. By 1934, the days on which the Bank of England closed had been reduced to four. The present Bank Holiday system resulted from an Act of Parliament of 1871. The Summer Bank Holiday used to be the first Monday in August, but this was changed a few years ago to the last Monday.

Seaside holidays grew in popularity at the beginning of last century, though it was only a very small number who could enjoy them. Some places became popular because of royal patronage. Weymouth grew from a small fishing village after visits by King George III, whilst the little Sussex village of Brighthelmstone, visited by the Prince Regent, began its development into the Brighton we know today, with such buildings as the Royal Pavilion dating from that time.

During recent times, more and more people have taken to the water for their holidays. Marinas and boat havens have been built alongside many rivers and canals. One popular boating area is the Norfolk Broads where, on the first Sunday of August, the Bishop of Norwich goes by boat to Horning for the annual Blessing of the Broads in St. Benet's Abbey.

In some parts of Britain it has been the custom for many years for all the factories to close down during the same period for holidays. So, in Stoke-on-Trent, for example, the city almost comes to a halt for the two weeks of the Potters' Holiday in July. In other places in the north of England and in Scotland most factories close for Wake Weeks.

The Wake Week was an extension of the wake, the vigil that was kept on the saint's feast day. After the vigil in church, no one was expected to work and so the day became a public holiday. This was a time for merrymaking and enjoyment as well as making a welcome change from a somewhat humdrum life with few comforts and little to enjoy.

The fun following the Wake was sometimes referred to as the Revel. One such Revel to survive is held each year on the Monday after 12 August in Marhamchurch, near Bude, Cornwall. It is on the day following the feast of St. Marwenne, who is thought to have taken Christianity to the village in the 6th Century. The Queen of the Revel, who has been elected from the village children, is crowned by Father Time. A band then leads a procession, with the Queen on horseback, round the village to the Revel ground where dancing, wrestling, competitions, sideshows and amusements can be enjoyed by all.

On most of the Wake or Revel days stalls were set up, often in the churchyard itself, for the sale of food, drink and all sorts of other things too. If a goodly number of people was expected, pedlars and others from elsewhere might come with an eye to business. So the occasion developed into an annual fair. Many of the present-day fun fairs originated in this way.

August is the month for some of the greatest of the horse fairs. For the Horse Fair at Brigg, Lincolnshire, on 5 August, gypsies gather several days beforehand and gallop their horses through the town so that prospective buyers can see them. Sales are confirmed by the traditional gypsy hand-slap. The Lee Gap Horse Fair in Yorkshire has been held for over 800 years. Once continuous from 24 August to 17 September, it is now held only on those two days.

Some of the once great horse fairs have changed in nature with the decline in the use of horses. At the Pony Fair, Barnet, there used to be a sale of over 40,000 animals: now the number is more likely to be in hundreds. Mitcham Fair, Surrey, on 12 August and the following two days, is one which attracts great crowds. It was once important for the sale of horses and cattle.

Most of the pony fairs, such as Barnet, are held during September. Sales of unbroken fell, dale and moorland ponies are held at Brough, Bridgewater, Tavistock, Widecombe and elsewhere (see *Autumn and Winter Days* p. 38).

August is a month in which many people like to enjoy outdoor pursuits of many kinds, either as individuals or at organised gatherings. One of the well-known events is in Cumbria. The Grasmere Sports, on the Thursday nearest to 20 August, has been held continuously for over a century.

For Welsh people, the great event of August, indeed the event of the year, is the Royal National Eisteddfod of Wales, held during the first week of the month. A different site is chosen each year and this alternates between North and South Wales. The great pavilion, erected on the Eisteddfod field, seats 9,000 of the many thousands who come from all parts of Wales and beyond.

There is an impressive opening ceremony, which has its roots deep in the past and which is enacted at the altar in the centre of the gorsedd circle of stones. A procession of Druids, bards and attendants moves to the altar, where the Druids, in turn, lay their hands upon the great Gorsedd Sword. The Arch Druid opens the eisteddfod with a speech from the Arch Druid's Stone, then partly unsheathes the sword and cries out three times, 'A oes heddwch?' (*Is it peace*?), to which the crowd responds, 'Heddwch!' (*Peace*!).

The eisteddfod is a great festival of Welsh culture, of music, singing, dancing and poetry, with prizes for the winners of the various competitions and the greatest honours, the bardic crown and bardic chair, awarded for different kinds of poetry.

In Scotland there are various Highland Gatherings, which are enjoyed by the Scots themselves and by holidaymakers too.

Long, long ago, the ancient Celtic people of Britain used to hold a festival on this day. It was known as Lughnasa, which was the festival of Lug. This was a harvest festival at which a play was performed in which a young warrior, representing Lug, fought a giant to get food for his men.

In Anglo-Saxon times, this day was also a harvest festival, not to give thanks for a harvest safely gathered in, but to offer the first fruits of the harvest to God. Some of the first grain to be reaped was made into a loaf to be broken and used at the Mass (Holy Communion). So this became the Loaf-Mass — or in the Old English language Hlaf-Maesse, which, in course of time, became Lammas, the name by which this day has been known ever since. It was also the day, hundreds of years ago, when people were expected to pay to the priests money known as Peter's Pence, to be sent to the Pope in Rome.

For many village people, Lammas Day was important for another reason. Certain land in the village was available for anyone to use. During the summer, hay was grown for cattle food on this land but, after 1 August, when the hay had been harvested, people could turn loose their animals on these Lammas lands. The day itself was a holiday with fairs and amusements. Some Lammas fairs still exist but in a somewhat different form.

On or about this date, there is an annual event on the River Thames. It is the Doggett's Coat and Badge Race, which was first held on 1 August 1715. Thomas Doggett was an Irish actor who left money for the race to be held each year. It is now run by the Fishmongers' Company. This is the oldest rowing race in the world and is open only to watermen who have just completed their apprenticeship. The race starts near London Bridge and finishes near Chelsea Bridge, a course of 4½ miles (7¼ km) rowed aginst the tide. The winner receives a scarlet coat with a large silver badge on the sleeve.

Mention of London Bridge is a reminder that the 'new' London Bridge opened on 1 August 1831. Designed by the Scottish engineer, John Rennie, it replaced the old bridge cluttered with buildings. It was dismantled and taken to Arizona, America, in 1967–73, as a new wider London Bridge replaced it.

A little down-river from London Bridge, the Regents Canal runs into the Thames. Opened on 1 August 1820, it is part of the Grand Union system and one of many canals which form the inland waterways of Britain, once very important for trade and now for pleasure cruising.

The boy stood on the burning deck
Whence all but he had fled

These words from *Casabianca* by Mrs. Felicia Dorothea Hemans are familiar to many people but the circumstances are not so well known. The boy was the ten-year-old son of Commodore Casabianca, commander of the French admiral's flagship *L'Orient*. On 1 August 1798, the French fleet was at anchor in Aboukir Bay, Egypt, when the English fleet, under Lord Nelson, caught them unawares. In the Battle of the Nile which followed, *L'Orient* was set ablaze. Casabianca's son, true to his instructions, remained bravely 'on the burning deck' until five past ten that night when, after burning for an hour, the ship was blown to pieces by an explosion which was heard fifteen miles (24 km) away. This was one of the decisive sea battles in the naval struggles between Britain and France in the time of Napoleon.

Richard Henry Dana, who was born on 1 August 1815, was also a man of the sea. For health reasons he took voyages on sailing ships round Cape Horn and then attended law school. His book *Two Years Before the Mast* is one of the best known books about the sea. He also wrote a book about sea law entitled *A Seaman's Friend* so that seamen should know their rights.

Another well-known book of the sea is *Moby Dick*, the story of a fierce white whale and those who hunted him. This day was the birthday, in 1819, of Herman Melville, the author, who had gained ideas for the book whilst serving on whalers in the Pacific. He returned home via Cape Horn as a seaman on a naval frigate. Melville wrote several other books, of which perhaps the best after *Moby Dick* was *Billy Budd*, published over 30 years after his death.

It was on this day, in 1834, that slavery was abolished in all British possessions.

The landscape of Gainsborough is soothing, tender and affecting. The stillness of noon, the depths of twilight, and the dews and pearls of the morning, are all to be found on the canvases of this most benevolent and kind-hearted man. On looking at them we find tears in our eyes, and know not what brings them.

John Ruskin had this to say of the paintings of Thomas Gainsborough, the 18th Century landscape and portrait painter. Born in Sudbury, Suffolk, he painted local people and scenes but later moved to Bath, where he was much in demand. He was a very fast painter but unable to keep up with the numbers that sought his time. Not content with painting heads or head-and-shoulders, he painted full length figures dressed in the most exquisite costumes and had the art of capturing just the right expression. He died in London on 2 August 1788.

This day also marked the end, in 1921, for Enrico Caruso, one of the greatest and most popular of Italian tenors. He had a strong, easy and rich voice, which appealed to vast numbers of people. He had a magnetic personality, too. Who else could stand before a vast audience at the Metropolitan Opera House, New York, pat his stomach and tell his admiring fans they should go home because he was hungry and wanted his supper? He died after rupturing a blood vessel in his throat whilst singing.

William Rufus, King William II of England, was anything but popular. It was on 2 August 1100, that he was killed by an arrow whilst hunting in the New Forest. Was it an accident? Or was it assassination? Nobody really knew. . . and few people really cared.

These three were born on 2 August. . .
Joseph Sturge, in 1793. He was a Quaker philanthropist and reformer, who led the movement against slavery.
John Tyndall, in 1820. He was the physicist who, amongst other things, demonstrated why the sky is blue.
Sir Arthur Bliss, 20th Century English composer, in 1891.
. . . and President Hindenburg of Germany died in 1934.

The Stoke Mandeville hospital for the handicapped was opened on 2 August 1972, by Queen Elizabeth II.

Miriam Hargrave passed her driving test on 3 August 1970. That may hardly seem newsworthy because people are passing the test every day. This was different, however, because it was her fortieth attempt and she had taken 212 driving lessons, so creating a record for persistence.

Christopher Columbus was a persistent man. He believed he could reach India by sailing westward across the Atlantic. Most people thought he was mad but he managed to persuade Queen Isabella of Spain to finance his expedition and he sailed on 3 August 1492.

It was on this day, in 1610, that Henry Hudson discovered Hudson Bay and, in 1958, that the US submarine *Nautilus* passed under the North Pole. Life at sea and the battle against nature is the theme of many of the novels written by Joseph Conrad, who died on 3 August 1924.

Persistence, patience and hard work will often produce results that make all the effort worth-while. Think of all the effort that must have gone into the intricate wood carvings of Grinling Gibbons, who died on 3 August 1721, which adorn royal palaces and St. Paul's Cathedral. Sir Joseph Paxton, born this day in 1801, was a gardener who designed glass houses — including the biggest of them all, the Crystal Palace. Sir Richard Arkwright, who died on 3 August 1792, was another man determined to succeed. He invented a new textile machine, opened factories, employed 5,000 workers, was knighted and made a large fortune. Perhaps today he would have received the Queen's Award for Industry — which was created on this day, 3 August 1965.

Archbishop Makarios, who died on 3 August 1977, will be remembered for his persistence in seeking independence for his country, Cyprus. And, whilst on the subject of patriotism, this was the birthday, in 1887, of Rupert Brooke, the poet, immortalised by the opening words of 'The Soldier'.

If I should die, think only this of me:
That there's some corner in a foreign field
That is forever England.

This was the day, in 1944, when Anne Frank was arrested. As a child she had been taken from Germany to Holland by her parents who were fleeing from the persecution of Jews in their homeland. When the Nazis occupied Holland, the family went into hiding until betrayed in 1944. After her arrest, Anne was taken to Belsen concentration camp, where she perished. The diary, which she kept, was published in 1947, a moving account of hardship and suffering. Anne Frank became a symbol of persecution: her name was given to many refugee settlements in Europe.

President Idi Amin of Uganda had little time for people who were 'different'. On this day, in 1972, he ordered the expulsion of some 40,000 British Asians from Uganda. The Asians lost most of their possessions: Uganda lost many of its most able people.

The invasion of Belgium by German armies in 1914 was the last straw as far as Britain was concerned. The ultimatum given to Germany expired at 11 pm on 4 August 1914, and Britain was at war with Germany, fighting alongside France and other nations for the next four years.

The foundation of our form of democratic parliament is attributed to Simon de Montfort, leader of the barons in the reign of King Henry III. His parliament included knights from the shires and citizens of certain towns. However, de Montfort was not without his foes and, at the Battle of Evesham, on 4 August 1265, he was slain.

Percy Bysshe Shelley, born on 4 August 1792, was something of a rebel and his revolutionary ideas are expressed in many of his writings. He left behind, at his death, a large amount of poetry and prose.

Sir Harry Lauder, the Scottish music hall comedian, was born on this day in 1870. His well-known songs, such as 'Roamin' in the Gloamin'' and 'Keep Right on to the End of the Road', are remembered by many.

This was the birthday, in 1900, of Queen Elizabeth, the Queen Mother, wife of King George VI, a gracious lady and one of the most popular royal personages of the 20th Century.

Lord Thompson of Fleet, newspaper magnate, died in 1976.

For many years, Southampton has been the port from which luxury liners have sailed to America and many other parts of the world. There was nothing luxurious, however, about the *Mayflower* and the *Speedwell,* which sailed from Southampton on 5 August 1620. In fact the latter proved unseaworthy, leaving the *Mayflower* alone to sail the Atlantic after a call at Plymouth.

On the *Mayflower* were about 100 people, strict Puritans from Scrooby and Gainsborough, who had earlier fled to Holland. Having obtained permission to set up a colony in America, they intended settling near the Hudson River but, instead, landed near Cape Cod, where they formed the colony of New Plymouth. It had been a long and difficult voyage and there were many hardships to be faced after their arrival. About half of these Pilgrim Fathers did not survive the first winter.

When Richard Howe went to sea at the age of 13, he was fortunate to serve under Anson, though life at sea could be very hard even under the best of captains. Howe was destined for a very distinguished naval career. He became a post-captain at twenty and later held high offices including that of First Lord of the Admiralty. Created a Viscount of Great Britain and later Earl, he commanded the Channel Fleet when war broke out with France, in 1793. A year later, off Ushant, he gained 'the Glorious First of June' (p. 121). He died on 5 August 1799.

Thomas Newcomen was an ironmonger, who spent about ten years experimenting with steam engines. In 1712, he built the first practical steam engine, a pumping engine for a coal mine at Tipton, Staffordshire, belonging to the Earl of Dudley. It remained in use at the mine for over thirty years. Thomas Newcomen died on this day in 1729.

Friedrich Engels, who worked closely with Karl Marx in the founding of Communism, died on 5 August 1895.

This was the birthday, in 1850, of Guy de Maupassant, the French novelist and short story writer.

Traffic in Cleveland, Ohio, was brought to a halt on this day in 1914 — by the first electric traffic lights.

Today we remember three people who were born on 6 August and over 75,000 who died.

Matthew Parker was born on 6 August 1504. He was appointed Archbishop of Canterbury by Queen Elizabeth I in 1559 and set about getting the Church on a firm basis, so that he has sometimes been called one of the founders of Anglicanism. He was party to the issue of the Thirty Nine Articles and he published his 'Advertisements' not all of which, including the wearing of the surplice, were very popular, especially with the Puritans. He also introduced a new Bible translation, the 'Bishops' Bible'.

Sir Alexander Fleming also introduced something new — penicillin, one of the very important medical discoveries. Born on 6 August 1881, he qualified as a surgeon before becoming a research scientist. His discovery of the effect of mould on the germs of a common cold was accidental, yet led to the development of what has been described as 'the miracle drug'.

This was the birthday, in 1809, of Alfred, Lord Tennyson. He began writing poetry at an early age and was appointed Poet Laureate by Queen Victoria in 1850. He was very fond of the works of Shakespeare and died with his hand resting on a volume of Shakespeare's plays. He was buried in Westminster Abbey.

Also buried in Westminster Abbey was Ben Jonson, who died on this day in 1637. 'O rare Ben Jonson', is the epitaph to the great playwright, referred to as second only to Shakespeare in his time. Shakespeare's wife, Anne Hathaway, also died on this day, in 1623.

The Spanish artist, Diego Velazquez, who died on 6 August, in 1660, is regarded as one of the world's greatest painters, whose works inspired many others.

John Mason Neale, hymnwriter, died on 6 August 1866.

Over 75,000 people died on 6 August 1945. They were the inhabitants of Hiroshima, Japan, the first city on which an atomic bomb was dropped at the end of World War II. If one were to count the number that died later from the effects of radiation, it would be almost double this figure.

Robert Blake was one of the greatest seamen in British history. Nelson once wrote, 'I do not reckon myself equal to Blake.' A dedicated Puritan, he made a name for himself as a general in the Civil War. Later, Cromwell appointed him one of three 'generals at sea'. He destroyed the Royalist fleet of Prince Rupert; he commanded the English fleet in the Channel during the Dutch wars, winning three out of four engagements with the Dutch Admiral Tromp; he wiped out a fleet of Barbary pirates off Tunis, North Africa; and he destroyed a Spanish treasure fleet in the Canary Islands without the loss of a single ship.

It was on the way home from his last victory that he died at sea just before entering Plymouth. He is remembered for his *Fighting Instructions* and *Articles of War*, which laid the pattern for naval tactics and discipline for future years. A few days after his death, on 7 August 1657, the following lines were penned by George Harrison:

R *est here in peace the sacred dust*
O *f valiant Blake, the good, the just,*
B *elov'd of all on every side;*
E *ngland's honour, once her pride,*
R *ome's terror, Dutch annoyer,*
T *ruth's defender, Spain's destroyer.*

B *ring no dry eyes into this place;*
L *et not be seen in any case,*
A *smiling or an unsad face.*
K *indle desires in every breast*
E *ternally with him to rest.*

On 7 August 1664, Pepys wrote in his diary:

> Several poor creatures carried by, by constables, for being at a conventicle . . . I would to God they would either conform, or be more wise and not be catched!

Rabindranath Tagore, the Bengali poet and thinker, who won the Nobel Prize for Literature in 1913, died on 7 August 1941. He was a writer, teacher, composer and painter.

Oliver Hardy, the fat one of the Laurel and Hardy slapstick comedy films, died on 7 August 1957.

It was on this day, in 1864, that representatives of various countries met at Geneva, Switzerland, for the first Geneva Convention. They met in response to suggestions made by Jean Henri Dunant (p. 90), whose booklet, *Un Souvenir de Solferino*, told of the horrors of that battle and advocated a code of practice in any future conflicts. These included the setting up of the Red Cross and the principle that military hospitals and medical supplies should be safeguarded. Later Conventions added other principles so that reference today to the Geneva Convention includes such matters as the correct treatment of prisoners of war, the safeguarding of food supplies and protection of ancient monuments and buildings.

On 8 August 1296, King Edward I of England removed the old Scottish coronation Stone of Scone from Scotland and had it placed beneath the English Coronation throne in Westminster Abbey so that future kings would be crowned simultaneously as kings of both countries. For many years that proved wishful thinking.

On this day, in 1948, Mother Theresa began her work amongst the poor of Calcutta, which has since received world-wide recognition and for which she received a Nobel Prize.

On this same day, in 1963, a group of men sought to become rich. This was the day of the Great Train Robbery, when the Glasgow–London express was stopped by thieves who had altered the signals, then took about £3 million of old bank notes. Twelve men were sentenced in April 1964, but little of the money was ever recovered. The train driver suffered permanently from the injuries he received.

This was the birthday, in 1646, of Sir Godfrey Kneller, who became court portrait painter from 1680 and whose subjects included the heads of various states.

Some who died on 8 August. . . .

In 1471, Thomas à Kempis (*Of the Imitation of Christ*).

In 1827, George Canning, English statesman and Prime Minister.

In 1919, F. W. Woolworth, founder of Woolworth's stores.

In 1975, Dmitri Shostakovich, Russian composer.

In 1979, Nicholas Monsarrat, English novelist (p. 28).

There are some phrases which slip into our language and are commonly used. We may say that someone is 'as savage as a bear with a sore head'; we speak of matters that are 'six of one and half-a-dozen of the other'; or we suggest that 'every man paddle his own canoe'. All these have come to us from the writings of Captain Frederick Marryat. He had a distinguished naval career, from which he resigned, in 1830, to take up writing. His sea stories rank with the best and some of his children's books are regarded still as classics. He died on 9 August 1848.

Izaak Walton, who was born on 9 August 1593, is also remembered for his writing — *The Compleat Angler*, a discourse on angling and other aspects of the countryside.

Also born on 9 August, in 1757, was a man whose memorials are too many to recount. Thomas Telford, the son of a Dumfries shepherd, became a stonemason, then taught himself architecture and many forms of civil engineering. Many of his great works are to be found in the West Midlands and North Wales — bridges including the suspension bridge across the Menai Strait, canal works including the Pontcysyllte aqueduct, and fine roads. He was also responsible for the construction of St. Katherine's Dock, London, over 1000 miles of road in Scotland, the Gota Canal in Sweden, and the Warsaw frontier road, to name but a few of his achievements. He was buried in Westminster Abbey and the new town in Salop bears his name — Telford.

This was also the birthday, in 1788, of Adoniram Judson, the American missionary, who is remembered for his great work in Burma in spite of persecution and suffering (p. 56).

For sheer determination, there are few stories to beat that of Douglas Bader. In 1931, he lost both his legs in a flying accident and was discharged from the Royal Air Force. At the beginning of World War II, he proved that he was a very efficient pilot, even with artificial legs, and was allowed to rejoin. On 9 August 1941, he was shot down, became a prisoner of war — and even attempted to escape!

The 2nd atomic bomb was dropped on 9 August 1945 (Nagasaki).

A number of ships have been lost on their maiden voyage, but there can be few that have been lost before they even started theirs. One was the *Vasa*, the magnificent new flagship of the Swedish royal fighting ships.

She was a fine ship by any standards. She had a displacement of about 1,400 tonnes and she could carry 300 fighting men in addition to her crew of 133. She was a three-decked ship with 64 cannon pointing through the gun ports. Nothing was spared to make the king's ship as attractive as possible in appearance, with carvings of many kinds and the woodwork painted brilliantly in red, blue and gold. Many had looked at her with admiration as she lay in the harbour.

Crowds came to Stockholm on 10 August 1628. Word had been passed around that the *Vasa* was to sail that afternoon on her maiden voyage and it seemed that almost everyone in the neighbourhood wanted to be there. At the appointed time her sails were hoisted, salutes were given by firing guns from other warships and *Vasa* replied with hers. She made a fine picture as she moved slowly off.

Then the unexpected happened. A sudden squall blew up; the *Vasa* listed to port; her gun ports went under the water and in a few minutes the fine ship had gone to the bottom of the harbour, where she was to remain entombed for the next 333 years (p. 68).

Much more successful was the Royal Greenwich Observatory, which was founded by King Charles II on 10 August 1675, to increase knowledge of the positions of the stars. The Greenwich meridian, from which all distances east and west round the world are measured, passes through this site. After World War II the observatory was moved from London to Herstmonceaux, Sussex, because the brighter London lights made observation difficult. The original building, designed by Sir Christopher Wren, became a museum of astronomy.

Another institution to be founded on this day was the Smithsonian Institution, Washington DC, in 1846 (p. 148).

For Napoleon this was the end. On 10 August 1815, following his defeat at Waterloo, he was exiled to St. Helena.

In 1516, when money was needed for the building fund of St. Peter's in Rome, a Dominican monk, Johann Tetzel, who was a fine preacher, was sent to preach an indulgence, that is a forgiveness of sins in favour of those who contributed toward the building fund. Some people were pleased to be granted this indulgence: others were horrified at this use of religion, among them Martin Luther, who, as a result of this and other thinking, protested with his Ninety-five theses at Wittenberg and sparked off one aspect of the Protestant Reformation. Tetzel died on 11 August 1519, leaving behind a church that was to become even more divided as the Reformation gained in momentum.

One of the great men of religion in England during the 19th Century was John Henry Newman. He was an Anglican clergyman, Vicar of St. Mary's, Oxford, a fine preacher and a leading member of the Oxford Movement in the high church. Gradually he turned toward Roman Catholicism, resigned his living in 1843, became a Roman Catholic and set up a brotherhood in Edgbaston, Birmingham. In 1879, he was appointed a cardinal in the Roman Catholic church. He died on 11 August 1890, leaving a wealth of deep religious thoughts and writings, which have proved helpful to people of various denominations:

To obtain the gift of holiness is the work of a life.

Andrew Carnegie died on 11 August 1919. His poor Scottish parents had crossed the Atlantic to America, where Andrew worked hard and made some good deals which led to his becoming one of the richest men in the world with a fortune of about 500 million dollars, most of which he gave away for libraries, education and scientific research.

The first single-handed crossing of the Atlantic was completed on 11 August 1876, when the Danish sailor, Alfred Johnson, reached the coast of Pembrokeshire after sailing for 57 days.

The radio distress call SOS was first used on 11 August 1909.

This was the date, in 1711, on which the first Royal Ascot race meeting was held. It was to become a colourful meeting with top society dressing fashionably for the occasion.

This is the day when the grouse shooting season opens and those who wish to do so are free to go out in their shooting parties to see how many grouse they can 'bag'.

Thomas Bewick, who was born on 12 August 1753, liked his birds on paper, or maybe in a book. His illustrations for *A History of British Birds* were masterpieces. Bewick was a wood engraver, who rediscovered and improved upon wood engraving techniques. He carved his pictures so skilfully in the end of a block of wood that he was able to produce many variations of shading and tone. Many of his most charming drawings are the illustrations which conclude a chapter, some of them humorous, such as the cat which steals the food whilst its master is saying grace.

Thomas Bewick was a man who helped people become aware of nature, as he was himself. The American artist and naturalist, John Audubon, who visited Bewick, described him: 'warm in his affections, of deep feeling, and possessed of a vigorous imagination, with correct and penetrating observation, he was purely a son of nature.'

William Blake, who died on 12 August 1827, was also an engraver as well as being a poet, painter, and visionary. Some of his simple poems which feature animals are *The Tiger*, *The Lamb* and *The Shepherd*.

And whilst on the subject of shepherds, most people are familiar with the well-known carol, 'While shepherds watched their flocks by night.' It was written by Nahum Tate, who died on 12 August 1715. He was an Irish dramatist and poet, who became Poet Laureate in 1692.

This was the birthday, in 1774, of another Poet Laureate, Robert Southey, appointed as such in 1813. He spent much of his life living in Keswick, where he wrote a great deal of poetry and prose.

The 'Father of the Railways' died on 12 August 1848. He was George Stephenson, builder of famous locomotives such as the *Blucher* and the *Rocket*, and pioneer of passenger railways such as Stockton to Darlington, which opened in 1825.

'And everybody praised the Duke
Who this great fight did win.'
'But what good came of it at last?'
Quoth little Peterkin.
'Why that I cannot tell,' said he,
'But 't was a famous victory.'

So wrote Robert Southey in *The Battle of Blenheim*. This famous battle was fought on 13 August 1704. The Duke was the Duke of Marlborough, fighting with Prince Eugene of Savoy against the French under Tallart and Bavarians under Maximilian II Emanuel. His victory cost Marlborough 12,000 casualties compared with 18,000 enemy casualties and 13,000 taken prisoner. Although hailed as a great victory, very little was settled by it.

In 1961, the people of Berlin awoke on the morning of 13 August to find that a barricade had been erected aross the city during the night, separating East Berlin from West Berlin. Once the capital of Germany, the city was divided at the end of World War II, part administered by the Western Allies and part by the USSR. The barricade, enabling strict control of movement to and from East Germany, was replaced by a concrete wall topped with barbed wire, surrounding West Berlin.

Today's birthdays. . . .
In 1879, John Ireland, English composer of songs and other music.
In 1888, John Logie Baird, Scottish pioneer of television.
In 1907, Sir Basil Spence, architect of Coventry Cathedral, the University of Sussex and many other public buildings.

Sir Alfred Hitchcock, the great master of suspense, was born on 13 August 1899. He began working in films in 1920 and he directed his first film in 1925. Thereafter he made a name for himself writing and producing thrillers in Britain and then in Hollywood, making, on average, one film a year.

Life ended on 13 August for. . . .
Sir John Millais, English painter and illustrator, in 1896.
Florence Nightingale OM, 'The Lady with the Lamp', in 1910.
Octavia Hill, pioneer of housing and National Trust, in 1912.
H. G. Wells, novelist, journalist and sociologist, in 1946.

The greatest disaster in the history of yachting occurred on 14 August 1979, as 335 yachts, ranging from the most expensive in the world to tiny 21-footers, took part in the Fastnet Race, the climax of the Cowes Regatta Week. Quite suddenly they found themselves in the open sea at the mercy of 70 mph (113 km/h) winds and 40 ft (12 m) waves. Many yachts were sunk and others overturned. Lifeboats and helicopters went to the rescue but a couple of dozen yachts were lost and many yachtsmen drowned.

The Revd. Augustus Toplady was caught suddenly in a storm in Burrington Combe, Somerset. He took refuge in a cleft in a rock — and began thinking. Picking up a playing card that was on the ground, he wrote the words of the famous hymn:

Rock of Ages! Cleft for me!
Let me hide myself in Thee!

The hymn has brought comfort to a great many people: the card is preserved in America; and Augustus Toplady no doubt went to his Rock of Ages when he departed this life on 14 August 1778.

When John Vianney became a priest, he went to a little village called Ars-en-Dombes to be the Vicar, or Curé. In time he became very famous, for he was the kind of person to whom people liked to go and talk about their problems. At the end of his 41 years as Curé d'Ars, about 20,000 people a year were flocking to his village. He died on 14 August 1859.

John Galsworthy was born on this day in 1867. He was the novelist and playwright who received the Nobel Prize for Literature in 1932 for his 'distinguished art of narration which takes its highest form in *The Forsyte Saga*'. This was very popular as a television serial when produced, in 1967, by the BBC.

This day, in 1945, was VJ-Day — victory over Japan, when the Japanese surrender brought to an end the final phase of World War II.

It was on 14 August 1969, that British troops were first sent into Londonderry to try to keep the peace in Ulster.

On 15 August 778, Charlemagne, who had been campaigning in Spain, was leading his armies back to France. A few miles behind him, his rear-guard was attacked by some Basque guerillas and the whole body slaughtered. Among them was a young commander, Roland, who was to be immortalised as the hero of the epic poem *Song of Roland.*

Roland was Duke of the Marches of Brittany: his close companion in the rear-guard party was Count Oliver. Both were very brave leaders but their party of 20,000 could not match an enemy twenty times that size. Oliver was stabbed from behind and died. Roland wielded his famous sword Durendal to the end but died of wounds under a pine tree.

He is remembered, as one of the most attractive characters of the Middle Ages, not only for his bravery and courage but for his high sense of duty, absolute loyalty, love of his country and his fear of God — the values one has to admire.

Also slain in battle, on this day in 1057, was Macbeth, King of Scotland.

At 8 am on 15 August 1942, the tanker *Ohio* slipped into the Grand Harbour at Valetta, Malta, with three destroyers acting as tugs and one of them pumping water from the tanker to keep her afloat. It was nothing short of a miracle that the ship had reached Malta and this was a tribute to the courage and bravery of her crew.

This was wartime. Malta had been attacked constantly by the enemy and was desperately in need of supplies. Fourteen ships had sailed through the Straits of Gibraltar to face heavy attacks from aircraft and submarines. Warships and merchant ships were sunk. *Ohio* was badly damaged and under constant attack yet survived to carry her vital cargo of oil to enable Malta to recover, Captain Mason received the George Cross for gallantry and fourteen members of *Ohio's* crew also received awards for their courage.

People born on this day include. . . .

Napoleon Bonaparte, Emperor of France, in 1769.
Sir Walter Scott, author, in 1771.
Edith Nesbit, authoress of books for children, in 1858.
T. E. Lawrence, soldier, 'Lawrence of Arabia', in 1888.

This was the day, in 1513, of the Battle of the Spurs, so named because of the speedy success of Henry VIII's army against the French, who were routed in the Pas-de-Calais, France.

It was on this day too, in 1819, that a small body of troops routed as many as 60,000 in Manchester. It was, however, an unarmed, peaceful crowd, many being women and children. This was a political rally, to show discontent and listen to a speech on parliamentary reform. Local magistrates, nervous at the size of the gathering in St. Peter's Field, ordered troops to disperse it. By the time the area had been cleared, eleven people were dead and about 500 injured. It became known as the Peterloo Massacre, the name taken from the recent Battle of Waterloo.

Elvis Presley, the 'king of rock 'n' roll', who was idolised by fans of pop music, died on 16 August 1977, at the age of 42, at his home in Memphis, Tennessee. He was one of the greatest influences on the popular music of his day and he remained a legend long after his death.

This day also saw the passing of another who influenced a great many people with his teachings. Ramakrishna, who died on 16 August 1886, had spent his life teaching the unity of all religions:

> *There are, in a tank or pool, various steps to the water. The Hindus draw out the liquid and call it* jal. *The Muslims draw out the liquid and call it* pani. *The Christians draw out the liquid and call it* water, *but it is all the same substance, no essential difference.*

Thousands gathered near his Calcutta home to hear him speak. His followers are active to this day.

Greatly esteemed in Cyprus was Archbishop Makarios, who led the campaign for independence and became the country's first president when that was achieved on 16 August 1960.

Charles Beebe and Otis Barton entered a new world on 16 August 1934, when they made a then record descent of 3,028 feet (923 m) in their bathysphere near Bermuda.

A legend was born on 17 August 1786. Davy Crockett (real name David) was a frontiersman in the days of the Old West and fought against the Indians before entering the political scene. He had some political successes and some defeats, after the last of which he headed for Texas and joined up with the American forces. He was one of those slain by the Mexican army at the Alamo in San Antonio.

This was the birthday, too, in 1892, of another legendary American figure — Mae West. The platinum-blonde star, dressed bewitchingly in furs and feathers, liberal with her jewellery, and not averse to the suggestive saying, became the sex symbol of her day and remained so for many years. A star of vaudeville, stage, screen, radio, and television, she was still glamorous when filming in her seventies. Her ample proportions led servicemen in World War II to name their inflatable life jackets 'Mae Wests'.

Three Americans landed about 60 miles from Paris after a transatlantic flight on 17 August 1978. They had travelled over 3,000 miles (4,800 km) and had taken 139 hours 10 minutes to fly that distance. Ben Abruzzo, Max Anderson and Larry Newman had made the journey in *Double Eagle II*, which was a balloon. They had completed the first transatlantic balloon crossing, had made the longest ever balloon flight and had spent a record time in the air.

This day, in 1786, saw the death of one of the great rulers of Europe. Frederick the Great, Frederick II of Prussia, had raised his small country to the position of being able to lead a united Germany. Frederick's early years were not happy. He was brought up strictly within a very rigid system. He rebelled and narrowly escaped being punished with death by his father.

Frederick became king in 1740 and proved to be a wise ruler. He was austere but had a keen sense of justice. He allowed a considerable degree of freedom to his subjects. He enjoyed literature and music; he was a prolific writer; and, by various means, doubled the size of his kingdom.

William Carey, Baptist missionary to India, was born in 1761.

There are many people who have complained at the size of the telephone bill when they have received it. None of them, however is as large as the one received on 18 August 1975 by the landlord of the Blue Bell Inn, Lichfield. It was for £1,494,000,000. It was an error, the Post Office agreed.

So to something infinitely larger, a vast empire that spread across Asia in the 13th Century from the shores of the Black Sea to the Pacific Ocean. It began when a lad of thirteen named Temujin became chief of a tribe of nomadic herdsmen living on the grasslands of central Asia. He had a hard struggle but he was determined. He took the title of Khan (Ruler) and the name of Genghis ('Very Mighty'). Before long, he was master of all the mongol tribes. He then formed the horsemen into armies and set out on a systematic conquest of the whole of Asia. Genghis Khan was powerful and ruthless. Whole cities were destroyed and their inhabitants slaughtered with great cruelty. It is estimated that he was responsible for the death of many millions of people. However, he was not only a warrior but a good administrator, who conquered empires and set up a number of states across Asia. He died on 18 August 1227.

Also on the subject of large things, the Tay Road Bridge was officially opened on 18 August 1966. It is the longest road bridge in Britain, not a suspension bridge but built on a series of columns spanning the river.

Over a century earlier, Sir William Fairbairn was building bridges in conjunction with Robert Stephenson. They were the new tubular railway bridges spanning the Menai Straits and the River Conway in North Wales. The girders were riveted by a hydraulic machine designed by Fairbairn. Fairbairn was a Scot, who became a millwright in Manchester, then set up a ship-building yard at Millwall, London. Sir William, who was the first to use wrought iron for ships' hulls, bridges and beams, died on 18 August 1874.

Another engineer to die on this day, in 1809, was Matthew Boulton, who went into partnership with James Watt to construct steam engines. He also employed steam power for new machines used to make coins in the Royal Mint and elsewhere.

Jonathan Flamsteed was born on 19 August 1646. He was unfortunate as a lad to catch an illness which left him crippled for life. Had this not been so, we might never have heard of him. As it was, he sat at his bedroom window gazing at the stars and studying some mathematical tables that had been lent to him. Soon he had discovered that the tables were wrong and he began to draw up a new set showing the correct positions of the stars. These were of great value to navigators, who used the stars to find the positions of their ships.

Flamsteed's fame grew after he had presented King Charles II with a set of his tables and some instruments. The king ordered that an Observatory, where stars could be studied, should be built at Greenwich, and he appointed Flamsteed as the first Astronomer Royal. In spite of increasing pain, Jonathan continued working until his death in 1719, after which his work, cataloguing 3,000 stars, was published, under the title *Historia Coelestis Britannica*, by his assistant, Abraham Sharp.

19 August was also the birthday, in 1871, of Orville Wright. He had his eyes on the sky above but for a different reason. He wanted to fly. On 17 December 1903, he made history by becoming the first man to fly a machine that was heavier than air.

Yet another who set his sights high was King Edward I of England. He was crowned on 19 August 1274. But he was not content just to be King of England: he wanted to be King of Scotland and King of Wales too — perhaps even King of France. He earned himself the title 'Hammer of the Scots' and spent much of his reign at war.

Some famous people who died on 19 August are. . . .

Augustus Caesar, Roman Emperor, in AD 14.

Blaise Pascal, mathematician and theologian, in 1662.

James Watt, engineer and inventor of the steam engine, in 1819.

Robert Bloomfield, poet, in 1823.

Sir Henry Wood, conductor, composer and founder of the Promenade Concerts, in 1944.

Sir Jacob Epstein, creator of many well-known modern sculptures, in 1959.

On 20 August 79, there were ominous rumblings from Mount Vesuvius overlooking the Bay of Naples in Italy. The earth began to tremble — and so did the people who lived in Pompeii, especially those who remembered how buildings had collapsed in the tremors some seventeen years earlier. However, the noises subsided and people carried on with their business. Four days later disaster struck. Vesuvius erupted; molten lava and poisonous gases rolled down the mountain; and Pompeii, with many of its inhabitants, became buried, remaining so for centuries, until excavated in recent times.

The end came just as quickly on 20 August 1940, for Leon Trotsky, who was assassinated in Mexico, where he had been granted asylum. A Russian Jewish revolutionary (real name, Lev Davidovich Bronstein), he was a fine orator and visionary who supported Lenin in the Russian revolution. After Lenin's death, Trotsky was ousted by Stalin, exiled to Central Asia, and finally expelled from Russia in 1929. In exile, he continued to agitate against Stalin so that he was sentenced to death, in 1937, in his absence. That sentence, by a Soviet court, was carried out by the assassin in 1940.

It was on this day, in 1968, that Soviet troops moved into Czechoslovakia to put down those who wanted a more liberal way of life than that demanded by the Soviet leaders.

William Booth's soldiers were on the march in east London in the latter part of the 19th Century, determined to do battle against the evils of their time. They were members of the Salvation Army, founded by Booth as a Christian Mission. Under their banner, bearing the words 'Blood and Fire' (the blood of Jesus Christ and the fire of the Holy Spirit), the bands played and the Christian gospel was preached. At their citadels, practical help was given to the poor, the hungry, the homeless and others in need — a work continued to this day by the Salvation Army, many years after the death of its founder on 20 August 1912.

Today is the feast day of St. Bernard of Clairvaux, the founder of the Cistercian monastic order.

There was something different about the young Scotsman who was looking for a job as an engineer: he was wearing a hat that he had made himself out of a block of wood. The firm was that of Boulton and Watt at Soho, Birmingham, where new steam engines were being built and the young man, William Murdock was given a job working on the engines. Later he was sent to Cornwall to supervise the setting up of the firm's steam engines and tried unsuccessfully to build a steam road carriage.

Meanwhile he had been experimenting with coal gas as a means of lighting and his house in Redruth, Cornwall, was the first house ever to be lit by gas. After he had moved back to Birmingham, he made further experiments and, in 1802, gas lighting was installed in part of Boulton and Watt's Soho factory. Today was William Murdock's birthday — 21 August 1754.

Ettore Bugatti, who died on 21 August 1947, was interested in engines of a different kind and road vehicles that were far removed from Murdock's steam carriage. He was the builder of racing and luxury cars at the factory he established, in 1909, in Alsace. The low powered racing cars he built for the Le Mans race were very successful. His other cars were the height of luxury, meticulously built and very highly priced. Only about half a dozen were built.

Cars would have been of little use to George Grenfell, whose work took him to the jungles of West and Central Africa, where the rivers were the highways. George Grenfell, who was born on 21 August 1849, was an English Baptist Missionary, whose first assignment, in 1874, was to the Cameroons, which he explored. In 1878, he went to the Congo, where he started new mission stations and helped undo problems caused by the slave trade. A few years later, he made exploratory voyages up the Congo, which greatly increased knowledge of that river. In 1887, he received the Founder's Medal of the Royal Geographical Society.

Two birthdays today. . . .

Christopher Bracher, British athlete, was born in 1928.

Princess Margaret, sister of Queen Elizabeth II, born in 1930.

This day, in 1485, marked the end of the Wars of the Roses. Henry Tudor, a Lancastrian claimant to the throne, met the Yorkist Richard III in battle at Bosworth Field. Some of Richard's supporters deserted at the crucial moment but the king fought bravely to the death. Henry later married Elizabeth of York, uniting the two sides and introducing the Tudor line of monarchs as Henry VII.

It was on this day, in 1642, that civil war broke out in England. Relationships between king and parliament finally broke down and King Charles I raised his standard at Nottingham, calling supporters to the royalist cause.

Some who died on 22 August . . . . Jean Honoré Fragonard, one of the finest French 18th Century painters and engravers, died in 1806.

Warren Hastings, who died in 1818, is remembered particularly for his work as an English administrator in India.

Richard Oastler was an English reformer who was concerned with conditions in the factories and advocated a ten-hour working day. He died in 1861.

George Shillibeer, who introduced buses to London in 1829, died on 22 August 1866.

'Lord' John Sanger, who gave himself the title, as did his brother, George, died in 1889. They were proprietors of a well-known travelling circus.

Sir Oliver Lodge, English physicist, died in 1940. He was concerned with electricity and was a pioneer of radio telegraphy. He also spent much of his time in psychical research.

Lord Nuffield, who died in 1963, began life as William Morris. He began his career by making bicycles, then Morris cars. Much of his vast fortune was used to benefit hospitals, Oxford University and charities. He also established the Nuffield Foundation for medical, scientific and social research.

Jomo Kenyatta became President of Kenya when that country gained independence in 1963 and he held this office until his death, on 22 August 1978.

On this day, in 1932, the BBC introduced its first regular television service.

William Wallace holds an honoured place in Scottish history. A man of great stature and strength, he was filled with a spirit of patriotism and independence that enabled him to inspire the Scots, under his leadership, to fight against the English. At first he was very successful, driving the English out of most of Scotland but, at the Battle of Falkirk, on 22 July 1298, the best of his soldiers were slain and, from that time, he could do little more than carry out guerilla raids here and there.

Sir William Wallace became a man with a price on his head, but remained at large until betrayed by a fellow-countryman, Sir John Mentieth. On 5 August 1305, Wallace was taken prisoner and thereafter shamefully treated by his captors. On 23 August, he was taken to Westminster Hall and charged with treason. He protested that he had never been a subject of the English king and could not therefore be a traitor. Nevertheless he was crowned, mockingly, with a laurel crown, found guilty, dragged by horses to Smithfield and there executed with the greatest barbarity.

The rise of George Villiers was meteoric. Within a few years of coming to the notice of King James I, he had been knighted, then raised to the peerage as Duke of Buckingham. Offices and lands were bestowed in abundance until he became, with one exception, the wealthiest peer in England. In other ways he was not so successful and did not enjoy popularity. On 23 August 1628, when in Portsmouth preparing to lead a military expedition to France, he was assassinated by a discontented junior officer.

This day saw the passing of two men, each of whom played an important role in the world of the theatre and entertainment. Mikhail Fokine, the Russian dancer and choreographer, is regarded as the man who gave ballet its new look and vitality. *Firebird* and *Petrouchka* are two of his creations. He died in 1942.

Oscar Hammerstein II wrote the words, in collaboration with Richard Rodgers, who composed the music, for some of the finest musicals produced, including *Rose Marie, Oklahoma, South Pacific* and *The Sound of Music*. He died on 23 August 1960.

The World Council of Churches, the forum for over 200 Christian denominations worldwide, was formed on 23 August 1948.

As at St. Bartholomew's Day
So will all the autumn stay.

In the past, this was the day around which Bartholomew Fair was once held in Smithfield, London, near the Church of St. Bartholomew and the hospital founded by Rahere. Charles II extended it from 3 to 14 days but it became the haunt of many undesirable characters. Few people were sorry to see it come to an end in 1855.

The greatest of the provincial fairs at Sturbridge, near Cambridge began with a procession on St. Bartholomew's Day and continued until 14 September. It, too, was last held in 1855.

St. Bartholomew is the patron saint of bee-keepers and honey makers. It used to be customary for the honey to be taken from the bees on St. Bartholomew's Day. So, today, at Gulval in Cornwall, there will be the service of Blessing the Mead, the drink made from honey, with all the ceremonial of the Worshipful Company of Mead Makers.

This was the day, in 1572, of the St. Bartholomew's Day Massacre in France, when several thousand French Huguenots (Protestants) were slain in Paris alone.

William Wilberforce was born on 24 August 1759. He became a Member of Parliament at the age of 21 and was instrumental in passing various reforms, particularly regarding slaves and the slave trade. The latter was stopped in 1807 and the Slavery Abolition Act, for which he had fought so hard, was passed one month after his death in 1833.

This was the birthday of two great British artists. George Stubbs, who was born in 1724, is especially renowned as a painter of animals, particularly of horses but of such animals as he was able to observe in private menageries. More recently, Graham Sutherland was born in 1903. He is known for some of his surrealist landscapes but also for his portraits and the great tapestry in Coventry Cathedral (p. 7).

Colonel Blood, who once stole the Crown Jewels from the Tower of London (p. 91), died on 24 August 1680.

25 August

Gaius Plinius Secundus, better known as Pliny the Elder, had a short military career but became interested in the natural world and science. Thought by some to be the most learned man of his time, he was regarded up to the Middle Ages as the greatest authority on science. Nowadays some of his recordings are known to be inaccurate but he has still given information on many matters which otherwise might not have been recorded. On this day, in 79, he was in command of the Roman fleet near Vesuvius at the time of its great eruption. Anxious to study the volcano more closely, he landed nearby — but he went too close and was suffocated by the vapours.

Two other men of science died on 25 August. Sir William Herschel, astronomer, who discovered and catalogued stars and planets, died in 1822. Michael Faraday, physicist, chemist and inventor of the first dynamo, died in 1867.

It was on 25 August 1875, that Captain Matthew Webb stepped ashore in France, having become the first man to swim the Channel. Just over a century later, on this day in 1978, Walter Robinson 'walked' across the Channel in a water shoe. It took him 11½ hours, about half the time taken by Webb. This day also saw the Channel crossed in 1919, by an aircraft which flew the first day air service from London to Paris. The allied armies arrived in Paris on this day, too. It marked the liberation of that city in 1944.

Henry Morgan, a Welshman, became a buccaneer in the West Indies harassing Spanish ships and settlements. He was knighted, appointed Lieutenant Governor of Jamaica, and lived there in a fine house until his death on 25 August 1688.

This was the birthday, in 1530, of Ivan the Terrible, who ruled Russia wisely for some years but later became a tyrant, responsible for the deaths of many.

It was the birthday, too, in 1876, of Eglantyne Jebb, whose work amongst homeless children in Vienna after World War I led to the founding of the 'Save the Children' fund.

In 1768, Captain Cook sailed on his first Pacific voyage.

The Roman soldiers of Julius Caesar landed on the beach where Deal, Kent, now stands, on 26 August 55BC, having crossed the Channel from Boulogne. This was a reconnaissance trip. They only stayed about three weeks but learned enough to plan a much bigger invasion in the following year.

Many years later, in 1346, it was an English army that crossed the Channel in the opposite direction. King Edward III had taken 4,000 men-at-arms and 10,000 longbowmen to fight the French. The decisive battle of this part of the Hundred Years' War was at Crecy, when the English longbowmen won the day against the Italian crossbowmen and the French Cavalry. It was at this battle that the king's son, the Black Prince, fought so well that he 'won his spurs', receiving a knighthood.

Five hundred years later, it was the name of another prince that was on the lips of many people in Britain. Prince Albert of Saxe-Coburg-Gotha, who was born on 26 August 1819, had married Queen Victoria and soon made his mark on the country. One of his achievements was the planning of the Great Exhibition in the Crystal Palace in 1851.

Three leading administrators were born on 26 August. In 1676, Sir Robert Walpole was born. In the reign of George I, he chaired the cabinet meetings, because the king knew no English, and has been regarded as the First Prime Minister.

Henry Fawcett was born on this day in 1833. He was blinded as a young man in a shooting accident but succeeded in being elected a Member of Parliament at his third attempt. He made such an impression that, in 1880, Gladstone made him Postmaster-General, in which office he made several reforms.

John Buchan, born on 26 August 1875, was for a short while a Member of Parliament and, as Lord Tweedsmuir, a popular Governor-General of Canada. He is also remembered as a well-known author of over fifty books, including *Prester John* and *The Thirty-Nine Steps*.

Two solo travellers died on 26 August. . . .

In 1972 Sir Francis Chichester, round-the-world sailor.

In 1974 Charles Lindbergh, first to fly solo across the Atlantic.

On 27 August 1883, there was an explosion which rocked part of the world. A series of eruptions on the volcanic island of Krakatoa culminated in one huge explosion which blew the island to pieces. The explosion was so loud that it could be heard nearly 3,000 miles (4,800 km) away, ash and pumice fell nearly 1,000 miles (1,600 km) away; and many thousands of people were drowned by the huge waves set up by the explosion, which swamped villages on many of the neighbouring islands in the East Indies.

Nearly a century later, on 27 August 1979, there was a much smaller explosion, which shook the world in a different sense. It was a bomb that had been placed in a fishing boat by a member of the IRA (Irish Republican Army) and it killed Earl Mountbatten of Burma, a cousin of Queen Elizabeth II, and one of the most respected personalities in the world.

He had made the Royal Navy his career and had served with great distinction, holding posts as Commander-in-Chief during the latter part of World War II. As Viceroy of India, he played an important role in setting up the new governments of India and Pakistan. In later years, he was often called upon to help solve difficult problems. His death was mourned worldwide.

On the same day, 15 British soldiers were also killed by the IRA in Ulster, one of many incidents in recent years in which IRA terrorists have taken the lives of soldiers or civilians.

Today's birthdays. . .

In 551 BC, K'ung Fu'tzu (Confucius), the Chinese teacher of moral responsibilities in government, society and home.
In 1886, Eric Coates, British composer.
In 1908, Sir Donald Bradman, Australian cricketer.

Today's deaths. . .

In 1576, Titian (Tiziano Vecellio), Venetian Renaissance artist.
In 1879, Sir Rowland Hill, originator of Penny Postage in 1840.
In 1919, Louis Botha, South African soldier and statesman.
In 1975, Haile Selassie, Emperor of Ethiopia, 1930–1974.

On 27 August 1859, the world's first oil well was drilled, by Edwin L. Drake, in Pennsylvania, USA.

Sir Francis Chichester began his circumnavigation in 1966.

I have a dream that one day this nation will rise up and live out the true meaning of its creed: 'We hold these truths to be self-evident, that all men are created equal.

The famous speech, of which these words are a part, was delivered on 28 August 1963, by Dr. Martin Luther King, to 200,000 people who had marched to the Lincoln Memorial in Washington DC as part of the non-violent civil rights campaign. It was a very moving and peaceful demonstration. In the following year Congress passed the Civil Rights Act of 1964.

All, everything that I understand, I understand only because I love.

These words in *War and Peace* by Leo Tolstoy help express his thoughts about human relationships. Count Leo Nikolayevich Tolstoy was born on 28 August 1828, in Russia. He studied law and oriental languages before joining the army and taking part in the siege of Sebastopol during the Crimean War. He travelled abroad before settling on his estate as an enlightened landlord. Meanwhile, he had come to be recognised as an author, generally regarded as Russia's greatest. His *War and Peace,* a domestic story of Russia at the time of Napoleon, which took six years to write, is regarded by many as the greatest novel in the world.

On the Law of War and Peace was the title of a legal masterpice by the Dutch scholar, Hugo Grotius. In 1618, he was sentenced to life imprisonment for his politics but, three years later, he escaped from a castle hidden in a box of books. He then lived in France, being one-time Swedish ambassador to France. He also wrote Dutch and Latin poetry. He died on 28 August 1645.

Another of the world's literary masterpieces is *Faust,* the life's work of Goethe, who began writing it in 1775, published the first part in 1808 and the second part in 1832, the year of his death. Johann Wolfgang von Goethe, the literary genius of Germany (p. 28), was born on 28 August 1749, in Frankfurt-am-Main.

This was the birthday, in 1833, of Sir Edward Burne-Jones, painter and, in 1840, of Ira D. Sankey, American revivalist hymn writer, who sang at meetings led by his partner, Moody.

On 29 August 1973, Roger Chapman and Roger Mallinson had been working on the bed of the Atlantic Ocean, 150 miles (240 km) from Cork, in the midget submarine *Pisces III*, burying part of a new transatlantic telephone cable. As they surfaced, there was an accident which sent *Pisces III* plunging to the bottom of the ocean, 1,575 ft (480 m) below the surface. Rescue work was immediately put in hand and the two men were rescued after 76 hours — the deepest undersea rescue ever accomplished.

The crew of HMS *Royal George* were not so fortunate. The 100–gun battleship was at anchor at Spithead, near Portsmouth, taking on stores. To make underwater repairs, the starboard guns were run inboard so that the ship was keeled over. They tipped her just a little too far and water began splashing into the gun ports on the port side. No one took much notice. A carpenter, who warned the duty officer, was told to mind his own business. But it was soon too late. Water came rushing in, the *Royal George* turned turtle and sank, drowning more than 900.

The spirits of English cricketers sank in 1882, when an Australian team won a surprising victory against England in a Test Match. The *Sporting Times* recorded the death of English cricket and said that the ashes had been taken to Australia. So today is the anniversary of the institution of 'The Ashes', the imaginary trophy for each England-Australia Test series.

Today's birthdays. . . .
  Oliver Wendell Holmes, US physician and writer, in 1809.
  Charles F. Kettering, engineer, in 1876. His inventions for cars included self-starters, lighting and ignition systems.

Today's deaths. . . .
  Brigham Young, Mormon leader, in 1877.
  Rev. W. A. Spooner, originator of 'Spoonerisms', in 1930.

The German airship *Graf Zeppelin* completed a circumnavigation of the world on 29 August 1929.

It was on 29 August 1896, that Li Hung-Chang's chef in New York gave the world a new dish — Chop Suey.

One of the greatest physicists of this century, Ernest Rutherford (1st Baron Rutherford of Nelson), was born near Nelson, New Zealand, on 30 August 1871. His first experiments were concerned with magnetism and later ones with radiation, leading to revolutionary ideas describing the atom as a miniature universe with a nucleus surrounded by electrons. His many honours included awards by the Royal Society, a Nobel Prize for Chemistry in 1908, a knighthood in 1914, the Order of Merit in 1925 and a peerage in 1931. He was also a president of the British Association and of the Royal Society. After his death in 1937, he was interred in Westminster Abbey.

Another physicist who helped revolutionise the knowledge of atomic structure was Sir Joseph John Thomson, also a Nobel Prize winner. He died on this day in 1940.

Sir John Ross, who died on 30 August 1856, was a Scottish Arctic explorer, who had served in the navy with distinction during the French wars. In 1818, he went on an expedition to Baffin Bay to seek a Northwest passage but was unsuccessful. In 1829–33 he sailed again on a voyage sponsored by Sir Felix Booth, during which he discovered and named a peninsula 'Boothia Felix'. An expedition, in 1850, to find Sir John Franklin was unsuccessful.

On 30 August 1896, Raymond Massey was born in Toronto, Canada, destined to become one of the top actors of stage, screen and television. Some of his well remembered roles were as *Abe Lincoln* in the stage production by that name, as Dr. Gillespie in the *Dr. Kildare* television series and as a sinister character in many films. Vincent Massey, the Canadian statesman, was his elder brother.

The first trams appeared in Britain on this day in 1860. They were horse-drawn and ran on a tramway in Birkenhead. It was an idea that had been imported from America, where trams, the brainchild of John Stephenson, had run in Manhattan as long ago as 1832.

That invaluable domestic appliance, the vacuum cleaner, made its debut on 30 August 1901, when it was patented by H. Cecil Booth.

This was once known as *Dies Mala* — a very unlucky day.

Aidan was a man with a mission. He was a monk from the community at Iona, sent to Northumbria, at the request of King Oswald, to teach the people about Christianity. Aidan set up his headquarters on Lindisfarne, or Holy Island, and from there travelled widely, winning the hearts of the people by his simplicity, sincerity and humility. He died in 635 AD and 31 August is the feast day on which he is remembered.

In later years, John Bunyan was a man with a mission — to preach in the villages around Bedford about his Christian faith. In November 1660, he was arrested whilst preaching and was imprisoned in Bedford gaol for twelve years, during which he wrote several books. Released in 1672, he was again imprisoned the following year for six months and it was during this time that he wrote the first part of his best seller *Pilgrim's Progress*. He died at the home of a friend in London on 31 August 1688 and was buried in the nonconformist burial ground, Bunhill Fields.

Only a few years before this, London had become a city of death with many people dying of the plague. On 31 August 1665, Samuel Pepys wrote in his diary: 'Every day sadder and sadder news of its increase. In the city died this week 7,496, and of them 6,102 of the plague.'

This was the birthday, in 12AD, of the Roman emperor Caligula, who was assassinated in the year 41. In three years he had spent some £27 million, had confiscated private property, declared himself to be a god, appointed his horse a consul and showed great delight in executions and tortures. People were relieved at the death of their mad ruler.

One who made a considerable contribution to mankind, yet whose name is not as well known as some, was Sir John Bennet Lawes, who died on 31 August 1900. Born at Rothamsted, in Hertfordshire, he carried out many experiments on plants and crops, which resulted in the development of the artificial fertiliser industry. His scientific researches into agriculture led to his estate becoming the Rothamsted Experimental Station, now controlled largely by the government and internationally recognised for its great contribution to world farming.

Some August Events and Commemorations

(see also pp. 193–5)

First week Meriden, West Midlands: Great Wardmote of the Woodmen of Arden. Archery contest on mediaeval lines.
First weekend Ripon, Yorkshire: Feast of St. Wilfrid. Parade with bands. City Hornblower.
5th Guisely, Yorkshire: Clipping (Encircling) the church on the day of the patron saint, St. Oswald.
5th or nearest Saturday Grasmere, Cumbria: Rushbearing to church. Distribution of gingerbread.
Second Sunday Macclesfield Forest, Cheshire: Rushbearing.
Souden, Borders: Battle of Otterburn (1388) Commemoration.
15th and following Sunday Walsingham, Norfolk: Pilgrimage (p. 156).
Monday after 15th Frampton-on-Severn, Gloucestershire: Feast with deer roasting on village green (Mediaeval feast day).
Third week Innerleithen, Border: Cleiking the Devil. Expulsion by St. Ronan enacted. Procession, festivities, pipes and games.
24th Sandwich, Kent: Distribution of buns and biscuits to children who have run round the church of St. Bartholomew.
Last Sunday Eyam, Derbyshire: Plague Sunday. Service in Cucklet Delf commemorating Rev. William Mompesson and self-sacrifice of villagers in containing the plague within the village.
Some time in month Whitstable, Kent: Blessing the Sea.
Cranham, Gloucestershire: Feast and deer roasting.
Hastings, Sussex: Town Crier Contest.
Barlow, Bonsall, Bradwell, Eyam, Stoney Middleton and Wormhill, Derbyshire: Well dressings.

SOME AUGUST FAIRS

In many places: Bank holiday fairs and feasts.
Barnsley, South Yorks and Bingley, West Yorks: Annual Feasts.
5th Brigg, Lincolnshire: Horse Fair.
2nd Thursday Wilton, Wiltshire: Sheep Fair.
Sometime Ipswich, Suffolk: Sheep Fair.
24th Lee Gap, Yorkshire: Horse Fair.
Late in month Preston, Lancashire: Pot Fair.

SOME AGRICULTURAL SHOWS

Bakewell, Bingley, Cricklade, Denbighshire & Flintshire, Dumfries and Lockerbee, Keith, Mid-Somerset, Monmouthshire, New Forest Pony and Cattle, Orkney, Pembrokeshire, Royal Jersey, Royal Manx, Rutland, Thame, Turriff, United Counties (Carmarthen), Westmorland, Dublin Horse Show.

Index of related themes

Entries are listed under main headings. For other themes, check in the General Index where an indication will be found of the main heading in this index (e.g. Balloons is a sub-heading of AIR TRAVEL).

ASTRONOMY

CHANNEL CROSSINGS

CHRISTIAN CHURCH

FESTIVALS

INDUSTRY AND TRADE

INVENTORS

MUSIC

STATESMEN AND POLITICIANS

SUPERLATIVES (see also SPEED)

TRANSPORT

WRITERS

General Index

Entries marked with an asterisk * in this index are indexed more fully in the Index of Related Themes (pp. 229-245) under the heading that is indicated beside the asterisk if different.